# PROFIT GOALS
## AND
## CAPITAL MANAGEMENT

# PROFIT GOALS

# AND

# CAPITAL MANAGEMENT

JOHN F. *Farnsworth* CHILDS

PRENTICE-HALL, INC., Englewood Cliffs, N. J.

PRINTED IN THE UNITED STATES OF AMERICA

B & P

**Photo by Jean Raeburn, N.Y.**

The author is well known in the field of finance as a lecturer, writer and corporate financial advisor. He has worked in Wall Street for 30 years. The first four years of his business career were with an investment banking firm as a financial analyst. He subsequently joined one of the major New York banks, where he has spent his time largely in the area of long-term corporate financial policy. He is now a Senior Vice-President in charge of the bank's Corporate Services Division, which includes the Corporate Financial Counseling Department.

His book, *Long-Term Financing*, published in 1961 by Prentice-Hall, Inc., is in its sixth printing and has been accepted as one of the most important practical books in its field. In addition, he has written numerous articles on various financial subjects. He was a contributor to *Corporate Treasurer's and Controller's Handbook*, Prentice-Hall, Inc., 1958, and to *Investor Relations: The Company and Its Owners*, American Management Association, 1963.

Mr. Childs lectures regularly throughout the country before such groups as the Financial Executives' Institute, National Association of Accountants, Administrative Management Society, Budget Executives' Institute, American Paper Institute, American Institute of Chemical Engineers, Atomic Industrial Forum, Southeastern Electric Exchange, and the American Management Association. He is a Vice-President of the American Management Association, Finance Division, and a Director of that institution.

He has testified before a number of regulatory authorities on Cost-of-Capital and also before the Joint Committee on Atomic Energy, Congress of the United States.

The financial seminars he originated for senior executives of industrial companies, banks, and utility companies have earned a unique reputation for their practical approach to finance. He has been active in the New York Society of Security Analysts and at one time was Secretary and Chairman of the Program Committee.

A member of the New York Bar, Mr. Childs is a graduate of Trinity College, B.S. '31 and M.S. '32; Harvard Graduate Business School, M.B.A., '33; and Fordham Law School, LLB '46.

v

My previous book, *Long-Term Financing,* was dedicated as follows:

> To Susan, my wonderful ten-year-old daughter, whose strong feeling about this book was that it took too much of Dad's time.

This book I also dedicate to her, but things have changed. At 16, she is so interested in her horse, that it is less important how Dad spends his time —but she is still just as much fun.

# *ACKNOWLEDGMENTS*

The author wishes to acknowledge the help of—

Dr. Victor H. Brown, Partner, Touche, Ross, Bailey and Smart, who contributed Chapters XV, XVI, and Appendix E, and Dr. Brown and Anthony H. Meyer, Vice-President, Irving Trust Company, for their many valuable suggestions throughout the book.

# CONTENTS

# EXHIBIT LIST

EXHIBIT

# PROFIT GOALS
## AND
# CAPITAL MANAGEMENT

# CHAPTER I

# What and Who—
# The Aim of the Book

## MANAGEMENT'S TASK

Today, the success of your company depends to a great extent on correct decisions on total capital management. They are vital to:

*Your stockholders*—because of the direct effect on profits through the return realized on the capital.

*All companies in an industry*—because over-expansion by one company will hurt prices in the entire industry and have a corresponding effect on profits.

*Our entire economy*—because capital directed where it is not needed means production of the wrong goods and a resulting reduction in our standard of living. Furthermore, if excessive expansion occurs in a prosperous period, it will accentuate the business cycle and the unemployment problem.

It is a tribute to American management that capital has been so well-handled that our nation has by far the highest standard of living in the world. However, management faces an increasingly difficult task in handling capital:

The amount of capital involved is staggering. Total capital of all U. S. Corporations now amounts to $700,000,000,000; it represents about $25,000 [1] per employee. Continued capital growth is necessary to raise our standard of living.

Raising capital is becoming more complex; new capital has to be drawn from an ever broadening group of investors.

The effects of the use of capital spread in an ever widening circle.

Management is distracted by other pressing problems.

These are the conditions under which management must operate in its efforts to do a better job. A company which handles capital poorly may be doomed to mediocrity or failure.

[1] Estimates based on statistics of Internal Revenue Service, Securities and Exchange Commission, Department of Labor, and National Industrial Conference Board.

## DO YOU NEED ANSWERS
## TO THESE QUESTIONS?

This book suggests answers to such perplexing questions about capital management as:

What should be the magnitude of an expansion profit goal?

What affects its size?

On what basis should it be determined?

Why is increasing present earnings per share of common stock a false goal for an expansion program or an acquisition?

Does the source of funds affect the amount that a company can spend on an expansion program or an acquisition?

How should an acquisition be priced?

What do changes in return on capital mean?

How can capital costs be reduced?

How should the profitability rate of a project be figured?

How should plant liquidation calculations be made?

How do you set profit performance standards by divisions for your company?

## WHO SHOULD BE THINKING?
## SHOULD YOU?

Large capital outlays call for decisions by top management—the Chairman, the President and other senior officers. The Financial Vice-President, or whoever carries out his responsibilities, plays a major part. He must have the knowledge to establish and justify minimum Profit Goals and be able to apply them. The directors must understand the subject in order to give their approval to projects intelligently.

In a large company, many staff people will have to do the preparatory work. If they are incorrectly oriented, they may present data to top management which will appear correct on the surface, but which may have serious underlying errors.

In fact, we suggest that if a company is to function properly, the general ideas expressed in this book should become second nature to everyone in management having to make decisions regarding total capital management.

Furthermore, a whole company will operate better if top management sees to it that plant managers, engineers, and others on the firing line are conversant with the subject. They will recognize the importance of striving to avoid capital waste, rather than being irritated when they fail to receive approval of projects which look good to the uninitiated. This understanding will make them better members of the team. This subject should be part of a company's training program.

The same principles apply to a privately-owned company as to one publicly-owned. The owner of a privately-owned company can run his company at a loss if he chooses to do so, since it is his property. Presumably, he will wish to run it so as to make the same profit as though his capital were invested in a similar type of publicly-owned company. Thus, a privately-owned company should apply the same principles. As will be seen later, a privately-owned company may have to seek different sources of evidence in order to arrive at a minimum goal, but this does not change the principles.

The return on capital of the public utilities, air lines, and railroads is regulated by local, state or federal agencies. Such companies should be allowed the opportunity to earn an adequate return. Their investors and their consumers are dependent on enlightened government regulation. Regulators must understand the principles which determine an adequate return. Basically, the same principles apply to regulated industry as to unregulated, since regulation is supposed to be a substitute for competition.

With the vast amount of government work which private industry is performing today, there is an increasing number of government officials who must pass on the reasonableness of prices paid to industry. This involves, in one form or another, a consideration of the profits which companies should make on capital. Officials cannot hope to be fair without some understanding about profits.

Whether right or wrong, more and more politicians, our elected representatives, are looking over the shoulder of management with regard to prices and profits. They must be helped toward a better understanding.

Investors should understand the subject thoroughly. They should be able to ask searching questions about a company's policy regarding return on capital, capital expenditures, acquisitions and profit goals.

Labor should receive its just rewards in terms of an increasing standard of living and more stability of employment. To achieve this goal, labor must understand that companies will do better if they are profitable—it leads to better pay and more jobs. In wage negotiations, labor leaders must be sympathetic to the need for a satisfactory profit rate.

The press, which is such a vital link in keeping our society informed, needs understanding in order to tell the story correctly to the average citizen and voter.

The fact is that if our system of private capital is going to function properly and survive, practically everyone should have some knowledge of the subject. Unfortunately, the large majority of our population does not have any clear concept of how our profit system works and its advantages over other systems. Businessmen should seek opportunities to create a more knowledgeable atmosphere for business to live in. Our schools, from high school through college, are a field where help is badly needed.

## FOR YOU, THE MANAGEMENT

The last few paragraphs sound as though we were getting ready to mount a soap box. Not so! This book is designed for you, the management. It is strictly a practical book to use in decision-making.

Insofar as possible, every effort has been exerted to make this book more readable. With this in mind, we have included introductory material at the start of four of the more difficult chapters for those who wish to obtain a quick general picture. From these introduc-

tions, you should be able to tell how much you need to read in those chapters. Furthermore, in order not to clutter up the main part of the book, we have relegated some details to the Appendix. You can refer to this material as your interest indicates.

This book is written so that those only slightly acquainted with finance may obtain an understanding of the subject. Nevertheless, the greater a person's financial knowledge, the more readily this book can be absorbed because the subject is truly a part of finance. Some understanding of security analysis is helpful. As will be seen later, we will be dealing with rates for securities and their quality in the competitive capital market. These are both determined by security analysis.

We do not suggest that this book is easy. On the contrary, many of the concepts may be new to you and some are complicated. Therefore, it will only be fun and a benefit if you are willing to put on your thinking cap and do two things:

Follow through some ABC types of explanations. This is necessary in order to be able to see the ultimate effect of the principles involved.

Have the patience to review the concepts until their significance is etched into your mind.

## THE AIM OF THE BOOK

Since this book is concerned with capital management, it will cover both existing capital and also new capital expenditures.

With regard to existing capital, management must try to maximize profits, have some way to measure performance, and be willing to weigh the advisability of liquidation. For new capital expenditures, management must measure the potential profit rate correctly and have a Profit Goal to use as a basis for a go or no go decision.

The book covers three topics. There is given below a brief comment on each one in order of presentation.

*Profit Goals*

This is concerned with the whole area of establishing a Profit Goal to use for capital expenditure decisions, the basis for the Goal and its size. Other related subjects are included: industry's earnings record, false ideas in evaluating acquisitions, the ways in which earnings per share increase, etc. In all its aspects, this is the principal topic of the book, and occupies the material in 14 out of 16 chapters.

*Profitability Rate*

This deals with the methodology for determining the profit rate on a new venture. Calculations for plant liquidation involve many of the same principles and they are also touched on.

*Profit Performance Standards*

This discusses some of the considerations involved in establishing profit performance standards for existing plants by divisions.

The techniques of corporate management have greatly improved in many areas. However, capital management is the foundation of sound corporate management and with the increasing dependence of industry on capital, capital management requires ever greater understanding and continuing improvement in its application. That is the reason for this book.

*CHAPTER II*

# Profit Goals:
# Framework for Thinking

## PROFITS THE KEY

Profits perform a major function in our system of private capital: they are the catalyst, the incentive, or the "carrot." They must and do fit into the ultimate purpose of our economic system. This purpose is to produce the most goods and services so as to improve our standard of living. In spite of its faults, there is no doubt that our free enterprise profit-incentive system has proven to be the most productive in the world. Improvement in handling of profits as a guide and as an incentive will improve our entire society.

Profits are dependent on prices and we cannot duck the elementary economic principle that prices are determined by supply and demand. Once plants are built, the potential sup-ply of goods from these plants is relatively fixed. New supplies, however, are determined by capital expenditures. If a company has an adequate Profit Goal it will avoid adding to the supply of goods unnecessarily and forcing prices and profits down below a satisfactory rate.

In 1924, Donaldson Brown, a Vice-President of General Motors, stated in an article entitled, "Pricing Policy in Relation to Financial Control":

> . . . a sound pricing policy must be founded upon a clear conception of what might be implied in the phrase, economic return attainable upon the capital required.[1]

[1] *Management and Administration*, Volume 7, No. 4, April 1924.

Therefore, it should be appreciated that the amount of expansion affects supply, and thus prices. And to the extent that a certain profit is looked upon as a required cost, the contemplated return is one of the determinants of price in an expansion program.

Many factors have to be weighed in an expansion program, but prospects of profits are the final guide. The management of a leading corporation put it this way:

> . . . Management's principal control over capital outlays involves rigorous attention given before authorization to the expected profit return after tax on the capital to be employed.[2]

This book proceeds on this premise and first tries to answer the question: What should be your after-tax Profit Goal to justify expansion —10%, 15%, 20% or more?

## WHAT SHOULD BE THE BASIS FOR A GOAL?

If you are one of the senior officers of a company, you know the Profit Goals for your

[2] *Variability of Private Investment in Plant and Equipment,* Materials submitted to the Joint Economic Committee Congress of the United States (87th Congress, 2nd Session). Part II, "Some Elements Shaping Investment Decisions." Appendix A, page 25, "Capital Expenditure Policies and Procedures" submitted by executives of the Armstrong Cork Company.

company. You may have questioned whether they are too low or too high. Have you ever asked yourself on what basis the goals were established? You must be able to answer this question before you can decide on the propriety of these Profit Goals.

Before we suggest the direction in which you might look for a goal, we will review the various goals that some managements believe have value, but which are actually unsound. Some of them are so obviously wrong that you will not consider them worthy of a second thought. Others may seem reasonable and their error only becomes apparent after complete discussion of the subject. In fact, you may be inclined to say that questioning the validity of the last goal mentioned below—increasing present common stock earnings per share—shows that this book itself must be incorrectly oriented. This review may help to challenge your thinking on the subject.

### Profit as a Per Cent of Sales—No

This is a pet approach by some people in the retail field. Since they are merchants, they have been trained in terms of markups. They find it difficult to orient themselves to the fact that in the final analysis profits must be related to the amount of capital employed.

For example, if two plants, such as A and B shown in Exhibit 1 (II), are similar in all re-

## EXHIBIT 1 (II)

### PROFIT ON CAPITAL VERSUS PROFIT ON SALES

|                   | Plant A      | Plant B      |
| ----------------- | ------------ | ------------ |
| Sales             | $10,000,000  | $10,000,000  |
| Profit after taxes | $    400,000 | $    400,000 |
| Profit on sales   | 4%           | 4%           |
| Capital           | $4,000,000   | $5,000,000   |
| Profit on capital | 10%          | 8%           |

spects except for the amount of capital investment, they represent quite a different picture as far as profitability is concerned.

Profit on sales may be a helpful management tool for some purposes, but it is wholly inadequate as a guide to expansion. Expansion requires capital, and it is capital that ultimately requires profits.

## Interest Rate on Long-Term Debt—No

It is fairly natural to think of the minimum Profit Goal as the cost associated with the interest rate that has to be paid on some form of borrowed capital such as a bond—say 5% or 6%. This is probably the most popular false goal.

A goal based on this idea will produce disastrous results. What about the common stockholders if the company only achieved such a minimum goal and just earned its interest or slightly over its interest—would this be adequate? The interest-cost concept overlooks the rate that should be earned on the common stock so that there will be an adequate return to the stockholders.

## Interest Rate on Long-Term Debt and Dividends on Common—No

If you believe that a company should pay some dividends to its stockholders as well as the interest on its debt, then at least you do not overlook the common stockholders completely. However, this criterion is totally inadequate as a measure for a goal. Dividend policy can be changed at the will of management. If two identical companies had different dividend policies, their goals would be different. And suppose a company had no debt and paid no dividends—what then, a zero goal? Of course, one of the real reasons dividends are no measure of a goal is the fact that they ignore the importance of earnings to the stockholders.

## Company's Experienced Return on Capital—No

The per cent return of profits on capital that a company has experienced is an interesting figure to study in evaluating how well a company has performed. However, should this historical return on capital be used as a minimum goal? Again no! It represents what has occurred; it is a result, not a goal. If a company has had poor earnings, it would correspondingly have a low goal and tend to perpetuate its failure. On the other hand, if it had high earnings, it might think it should forego profitable investments unless the past high rate were duplicated. Thus, a company's record of earnings in relation to capital leaves unsolved the problem as to what rate of return is correct as a minimum goal. Neither can the record of other companies in the industry be used directly as the basis for a goal, although they may be of real interest for comparative purposes.

Carrying this one step further, some managements seem to feel that the goal for new capital expenditures should be to improve the experienced return on capital. This fails for the same reason already discussed. Supposing that the experienced return is totally inadequate, a goal which will produce a small improvement will still be inadequate. The problem of what the goal should be is still unsolved.

## Increasing Present Common Stock Earnings Per Share—No

This is one goal which many businessmen, as well as financial analysts, consider sound. Managements reason that they are working for the common stockholders and that any increase in present earnings per share is worthwhile. We do not dispute the fact that management should watch this figure carefully and attempt to increase earnings per share, but it is not that simple. Suppose an industrial company, earning only 6% on its total capital and $1.00 per share on its common stock, is considering an expansion program which will increase earnings per share to $1.10. The question immediately arises as to whether this is a sufficient increase to justify the project. Merely increasing present earnings per share in itself is not the answer. There must be an adequate increase in earnings per share, but what is adequate? If you hesitate to believe that increasing present earnings per share is an unreliable goal, we will cover this subject in Chapter XI, after we have presented the material necessary to understand the basis of our reasoning.

## A SIMPLE STATEMENT OF THE BASIS—COST-OF-CAPITAL

Where will we look for the answer to a Profit Goal? We suggest that Cost-of-Capital is the starting point.

It is interesting to note that Donaldson Brown, in the 1924 article about pricing policy mentioned earlier, stated that ". . . the fundamental consideration is the economic Cost-of-Capital to the individual business."

By Cost-of-Capital, we do not mean just an interest-cost. A company obtains its capital through various types of long-term securities, such as bonds, preferred stock, and common stock. There is a competitive market for all types of securities, just as there is a competive market for goods and services. Furthermore, each type of security has an economic cost. If a company uses more than one type of security, it is necessary to obtain a weighted average cost, or in other words, a composite cost. As a mark of success, a company's earnings should exceed the minimum cost rate which investors require to induce them to purchase each type of security, including common stock.

Cost-of-Capital includes two elements:

1. One element is the amount necessary to induce people to invest and save their money rather than hold it idle or spend it. This is what is known as pure interest.

2. The other is the amount necessary to compensate investors for the risk of the investment.

Therefore, our problem is essentially one of assessing *the risk of an enterprise as it is judged in the competitive capital market through Cost-of-Capital.* You must focus on the capital market because that is where capital has to be obtained.

The idea would be easy to understand and calculate if all capital consisted of debt. Debt obviously has a cost; the cost is the interest rate. The problem becomes difficult because of the common equity part of our capital. This is the real teaser with which we will have to struggle.

An understanding of the concept of Cost-of-Capital and, equally important, the principles which flow from it, is absolutely essential to correct decision-making in the entire area of capital expenditures, acquisitions, and plant abandonment. There is no other way in which management can be sure that its capital decisions will prove consistently beneficial to its stockholders in the future.

## WHERE DO WE START?

In order to have a base for our thinking, we will start with a look at a balance sheet and an income statement. Our purpose will be to illustrate how capital flows into our corporations. Also, since we will be working with capital, we want to show at this point on what parts of capital we will be focusing our attention. This may seem elementary, but it is often lost sight of.

There is shown in Exhibit 2 (II) a balance sheet in summary form with long-term capital equal to 100. Any balance sheet can be treated in a similar fashion. So that you will not think we are dealing in theory, and so that you can apply the idea to your company, there is given in Appendix A an actual balance sheet in complete detail, a summarized version, and a version adjusted so that long-term capital equals 100. There is also included in Appendix A an actual income statement and an explanation of how it can be summarized so that it ties in with the balance sheet with long-term capital equal to 100.

We show "Other Items" as "0." If they are large, they will have to be given special consideration in order to decide how to handle them. Generally, they are small and can be disregarded.

We could spend hours talking about all of

## EXHIBIT 2 (II)

### BALANCE SHEET SUMMARIZED WITH LONG-TERM CAPITAL EQUAL 100

| Assets | | | Liabilities | | | |
|---|---|---|---|---|---|---|
| Current Assets | $100 | | Current Liabilities | | | $ 50 |
| Plant, net | 50 | | Long-Term Capital | | | |
| | | | Debt | $20 | | |
| | | | Common Equity | 80 | 100 | |
| Other Items | 0 | | Other Items | | | 0 |
| Total | $150 | | | | | $150 |

the different types of long-term securities that can be used to raise capital. However, we can simplify our thinking at this point if we boil them all down to two basic types: debt and equity. The debt category includes mortgage bonds, debentures, long-term notes, etc. There are two divisions of equity: preferred and common stock. For the present we will skip

preferred stock. There are various parts to common equity: the stated or par value, capital surplus and earned surplus. They should all be lumped together. We will have more to say about this in Chapter V.

The relationship between the two sides of the balance sheet must be clearly visualized. This is illustrated in Exhibit 3 (II). It is im-

## EXHIBIT 3 (II)

### COMPANY LONG-TERM CAPITAL - SOURCE AND USE

| You use long-term capital here: | | You obtain long-term capital here: | | |
|---|---|---|---|---|
| Working Capital | $ 50 | Long-Term Capital | | |
| Plant, Net | 50 | Debt | $ 20 | |
| Total | $100 | Common Equity | 80 | |
| | | Total | $100 | |

Working capital is the difference between current assets $100 and current liabilities $50.

In effect, part of current assets are provided by current liabilities and the difference, which is working capital, by long-term capital.

This is how the savings of our nation flow into corporations through the sale of securities and through the retention of earnings in earned surplus, which belongs to the common stockholders.

When we calculate Cost-of-Capital we will be working with long-term capital.

portant that the rate obtained on the right-hand side for long-term capital be correctly applied to the assets on the left. Some managements seem to think that they only need to earn an adequate return on fixed assets—that is, on plant. Not so! In order to operate, practically all companies need some working capital. The working capital is obtained from the same source as plant—long-term securities. More will be said about this subsequently.

## AN ALL-DEBT CAPITAL STRUCTURE TO ASSIST IN EXPLANATION

To get into the explanation of Cost-of-Capital, let's take a unique view. For the mo-ment let's reason in terms of debt securities since we can probably agree that debt has an actual cost. This will permit us to avoid at this point the intricate question of the cost of common stock. Furthermore, this gymnastic will illustrate that all capital has a cost.

We will carry out this idea in three steps. In Step 1, we will start with $20 of debt and $80 of common equity. Let's say that this first layer of debt consists of mortgage bonds. If we assign an interest rate of 5% to them, the picture would be as shown in Exhibit 4 (II).

Forget about the tax savings that interest produces; we are now talking only about the rates that investors require, and they do not pay the corporate tax; that is taken care of

EXHIBIT 4 (II)

STEP 1, ALL-DEBT CAPITAL STRUCTURE ILLUSTRATION

|  | Amount | Rate | Cost |
|---|---|---|---|
| Debt (mortgage bonds) | $ 20 | 5% | $1.00 |
| Common Equity | 80 | | |
| Total | $100 | | |

by the company. We will cover the effect of interest on corporate taxes subsequently.

As a second step, let's change the composition of our capital structure and substitute a layer of $30 of junior debt in place of $30 of the common equity. This second layer of debt we will call unsecured debentures. Since the added debt would be junior to our first layer and in a more risky position, it would require a higher interest rate. For illustrative purposes we will use 6%. Then the picture would be as shown in Exhibit 5 (II).

EXHIBIT 5 (II)

STEP 2, ALL-DEBT CAPITAL STRUCTURE ILLUSTRATION

|  | Amount | Rate | Cost |
|---|---|---|---|
| Debt (mortgage bonds) | $ 20 | 5% | $1.00 |
| Junior Debt (unsecured debentures) | 30 | 6% | $1.80 |
| Common Equity | 50 | | |
| Total | $100 | | |

For an industrial company, we have already added much more debt than would be wise from the point of view of sound financial pol-icy, but purely for the purpose of illustrating the idea of Cost-of-Capital, let's go one step further and substitute a third layer of subordinated junior debt for $49 of common. This third layer we will call subordinated unsecured debentures. It ranks below both the $20 of debt (mortgage bonds) and $30 of junior debt (unsecured debentures).

We have referred to the three different layers of debt in rather elaborate terms to make it clear that the second layer is in a junior position to the first, and that the third layer is junior to both the first and second. Each junior layer has more risk than the preceding one and for this reason requires a higher interest rate.

Now all our capital structure is in the form of debt, except for $1 of common. We will leave $1 of common equity because someone has to own the company.

No ordinary investor would purchase such risky debt as the third layer of subordinated junior debt with only 1% of common equity to protect it. Any interest rate we assign to it would be a pure guess. But, if we did try to sell it, the type of investor who might be interested would be a so-called "money-lender." If you have ever heard about the rates they charge, you are aware of their exorbitance. At least, it is not inconceivable that with 99% debt the rate on the third layer of subordinated junior debt might be between 10% and 20%; let's use 15%. Then the cost of our capital would be as shown in Exhibit 6 (II).

Leaving out any cost for the $1 of common and using merely the debt costs as above, the

## EXHIBIT 6 (II)

### STEP 3, ALL-DEBT CAPITAL STRUCTURE ILLUSTRATION

|                                                              | Amount | Rate | Cost |
|--------------------------------------------------------------|--------|------|------|
| Debt (mortgage bonds)                                        | $ 20   | 5%   | $1.00 |
| Junior Debt (unsecured debentures)                           | 30     | 6%   | 1.80 |
| Subordinated Junior Debt (subordinated unsecured debentures) | 49     | 15%  | 7.35 |
| Common Equity                                                | 1      |      |      |
| Total                                                        | $100   |      | $10.15- Approx. 10% |

weighted average cost for 99% of our capital is over 10%.

Why did we use this approach as a start at explaining Cost-of-Capital? To show the following:

1. All capital has a cost, whether it be debt or equity. In the three capital structures mentioned, with different amounts of debt there were different debt costs, but it should be clear that merely substituting debt for equity or vice versa does not change the fact that there is a cost to all capital. Observe the illogical position in which we would be placed if we

maintained that only the debt part of capital structure had a cost. With 50% bonds, and 50% equity, would we then have a cost for only 50% of our capital? If bonds were reduced to 20% and the equity increased to 80%, would we then have a cost for only 20%? If we changed the capital structure to all common stock can we say that capital has no cost? That would be ridiculous. Common equity does not have an interest cost as debt does, but it does have an economic cost. It is merely measured differently and with more difficulty.

2. Capital is not cheap. As the debt becomes

more junior, the interest rate must rise because of the added risk. Common stock has all the risk with no junior security protecting it, and, in fact, it must provide protection for the senior securities. Therefore, when we calculate the common cost, we should be prepared to expect a relatively high rate.

3. The rate we are seeking for a Cost-of-Capital is the weighted average cost of all capital. It is referred to as the "composite cost." It is the composite rate which must be used as a basis for setting a Profit Goal. Even if a particular project is financed with debt, the composite rate still must be used because, as a practical matter, debt money cannot be raised without equity for protection. In other words, in applying a rate to assets, we cannot say that some assets were supplied with debt money and some with equity, regardless of how they were financed.[3]

Finally, it is interesting to visualize what would happen if all capital for every company were in the form of debt. Then managements would readily be able to calculate their Cost-of-Capital. They would have to set Profit Goals above Cost-of-Capital when they expanded. If they did not earn the Cost-of-Capital they would be bankrupt. If they just earned their Cost-of-Capital they would show no profit. Such a type of capital structure would

mean real discipline for managements. Of course, this is impractical, and in fact, a conservative financial policy is far better than too much debt. However, because capital structures must include common equity, on which there is no fixed or obvious cost, managements may become confused as to the basis for a Profit Goal. Furthermore, they can continue to expand without achieving an adequate return.

Subsequently, we will discuss these points more fully.

## BACK TO OUR ORIGINAL CAPITAL STRUCTURE

In order to see the outline of the picture before we try to explain it, let's switch back to our original capital structure which included common stock. We will arbitrarily assign rates of 5% interest to the debt and 11% to the common stock. Then the composite Cost-of-Capital would be about 10%, as shown in Exhibit 7 (II). This approximate figure of 10% might apply to a large, well-situated industrial company.

If, as shown above, we represent the parts of long-term capital as percentages of 100%, and apply cost rates to each component, and then total the products, we obtain a composite rate for the entire capital structure. The result

### EXHIBIT 7 (II)

### COMPOSITE COST-OF-CAPITAL

|  | Amount | | Rate | Cost |
|---|---|---|---|---|
| Debt | $ 20 | 20% | 5% | 1.00 |
| Common Equity | 80 | 80 | 11 | 8.80 |
| Total | $100 | 100% | | 9.80- |
|  |  |  |  | Approximately 10% |

[3] This is different from the question of comparing the relative merits of different types of securities such as lease financing versus debt financing. For that purpose, we must compare like securities, or, if unlike, then allow for the difference.

is the same as if we applied cost rates to the dollar amount of each part of long-term capital and divided the total by the total long-term capital to get the composite rate. We will generally use the former procedure through-out this book.

## THREE RATES

Throughout the book we will be talking about three rates as outlined below.

### Cost-of-Capital

This rate we have already discussed. It is the basis for the other two rates.

### Return on Total Capital Target

This is the return which a company sets as its target for its total long-term capital. It represents what a company hopes to achieve.

A company should earn something above Cost-of-Capital in order to show a true profit above all costs. This is an incentive for management to do a good job for the investor.

For industrial companies, good managements may try to achieve a rate above strict cost—1%, 2%, 3% or more. Of course, a company should attempt to earn as much as it can on existing investment in keeping with good business judgment and the competitive situation.

### Profit Goal for Expansion

The Profit Goal for Expansion, which is also referred to simply as the "Profit Goal," is used as a cutoff rate for expansion projects or acquisitions. It will vary depending on the risk in each project.

Managements of industrial companies will have to set the Profit Goal higher than either of the other two rates for many reasons. How high the Profit Goal should be above Cost-of-Capital will vary with the circumstances. It has been reported [4] that some major companies have used as high as 20% after taxes as a Profit Goal in some situations. The question of the spread between the Profit Goal and Cost-of-Capital will be reviewed in detail in Chapter VI.

[4] *Variability of Private Investment in Plant and Equipment,* Materials submitted to the Joint Economic Committee Congress of the United States (87th Congress, 2nd Session). Part II, "Some Elements Shaping Investment Decisions," page 14.

## SOME COMPOSITE RATES BEFORE THE EXPLANATION

In order to give you an idea of the end result that we will be working towards, we present in Exhibit 8 (II) figures in summary form for three different types of businesses which have distinctly different risks. They are for large, well-established companies. Two regulated industries, electric and telephone utilities, are included because much work has been done in the utility field and, because of their more stable nature, they give us good reference points for our thinking about companies with greater risk. In the case of the utilities the figures given are for the Return on Total Capital Target. These companies are regulated on the basis of their return on investment, and these are the figures with which they are primarily concerned. When the utilities consider an individual project, they will generally use the Return on Total Capital Target as the rate they require because of the similarity of risk from project to project.

In general, the rates shown in Exhibit 8 (II) apply to total capital after taxes for investors. We refer to them as To Investor Rates; we will discuss how taxes apply in Chapter VI.

We will be concentrating our efforts primarily on unregulated types of businesses. Therefore, before leaving these figures, we will say a few words about the nature of the risks of the electric and telephone utility industries which justify their lower rates as compared with industrial companies.

The electric industry is one of the most stable types of businesses and has many favorable economic characteristics. Its earnings record has been good. It has been able to go through the entire inflationary period subsequent to World War II with only minor increases in rates. It has withstood business recessions remarkably well. Relatively, it represents the type of business which falls in the lower risk group. Some regulatory commissions have indicated that they believe that the return on total capital should be about 6%. To provide a satisfactory profit, it should be

## EXHIBIT 8 (II)

## SOME COMPOSITE RATES

| | Cost-of-Capital | Return on Total Capital Target[a] | Profit Goal for Expansion |
|---|---|---|---|
| Industrial companies average | 10% | 10% Plus 1%, 2% 3% or more | Up to 20% |
| Telephone utility | | 8% | |
| Electric utility | | 6 3/4% to 7% | |

[a] These returns are based on average interest rates for debt securities. There has been a substantial increase in the general level of interest rates in recent years. If this increase continues, it will increase the composite rates which will be required. This will have the most effect on the utilities because a higher proportion of their long-term capital consists of debt. Also it is possible that a prolonged high level of interest rates may have some effect on increasing the rate that common stockholders require because of the alternative investment considerations.

higher, in the neighborhood of 6¾% to 7%.[5]

The telephone industry is not as attractive economically as the electric industry. Wages absorb about 40% of revenues, which is about twice the percentage of the electric industry. The telephone industry has some aspects of increasing costs. It has only one type of appliance to promote as compared to the many types of appliances which use electricity, and it must do all the promotion itself. Consequently, the telephone industry has more inherent risk than the electric industry. The American Telephone & Telegraph System has done much work on this subject and feels that, because of the greater risk as compared with an electric utility company, it should earn in the neighborhood of 8%[6] on total capital.

[5] A public utility should be allowed to earn a fair return on a rate base giving effect to present reproduction cost or, at least, fair value in order to allow for any change in the value of the dollar.

[6] *New York Herald Tribune,* June 2, 1965. Article covering speech made by Mr. John Scanlon, Vice-President and Treasurer of American Telephone & Telegraph Company, before the New York Society of Security Analysts: ". . . AT&T has earned on the average of about 7½% on its capital annually since 1958. . . . He said about 8% would be a reasonable return."

The point illustrated here is the step-up in rate from electric to telephone with the added risk. If you are at all familiar with the nature of these two industries, you should expect an increase in Cost-of-Capital for industrial companies because of their greater risk.

## TOUGH QUESTIONS
## WE WILL NEED TO ANSWER

We have alluded to some of the difficulties encountered in determining Cost-of-Capital. Undoubtedly, major questions for which you require answers are:

Does common really have a cost?
How can common cost be measured?
What capital structure should be used?

With these first two chapters to point the way, we are now ready to focus more closely on our subject. In the next four chapters we will develop the concepts of Cost-of-Capital and Profit Goals. While this may seem to be a lot of territory to cover in order to build your working tools, it is essential if you wish to use them in decision-making.

*CHAPTER III*

# Common Cost

## PART I—WHAT IS IT?

## PART II—MEASUREMENT

# Part I—What Is It?

## INTRODUCTION

From what has already been said it is clear that determining a composite Cost-of-Capital requires first establishing a capital structure, then determining the rates for the senior securities and the common equity and finally combining these rates on a weighted average basis. Since our major problem is common cost and it has the highest cost, we will reverse the process and start with it. It is the essential ingredient. In fact, this chapter is basic to understanding capital management.

The rate for the common stock, and in fact for each type of security, should be representative of how investors evaluate the risk for the security as effected by:

The business itself.

The amount and terms of the other securities of the particular capital structure.

### Does Common Have a Cost?

Your reaction may still be: "Who ever heard of common stock having a cost?"

We reply: "It does not have an accounting cost, and it does not have a cost in the sense that debt has an interest cost. However, common stockholders have to be satisfied and common stock does have a cost in the economic sense. The rate can be expressed as a percentage, just as the debt cost is expressed as a percentage interest rate."

Some people contend that it is a misnomer and confuses the picture to use the term "cost." They prefer to say that common has an "earnings requirement." Whatever terminology you prefer, you must arrive at a rate to apply to the common equity.

### Importance of Future Earnings

For a debt security, such as a bond, it is the expectation of receiving interest payments in the future and repayment of the principal amount at maturity that attracts investors to pay a price for a bond. We emphasize that it is the prospect of future interest payments which induces investors to buy a bond. Past payments are over the dam.

What is it that attracts common stockholders to pay a price for common stock? In essence, stockholders receive two things: future dividends and market appreciation—the difference between the price at which they buy the stock and the price at which they sell it. It is these two elements, both in the future, that induce investors to pay a price for common stock.

Where do both dividends and market appreciation come from? They both derive from future earnings per share. In total, it is the expectation of future earnings per share which induces investors to buy a stock and which determines the price they will pay. It is the relationship of market price to the expected future earnings per share that is the guide to the common cost. We will try to build up gradually to the full meaning of this concept.

On the basis of what has been said, if a stock earns $10 per share and sells at $100 per share, the apparent cost rate for the common would be $10 divided by $100 or 10%. This is similar to the situation for a bond which sells at $100. If it pays $5 interest, the cost rate would be 5%. Presumably, in this simple example, if the company continued to earn $10 per share the stock would continue to sell at $100. The company would be just earning the rate that investors required in the competitive capital market. Unfortunately, it is not quite this simple.

Suppose we have a bond which matures in two years and pays 4% interest the first year and 6% the second year. What would be the cost rate for the bond? Would it be 4%—the relationship of price to interest being paid immediately? Hardly. It would be the relationship of price to a combination of all future payments. A simple average of future payments would give us 5%. Similarly, if a stock were expected to earn $8 next year and $12 the year after, it would be some combination of the two figures which would determine the price of the stock. This would be the basis to use as the cost rate.

The important point we are stressing is that the common cost is the relationship of market price to *future* earnings rather than to present earnings per share. Present earnings are past

earnings once a stock is purchased; all gain to the stockholder comes from future earnings. Past and present earnings may be some guide to future earnings, but they are not what benefits the common stockholder and they are not what he buys. This idea is summarized in Exhibit 1 (III).

Without going into minor refinements, it is the future earnings in Column 3 and not the present earnings in Column 2 which determine the market prices and thus the cost rates shown in Column 4.

EXHIBIT 1 (III)

COMMON COST DEPENDS ON EXPECTED EARNINGS

| Column<br>Company | 1<br>Market Price<br>of Stock | 2<br>Present<br>Earnings<br>Per Share | 3<br>Expected<br>Future Earnings<br>Per Share | 4<br>Common<br>Cost |
|---|---|---|---|---|
| A | $100 | $ 5.00 | $10 | 10% |
| B | $100 | $10.00 | $10 | 10% |
| C | $100 | $20.00 | $10 | 10% |

*Investors' Expectations*

There is another more subtle point with regard to the common cost. There are actually three earnings per share from which we have

to choose in order to arrive at a definition of the common cost. This can be illustrated by the simple figures shown in Exhibit 2 (III).

For items C and D, that is, $8 and $10, we

EXHIBIT 2 (III)

INVESTORS' EXPECTATIONS

| | | |
|---|---|---|
| A. | Price of stock | $100 |
| B. | Present earnings per share | $ 5 |
| C. | Potential earnings per share<br>estimated by company | $ 8 |
| D. | Potential earnings per share<br>expected by investors | $ 10 |

have used single figures to represent future earnings per share. Actually, future earnings will be a stream over a period of years rather than one single figure.

What is it that makes investors pay $100 per share for the stock—the $5, $8 or $10?

The stock sells at 20 times the present earnings per share of $5. The reciprocal, or earnings-price ratio, is 5%. The greatest misconception about the common cost is that it is this 5% figure. Such a misconception leads managements to believe that the common stockholders will necessarily be benefited if the earnings per share of $5 are increased, even a small amount, by an expansion program or an acquisition. This might not be true. The $5 reported present earnings per share is already history when a stock is purchased.

It is not the $8 per share estimated by the management which determines the market price of the stock because that estimate is known only to management. It is a secret: managements generally do not give out such forecasts. Secrets cannot affect public market prices. It is the investors who buy and sell the stock who affect the market price.

The investors' expectation of $10 is what makes market price. Thus, the cost rate for common has to be based on the price *investors* pay for a stock related to the earnings that *they* expect to receive in the future. The approximate rate based on Exhibit 2 (III) is as follows:

$$\text{Common Cost} = \frac{D}{A} = \frac{\$10}{\$100} = 10\%$$

We qualified this rate by the word "approximate" because we have to allow for financing costs, which will be discussed shortly.

Eventually, if the company's estimate proves to be correct, investors will revise their expectations from $10 to $8. Consequently, the price of the stock will fall to $80 per share. The common cost will still be 10%.

As to the size of the common cost, it must be substantially higher than debt cost because the common stock is in the more risky posi-

tion in the capital structure. Debt is protected by the common stock and has its risk reduced thereby. A common stock of a well-established large company with a conservative capital structure may have a minimum cost in the neighborhood of 11%.

If your business is very risky, your common cost as well as your overall cost will be higher. So will the common cost be higher for a company with a large proportion of senior securities, or for a small company. Foreign investment adds substantially to the risk.

If you do not have time to read the rest of this chapter, that will be fine, providing you can accept the idea that common cost is large. Furthermore, you should be able to switch away from the concept of accounting profit and accept the fact that a company is losing money for its stockholders if it expands and does not earn the common cost. To make a profit it should earn more. We admit that these are categorical statements. If you question their validity, you will want more than just this introduction. The remainder of this chapter provides explanations and statistical data.

## FINANCING COSTS

Getting deeper into the subject of common cost, we have to add another point. Thus far, to simplify the picture, we have left out financing costs. If a common stock sells for $100 per share in the market and the company sold some new stock, the net amount it would receive per share would be less than the $100 because of such factors as financing costs and the pressure of the new issue.

There are two methods of selling common stock: direct offerings to the public, or through rights to existing stockholders. Somewhat different costs are associated with each method, but in determining Cost-of-Capital it seems appropriate to allow for sufficient cost so that the company would be able to use the rights method if it were required to do so by statute or charter, or if it chose to do so for the good of the stockholders where it had the alternative.

The measurement of financing costs in a rights offering is complicated. One consideration is the need to set the subscription price sufficiently below the market price so that the rights will have some value. Also, allowance has to be made for financing expenses such as printing the prospectus, legal and accounting fees, etc., and the investment banker's charge if the issue is underwritten. The size of the overall financing cost may vary depending on many factors such as the condition of the stock market, the nature of the company, and the quality and size of the issue.

As a rough rule of thumb, for Cost-of-Capital purposes we can use a figure of 10% of the market price for a large, relatively stable company like an electric utility and a slightly higher figure of 15% of the market price for a large well-situated industrial company. Financing costs for a small company will generally be higher. A new venture may require all kinds of payments for financing costs, including special compensation to the underwriter in the form of stock options, warrants, etc. It is hard to give any specific figures for such situations. Throughout the book, we will use either 10% or 15%, as seems most appropriate, in calculating the financing costs for the common cost.

Our illustration above for common cost would have to be modified for financing costs as shown in Exhibit 3 (III).

## EXHIBIT 3 (III)

### COMMON COST

| | | |
|---|---|---|
| A. | Market price of a company's stock | $100 |
| B. | Less 15% allowance for financing costs | $ 15 |
| C. | Net proceeds to company | $ 85 |
| D. | Present earnings per share | $ 5 |
| E. | Potential earnings per share estimated by company | $ 8 |
| F. | Potential earnings per share expected by investors | $ 10 |

$$\text{Common Cost} = \frac{F}{C} = \frac{\$10}{\$85} = 11.8\%$$

## INVESTORS' TAXES?

Before we go further, we should eliminate an argument about taxes that is sometimes presented in rather vigorous fashion; that is, that taxes paid by investors should be taken into account in calculating the Cost-of-Capital.

Taxes which investors pay may affect the supply and demand for various types of securities. However, the effect is registered in the market prices. The company must meet the market rates.

A further point sometimes raised is, that earned surplus should be treated differently from earnings paid out in dividends because investors pay the full tax rate on dividends but none on the earnings that are retained. This, of course, is not completely true. Retained earnings build up the earnings base which should result in higher earnings. This in turn should result in market appreciation, on which some taxes have to be paid when the appreciation is realized. But, again the effect of taxes paid by investors will be reflected in the market price of the stock as a result of their appraisal of the worth of the returns to them giving effect to the taxes they pay. In any event, we are seeking to find the rates that the company must earn based on the market, not the rates adjusted by investors for the taxes they pay to obtain their effective net income.

To clarify the idea that we do not have to allow for the taxes paid by investors, consider the following example.

Interest on municipal bonds is exempt from Federal income taxes. Consequently, the interest rate investors require is relatively low. If the tax law were changed so that such interest were taxable, the interest rate that municipalities would have to pay on new financings would be increased through investors' reaction and corresponding change in demand. Let's put this in terms of figures. We will assume that a municipality could sell a tax-exempt bond to yield 3½% with the interest exempt from income taxes. Now assume that the tax laws are changed so that investors would have to pay income taxes on such interest. Then the interest rate that investors would be willing to accept would increase on the basis of supply and demand to reflect the rate they could get on similar quality corporate bonds subject to income taxes. Assume that this resulted in a 5% rate. The net income which investors obtained, after the tax law was changed, might be roughly the same as their return of 3½% when the bonds were tax-exempt. However, it would not follow that a municipality would only have to pay the net income that investors obtained; it would have to pay the full interest rate of 5%. Likewise a company has to determine the rates it has to pay investors without regard to the taxes the investors pay.

## IS RATE DETERMINED ON MARKET PRICE OR BOOK VALUE?

Even after there is an understanding of common cost, some confusion seems to linger regarding the relationship of market price and book value as the base for figuring the cost and how the rate figured on one ties together with the other.

The common cost must be based on market price because we wish to obtain the rate investors require in relation to the price they will pay. But this statement does not always clear up the matter. The question still remains: "How can the rate be obtained from the market price and then applied to book value?"

A simple example may help:

A company's capital structure consists solely of one share of common stock with a book value of $100 per share. Assume that the book value represents a true present value of the company's assets.

It earns 20% or $20 per share on the book value.

The stock sells for $200. If we assume that investors do not anticipate any growth, the common cost is 10%, leaving out financing costs to simplify the picture.

A company can earn only on the capital with which it has to work. It has $100 to work with, not the market price of $200.

In order to meet its Cost-of-Capital it would only have to earn 10% on the book value. In fact, it is doing much better so the stock sells well above book value.

The company needs to increase its capital for expansion purposes and sells one new share for $200. The book value will now be as follows:

|  | *Book Value* |
|---|---|
| Original Share | $100 |
| New Share | 200 |
| Total | $300 |
| Per Share | $150 |

If we assume that the company continues to earn 20% on the original $100 investment and just earns its 10% Cost-of-Capital on the new investment of $200, the earnings would be as follows:

|  | Book Value | Rate | Earnings |
|---|---|---|---|
| Original Share | $100 | 20% | $20 |
| New Share | 200 | 10 | 20 |
| Total | $300 | 13⅓% | $40 |
| Earnings Per Share |  |  | $20 |

With no change in risk as appraised by investors, the stock will sell at 10 times earnings or $200 per share.

So we conclude that the common cost must be obtained from the market price and not the book value the company must earn on assets. Note that at the beginning of the example we said that the book value represented a true present value of the company's assets. We will have more to say about the significance of return on book value later on.

Our example may raise a question in your mind as to what would happen if the original part of the business making 20% is gradually liquidated through depreciation. What happens is obvious. This lucrative investment will gradually be reduced to zero and the market price of the stock will fall.[1] Now the company has to decide what to do with the cash as it flows back. If the company invests it at the Cost-of-Capital rate, the stockholders will receive a return equivalent to the risk and the investment recaptured through depreciation will be preserved.

A company should earn more than the Cost-of-Capital, and to the extent that the investment of funds derived from depreciation does earn above the Cost-of-Capital, the stockholders' position would be improved. Only if the return on that investment reaches 20% will they be as well off as before. But the company

[1] It is possible that investors' appraisal of risk may be affected by a change in the rate earned on total capital depending on all the circumstances.

cannot be limited in its use of the cash by the 20% rate which was earned on a previous investment. Once the cash flows back the next step is a new and independent decision.

## DEFINITION OF COMMON COST

At this point, we will pause to give a comprehensive definition to common cost.

Our definition is more in the nature of an explanation and review in the hope of clearing up questions which may be plaguing you.

The common cost is determined as follows:

$$\frac{\text{Future earnings per share expected by investors}}{\text{Market price of stock, adjusted for financing costs}}$$

The figures which we have used to describe the common cost are shown in diagram form in Exhibit 4 (III). For comparative purposes, the bond cost, which we will cover in the next chapter, is also included.

The common cost should be calculated over a period of years, including both favorable and unfavorable market conditions. This will give a representative average current cost. Spot or short-term figures should be avoided. The period to use in determining cost rates is discussed in Chapter IV, Senior Capital Cost.

The common cost represents what investors require on the average in the way of future earning power in order to justify their paying the specific market prices they pay in view of their appraisal of the risk of the stock.

Throughout the book, we will use many examples involving common cost. They have to be based on investors' expectations. We will use a single figure for earnings per share to represent this concept. Actually, as already mentioned, investors' expectations consist of a stream of earnings rather than one figure and, generally, the stream will be on the increase. Using a single figure, with no growth, may seem unrealistic, but it is perfectly satisfactory for the purpose to which it will be put. So expect to see example after example with a heading "Earnings Per Share Expected By Investors" and a single figure underneath.

## EXHIBIT 4 (III)
## COST RATE ILLUSTRATION

### COMMON

Market price is a result
of investors' appraisal of
potential earning power,
not present earning per
share, or company estimates.

COMMON COST
$$\frac{\$10}{\$85} = 11.8\%$$

Potential earnings expected
by Investors — ($10)[a]

Potential earnings estimated
by Company — ($8)[a]

Market price
of stock               $100

Allowance for
financing costs        $ 15

Net proceeds to
company from
sale of new stock      $ 85

Present Earnings Per Share  $5

### BOND

BOND COST
5.13% yield to maturity

Market price
of bond                100%

Allowance for
financing costs        2%

Net proceeds
to company             98%

Future Interest Coupon 5% Payment at 100%
at maturity in 30 years

[a] The $10 and $8 figures are each supposed to represent in one figure the potential stream of future earnings per share.

## WHAT FOLLOWS FROM OUR DEFINITION?

If a company with long-term capital consisting only of common stock sells stock and uses the proceeds in an expansion program so as to earn the rate investors expect, the price of the stock will appreciate in keeping with the retained earnings. If the company earns less and investors' appraisal of the risk remains the same, the stock will ultimately fall in market price, regardless of the short-range action. The company will have misdirected capital so as not to provide a return commensurate with its cost.

By way of further explanation, let us think of this idea in terms of bonds. If a company sells bonds to investors it will have to offer an interest rate which will satisfy investors' appraisal of the risk in the bond. If the company sells a 30-year bond at $100 with a 6% interest rate, the bond will continue to sell at $100 (assuming stable interest rates in general) as long as the company continues to pay 6% and there is no change in investors' appraisal of the risk. Assuming, hypothetically, that the company could cut the interest rate at will and reduced it to 5%, the price of the bond would fall to about $86 so that the yield at the new price would be 6%. Investors would have lost money. The same idea applies to a common stock when a company fails to earn the common cost as measured in the competitive capital market by the relationship between market price and investors' expectations.

You may feel that investors' expectations are limitless and that a company could not hope to earn enough to satisfy them. If this troubles you, we have failed to make the point clear. If investors' expectations are high, then they will pay a correspondingly high price for the stock. To illustrate, suppose that investors would buy a 30-year bond at $100 with a 4% interest rate on the basis of their appraisal of the risk. For no good reason, let us suppose that the company decided to pay 6% interest.

Then in the competitive capital market the company could sell the bond at a price of about $135. The price would go up in proportion to their expectations. The yield to maturity to investors would still be the 4% rate they required in terms of their risk appraisal. Likewise, with common stocks, if investors' expectations are high, prices of stocks will be high. During a bull stock market the common cost may not decrease. The increase in the prices of stocks may be due to investors' optimism and an increase in their expectations.

By now, you should have a feeling as to why merely increasing present earnings per share is not necessarily the right goal for management to use in deciding on expansion and acquisition policies. Present earnings do not focus on the rate that the capital must return in order to satisfy the cost in the competitive capital market unless investors expect no growth when they buy a stock.

You may insist that, if a company's reported earnings per share increase, the price of the stock will increase. Therefore, we should concentrate on present earnings per share. You are right about the immediate market action. This is why we have to spend so much time on this point. Investors do have to place much reliance on trends in reported earnings to make their estimates of the future. However, regardless of past trends, if investors' expectations based on their appraisal of prospects for the company are not realized in the future, then the price of the stock will ultimately be bound to suffer.

If you go along with the explanation so far, we are over the worst of the hurdles. You may reply: "I agree with you about the importance of expected earnings in figuring the common cost, but now the hurdles look even more formidable. How can we ever measure investors' expectations and obtain a meaningful figure?" You are right, it is not easy! But we can come up with some pretty good figures. And now you have the background with which to face the figures.

# Part II—Measurement

So how the devil do we solve the mystery of determining investors' expectations?

What investors expect when they buy a stock may vary all the way from cold calculations based on long experience to pure fancy without any common sense. The market reflects all the different elements which bear on supply and demand. At any time it may be dominated by irrational actions. This is one reason why spot figures should not be relied on for a common cost.

Nevertheless, the only thing that investors receive from a stock is money, just as when they invest in a bond. The return they expect to receive and the risk they think they bear must determine the price they will pay. Over an extended period, the market price for common stocks must show some semblance of rationality; an investor always has the alternative of investing in bonds and receiving a protected return. We must seek our common cost on the basis of investors' rational appraisals of future expectations.

For some companies, we may be unable to measure the common cost because of the difficulty of discovering how investors view the prospects for future returns. Companies which fall into this category include privately-owned companies for which there is no public market for the stock, small companies for which there has been no sustained record, speculative types of companies for which no reasonable consensus of investors' expectations can be obtained, and so forth.

If we are unable to use a company's own securities as a source of data, we may be able to find securities of similar companies which are sufficiently comparable.

There may be situations for which we simply cannot find any satisfactory source of information. For such companies we must arrive at a figure for the composite Cost-of-Capital by judgment based on appraisal of risk of the business as a whole as compared with other companies for which we have Cost-of-Capital figures.

We may be able to obtain some help in such a comparative risk appraisal from a discussion with experienced financial analysts. We are seeking the risk as viewed in the marketplace for capital and not as appraised by management.

Now, let us notice some examples of arriving at a common cost where we can make an approximate appraisal of investors' expectations. The nature of the earnings—that is, whether they are stable or expected to grow—affects the approach that is used. We will refer to companies which have relatively sound capital structures.

We are concerned primarily with the techniques involved. The figures should not be considered to represent any final conclusions. Each example would require more detail than is presented here.

## COMPANIES FOR WHICH INVESTORS HAVE NOT EXPECTED GROWTH IN EARNINGS PER SHARE

If investors expect that a company is static in earnings per share, then the average earnings in the past are expected to be repeated. Under these circumstances, since past earnings represent what investors expect in the future, an average of ratios of past earnings per share to the market price of the stock in the same year will give a common cost. In other words, we are talking about non-growth companies. The ratio for any single year might be unrepresentative because of swings in earnings from year to year, but if we use an average of such ratios over a period of years, adjusted for financing costs, we should be able to obtain a reasonable result.

This is the easiest situation in which to determine the common cost, but there are pitfalls which must be avoided:

The fact that a company's earnings have exhibited no growth does not in itself mean that investors believe there is no growth. For example, a company which has spent large sums on research and development may not yet have reaped the benefit of those expenditures. Past earnings may have been disappointing. Nevertheless, investors may have bought the stock in anticipation of future growth in earnings when research and development reach fruition. Under these circumstances, ratios of earnings per share to the market price in the same year would not produce a common cost.

Furthermore, since most companies only pay out a part of their earnings in dividends and build up the common stockholders' equity with the balance, investors logically can expect some growth in earnings per share. Therefore, whenever we use this ap-

## EXHIBIT 5 (III)

## BUILDING TRADE COMPANY

| Column | 1 | 2 | 3 | 4 | 5 |
|--------|---|---|---|---|---|
| Year | Earnings Per Share | Average High-Low Market Price | Average Market Price Reduced by 15%[a] | Ratio Earnings Per Share to Adjusted Market Price | Return on Year End Common Equity |
| 1966 | $1.52 | $27.84 | $23.66 | 6.4% | 4.0% |
| 1965 | 2.72 | 30.95 | 26.31 | 10.3 | 6.7 |
| 1964 | 3.05 | 32.25 | 27.41 | 11.1 | 7.7 |
| 1963 | 2.46 | 23.54 | 20.01 | 12.3 | 6.5 |
| 1962 | 1.70 | 22.70 | 19.30 | 8.8 | 4.7 |
| 1961 | 1.79 | 22.13 | 18.81 | 9.5 | 5.1 |
| 1960 | 1.65 | 20.54 | 17.46 | 9.5 | 4.7 |
| 1959 | 2.70 | 23.54 | 20.01 | 13.5 | 7.8 |
| 1958 | 1.88 | 21.00 | 17.85 | 10.5 | 5.6 |
| 1957 | 1.94 | 21.29 | 18.10 | 10.7 | 7.0 |
| Average | | | | 10.3% | 6.0% |

[a]Reduction in market price to allow for financing costs for sale of new stock.

proach for companies which apparently have no prospects of growth, we must keep in mind that the resulting common cost may be on the low side. The same idea applies to a company with earnings at an abnormally low level; investors can expect that earnings will return to a more normal level.

## Company with No Growth Expected

There are shown in Exhibit 5 (III) figures representing a manufacturing company supplying products largely to the building trade. A check with financial analysts produced comments such as:

> We thought that the company was going to show some growth a few years ago, but it did not materialize. We look at the stock as cyclical rather than growth.

Of course, the market price reflects the various views of all buyers and sellers of the stock, but it is believed that such a comment is typical of the reaction to this company.

Because of the fluctuation in earnings per share, the ratio of earnings to price in any one year may not represent a measure of investors' expectations. When earnings were high they may have overstated investors' expectations, because a downturn may have been anticipated for the next year. The reverse may have been true when earnings were low. However, the average figure for the ten-year period may largely balance out these variations.

There is a reason why we believe that the average of 10.3% is too low for a common cost. This ten-year period included so many years of poor earnings that investors may well have expected better results than materialized, even though they did not expect a steady upward growth.

## Company Without Much Growth but Growth Expected

Figures representing a chemical company are given in Exhibit 6 (III). It has shown some growth in earnings per share, but the growth has not been spectacular.

Why the great difference in the relationship of earnings per share to adjusted market price for these two companies? There may be some difference in risk, but this is not the main reason. In the first place, the chemical company showed some growth and investors may have expected even more growth than the company achieved. Typical of their thinking is:

> This is a leading company in its field, spending heavily on research and development which should pay off in the future with improved earnings.

Therefore, when investors bought the stock they were not thinking in terms of past earnings: they were looking for higher earnings in the future. The average relationship of earnings per share to adjusted market price of 5.6% in no way measures the common cost for such a situation.

In other words, if we try to use past earnings to obtain the common cost, we must be particularly careful to determine that past earnings represented what investors expected.

## Department Store Stocks

Department store stocks for many years were not considered as having much prospect of growth and were bought primarily for yield. Exhibit 7 (III) shows that the ratio of earnings per share to average market price, reduced by 10% for financing cost, was 12.2% for the years 1950–1959 when growth was generally not expected.

Beginning about 1959, investors took a new look at prospects for department stores and decided that there were growth possibilities. Subsequently, earnings per share did increase, and there was an increase in price-earnings ratio and a drop in yield. For example, on March 8, 1967, the average price-earnings ratio for these five companies was 13 times based on the latest reported earnings and the average yield was 3.8%.

## High Income Stocks

Moody's Investors Service, Inc. provides a list of stocks in its *Stock Survey* which it recommends for income. Certain average fig-

## EXHIBIT 6 (III)

## CHEMICAL COMPANY

| Column | 1 | 2 | 3 | 4 | 5 |
|---|---|---|---|---|---|
| Year | Earnings Per Share[a] | Average High-Low Market Price | Average Market Price Reduced by 15%[b] | Ratio Earnings Per Share to Adjusted Market Price | Return on Year End Common Equity |
| 1965 | $2.81 | $50.34 | $42.79 | 6.6% | 16.7% |
| 1964 | 2.36 | 46.59 | 39.60 | 6.0 | 15.2 |
| 1963 | 2.00 | 41.77 | 35.50 | 5.6 | 14.2 |
| 1962 | 1.99 | 38.30 | 32.56 | 6.1 | 14.9 |
| 1961 | 1.77 | 48.75 | 41.44 | 4.3 | 14.0 |
| 1960 | 1.97 | 47.81 | 40.64 | 4.8 | 16.1 |
| 1959 | 2.14 | 50.81 | 43.19 | 5.0 | 18.5 |
| 1958 | 1.56 | 40.17 | 34.14 | 4.6 | 14.5 |
| 1957 | 1.67 | 40.22 | 34.19 | 4.9 | 15.9 |
| 1956 | 1.82 | 44.35 | 37.70 | 4.8 | 18.0 |
| Average | | | | 5.3% | 15.8% |

[a] Annual compound growth rate per share from 1956 to 1965 was about 4.5%.

[b] Reduction in market price to allow for financing costs for sale of new stock.

ures taken from one of these lists is shown in Exhibit 8 (III).

These stocks showed some growth in the past, and certainly investors would not purchase such stocks for a 5.4% yield if that were all they expected to obtain. They would be better off investing in bonds which would provide almost as much income and far less risk. *Moody's Investors Service, Inc. Corporate Bond Index* for June 24, 1966, showed a yield of 5.27%.

If a company's stock offers only yield with little growth prospect, it should be obvious that the stock must be of high quality and the dividend must be well protected by earnings. Reasoning on this basis, a common stock of a large well-situated industrial company with a conservative capital structure, which provided a 5% dividend yield based on the market price and had a dividend payout ratio about in line with the industrial company average of 50%, would have a minimum required earnings rate

## EXHIBIT 7 (III)

### DEPARTMENT STORES
### AVERAGE FOR FIVE NATIONAL STORES

| Column<br><br><br><br><br>Year | 1<br><br><br>Average<br>Earnings<br>Per Share | 2<br>Ratio<br>Earnings Per<br>Share to<br>Average<br>Market Price | 3<br>Ratio<br>Earnings Per<br>Share to<br>Average Market<br>Price Reduced<br>by 10%[a] | 4<br>Dividend<br>Yield<br>Based on<br>Average<br>Market<br>Price |
|---|---|---|---|---|
| 1959 | $4.30 | 8.2% | 9.1% | 4.3% |
| 1958 | 3.74 | 9.6 | 10.7 | 5.3 |
| 1957 | 3.68 | 11.5 | 12.8 | 6.3 |
| 1956 | 3.79 | 10.4 | 11.6 | 5.3 |
| 1955 | 3.55 | 10.0 | 11.1 | 4.9 |
| 1954 | 3.25 | 11.4 | 12.7 | 5.9 |
| 1953 | 2.97 | 12.4 | 13.7 | 6.9 |
| 1952 | 2.84 | 11.1 | 12.4 | 6.7 |
| 1951 | 2.27 | 8.4 | 9.3 | 6.2 |
| 1950 | 3.89 | 16.4 | 18.3 | 6.7 |
| Average | $3.43 | 10.9% | 12.2% | 5.9% |

[a]Reduction in market price to allow for financing costs for sale of new stock.

of 10% on the market price. For common cost purposes, this rate would have to be increased further for financing costs. This procedure is rather a backhanded way of looking at common cost, or perhaps we should say earnings requirements. It does not attempt to measure investors' expectations when they buy stocks, but perhaps it adds some understanding of the magnitude of earnings needed for the common.

## MARKET PRICE RELATED TO FORECAST EARNINGS PER SHARE

Financial analysts must make forecasts of earnings per share. Some of the financial services carry estimates of earnings per share at least a year ahead. For certain industries, analysts make forecasts a number of years ahead. We will now discuss the extent to which such forecasts may give a clue to common cost.

EXHIBIT 8 (III)

MOODY'S STOCK SURVEY
MIDYEAR STOCK SELECTOR, JUNE 27, 1966
COMMON STOCK SELECTIONS FOR HIGH YIELD
AVERAGES FOR TEN INDUSTRIAL COMPANIES

| Per Share Earnings | | Current Dividend Yield | Ratio Price to Est. 1966 Earnings |
|---|---|---|---|
| 1965 | Est. 1966 | | |
| $4.41 | $4.68 | 5.4% | 11.1 |

This idea may be applied to a study of the historical relationship of market price and earnings per share a certain number of years ahead, if we are able to determine how far ahead analysts have been looking. For example, we might examine the historical relationship of past market price, adjusted for financing costs, to earnings per share five years ahead. We could do this over an extended period of time to obtain an average figure. We refer to this method as the "lead and lag" approach—that is, the lead in earnings vs the lag in price. It should be used with extreme caution for these reasons:

1. The number of years which investors look ahead may vary. This was true in the case of the electric utilities. About 20 years ago, when analysts first became convinced that utilities had growth in earnings per share, they cautiously looked one or two years ahead; now they look at least five years ahead.

2. When we relate past market prices adjusted to actually reported earnings a number of years ahead, we are assuming that the actual earnings are the same as those which investors expected, and which actually affected the prices at the time. This may or may not be the case.

3. The worst error that may be made in this approach is the assumption that investors expect no further growth past the year

of the estimate. Such a measure is thus too low to the extent that further growth may be expected. This idea is illustrated in Exhibit 9 (III).

In spite of the many dangers inherent in using the ratio of market price, adjusted for financing costs, to analysts' forecast earnings, there are some companies for which this approach can give a clue to the common cost. It may work for a company which has had depressed earnings for a considerable period, but for which the future looks encouraging. The current market price may be largely affected by expectations of analysts that earnings will return to a more normal level. A discussion with analysts may give a gauge as to general level of their expectations.

*Steel Companies as an Example*

Earnings of the steel companies were restrained by uncertainties in 1966. Market prices of the stocks largely marked time looking toward earnings recovery to more normal levels. Examples of the estimates by one analyst for eight steel companies is shown in Exhibit 10 (III).

The estimate for 1967 gives a figure of 13% and, for five years ahead, 15%. On the basis of these figures alone, we suggest a judgment figure somewhere in between, but probably not less than 14%. However, this should not be considered as representing any final con-

## EXHIBIT 9 (III)
### CONTINUED GROWTH IMPORTANCE

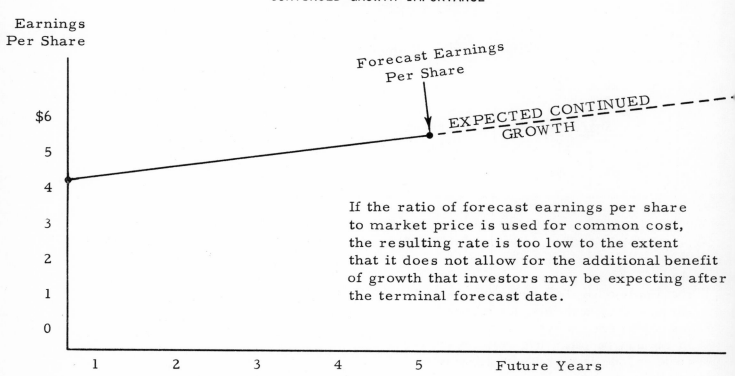

If the ratio of forecast earnings per share to market price is used for common cost, the resulting rate is too low to the extent that it does not allow for the additional benefit of growth that investors may be expecting after the terminal forecast date.

clusion for the common cost for the following reasons:

1. We do not give effect to further expected growth after the terminal forecast year, but it is felt that this is not as important as for companies which have a regular growth pattern.
2. The figures are spot and do not represent an average figure over a period of years.
3. There was no check made to determine whether the figures on potential earning power represented a fair cross section of market opinion. In other words, the point is not whether the estimates turn out to be right, but whether they represent the predominant thinking in the market at the time.

The figures do illustrate the approach to common cost through the use of expected earnings, and even with the reservations noted above they give some concept of the general magnitude of the common cost for such companies.

## GROWTH RATE APPROACH

There are more sophisticated approaches to the valuation of common stocks in terms of prospective returns. They generally involve an estimate of the combined return from future dividends and market appreciation, both of which are derived from earnings.

The simplest method assumes that the investor expects the stock can be sold at the same price-earnings ratio at which it is bought and that the dividend payout ratio will remain the same. An estimate is made of the growth rate the investor expects in earnings per share. On the basis of these facts, the approximate return to the investor, no matter how long he holds the stock, is the total of the present dividend yield plus the growth rate in earnings

EXHIBIT 10 (III)

COMMON STOCK DATA FOR STEEL COMPANIES
APPROXIMATE AVERAGES FOR EIGHT COMPANIES[a]

| Column 1 | 2 | 3 | 4 | 5 | 6 | 7 |
|---|---|---|---|---|---|---|
| Average High & Low Market Price First 3 Mos. 1967 | Market Price Reduced by 15%[b] | Earnings Per Share 1966 | Expected Earnings Per Share 1967[c] | Expected Potential Earning Power Per Share[d] | Ratio Expected Earnings Per Share for 1966 to Market Price Adjusted | Ratio Expected Potential Earning Power Per Share to Market Price Adjusted |
| $43 | $37 | $5.04 | $4.80 | $5.60 | 13% | 15% |

[a] Average debt ratio for the eight companies at December 31, 1966 was 20%.

[b] Reduction in market price to allow for financing costs for sale of new stock.

[c] The 1967 estimates assume a continued level of business activity for the balance of the year with relatively moderate liquidation of inventories during the fourth quarter.

[d] The estimates of potential earning power are for five years out. They are, of course, not a forecast, but merely a statement of possibilities under favorable conditions. Assumptions about the trend in the direction of capital spending vary, but they are generally around what appears to be an industry norm at this time of about a 3% net addition to invested capital per year.

per share. This is illustrated in Exhibit 11 (III).

When figuring the common cost, the figure of 10% would have to be increased for financing costs.

If you are not familiar with this method, you might wonder how it works out. This is shown in Exhibit 12 (III) which is based on the above figures.

The arithmetic annual average of 11.20% is not an exact representation of the return on the $100 invested because it does not give effect to the time value of money. Figured on a correct basis, the future return represents about 10% calculated by the Time Value Profitability Rate technique. This 10% figure is the same as we obtained above by adding the dividend yield of 4% at the start to the

compound growth rate of 6%. The Time Value of Money technique is explained in Chapter XV. You can check this figure by using the discount table in that chapter.

As we have already noted, the 10% figure which we have been discussing as the return to the investor would have to be increased for common cost purposes to allow for financing costs.

The limitations of this approach must be appreciated. The number of years does not affect the results, but the idea assumes that the investor expects a constant dividend payout ratio and believes that the stock can be sold at the same price-earnings ratio at which he bought it. This, of course, is a very broad assumption and one which materially affects the

## EXHIBIT 11 (III)

### GROWTH RATE APPROACH ILLUSTRATION

| | |
|---|---:|
| Present price-earnings ratio | 10 |
| Expected price-earnings ratio at which stock will be sold--same as at time of purchase | 10 |
| Present dividend yield | 4% |
| Expected dividend payout ratio | 40% |
| Expected growth rate in earnings per share | 6% |
| Total approximate expected return to investors: | |
|     Present dividend yield | 4% |
|     Expected growth rate in earnings per share | <u>6%</u> |
|     Total return | 10% |

final result. Furthermore, the values obtained are relatively insensitive to market prices when the yield is low, but highly sensitive to growth rate.

*Electric Utility Common Stock Index*

It is interesting to view electric utility stocks on the basis of the growth rate approach because this industry has shown a relatively steady growth. An index of electric utility stocks is shown in Exhibit 13 (III).

From 1957 to 1966 the compound growth rate was 7.1%. It is believed that financial analysts based their appraisal of electric utility company stocks expecting approximately this growth rate. Assuming that analysts did not expect any change in the price-earnings ratio, we can add the growth rate to the average yield of 3.7% to obtain a total return of 10.8%. Applying a 10% discount for financing costs (divide by 90%) would increase the rate to about 12%.

Actually, investors received a greater total return in this period because the stocks increased in value because of climbing price-earnings ratios. For example, the actual total return, using the Time Value Profitability Rate technique, for stocks in the index bought in 1957 and sold in 1966 would have been about 13% from a combination of dividends and market appreciation. Undoubtedly, some financial analysts were sufficiently astute to visualize that this would occur, but we have assumed that the majority were not relying on the added appreciation due to an increase in the price-earnings ratio.

A further refinement of the yield-plus-growth-rate method is based on the same assumptions as above, but covers estimates of price-earnings ratios at the time of sale of the stock different from that at the time the stock was purchased. Elaborate tables [2] have been

[2] One of the first major studies of this type was contained in a book published in 1931, *Stock Growth and Discount Tables* by Samuel Eliot Guild, Financial Publishing Co., Boston, Massachusetts.

## EXHIBIT 12 (III)

### RETURN ON COMMON STOCK FROM DIVIDENDS AND MARKET APPRECIATION
(Constant price/earnings and payout ratios)

| Column | 1 Earnings Per Share | 2 Dividend Payout Ratio | 3 Dividends Per Share | 4 Price-Earnings Ratio | 5 Market Price |
|---|---|---|---|---|---|
| Year | | | | | |
| At Time of Purchase | $10.00 | 40% | $4.00 | 10 | $100.00 |
| 1 | 10.60 | " | 4.24 | | |
| 2 | 11.24 | " | 4.49 | | |
| 3 | 11.91 | " | 4.76 | | |
| 4 | 12.62 | " | 5.05 | | |
| Estimated Sale Price | | | | 10 | $126.25 |

| Column | 6 | 7 | 8 |
|---|---|---|---|
| | | RETURN TO INVESTOR | |
| Year | Dividends | Market Appreciation | Total Return |
| 1 | $4.24 | | $ 4.24 |
| 2 | 4.49 | | 4.49 |
| 3 | 4.76 | | 4.76 |
| 4 | 5.05 | $26.25 | 31.30 |
| Total | | | $44.79 |
| Annual Average Return | | | 11.20% |
| Time Value Profitability Rate | | | 10.00% |

devised so that an investor can read off the estimated total return. However, this refined approach would be of value only in special situations because of the difficulty of finding out what terminal price-earnings ratio investors may have been expecting.

*A Hard to Interpret Example*

A striking example of the effect of a change in the price-earnings ratio on total return to investors occurred in the years 1960–1965 for a large manufacturing company. Figures representing this situation are shown in Exhibit 14 (III).

This company showed a good growth in earnings per share, but in spite of this fact it can be seen from the table that the total return to investors who bought the stock in 1960 was not great. They could hardly feel disappointed in the company's growth in earnings per share; undoubtedly, they were disappointed that they did not foresee what would happen to the price-earnings ratio. The figures for this company highlight the importance of knowing how investors actually view a stock at any particular time in order to make an estimate of their expected return and thus the common cost.

## EXHIBIT 13 (III)

### ELECTRIC UTILITY COMMON STOCK INDEX
### MOODY'S INVESTORS SERVICE, INC.

| Column | 1 | 2 | 3 | 4 | 5 | 6 |
|---|---|---|---|---|---|---|
| Year | Earnings Per Share[a] | Dividends Per Share | Dividend Payout Ratio | Dividend Yield | Average Market Price | Average Market Price-Earnings Ratio |
| 1966 | $6.30 | $4.18 | 66% | 4.0% | $102.90 | 16 |
| 1965 | 5.92 | 3.86 | 65 | 3.3 | 117.08 | 20 |
| 1964 | 5.41 | 3.43 | 63 | 3.2 | 108.76 | 20 |
| 1963 | 4.99 | 3.21 | 64 | 3.1 | 102.79 | 21 |
| 1962 | 4.73 | 2.97 | 63 | 3.2 | 91.50 | 19 |
| 1961 | 4.33 | 2.81 | 65 | 3.1 | 90.55 | 21 |
| 1960 | 4.12 | 2.68 | 65 | 3.8 | 69.82 | 17 |
| 1959 | 3.82 | 2.61 | 68 | 3.9 | 66.35 | 17 |
| 1958 | 3.63 | 2.50 | 69 | 4.3 | 57.96 | 16 |
| 1957 | 3.41 | 2.43 | 71 | 4.9 | 49.42 | 14 |
| Average | | | | 3.7% | | |

[a]Compound growth rate in earnings per share for 1957 to 1966 was about 7.1%.

## Other Approaches to Growth Situations

There are various other approaches to the valuation of common stocks based on estimated future returns. One such approach proceeds on the assumption that the only stream of value which flows from a company to its stockholders over an indefinite period of time is the cash dividends. Viewed another way, the individual stockholders may change from time to time with sellers and buyers, but as a whole the entire mass continues intact. The only benefit they receive as a whole from the company is cash dividends. This method attempts to place value on stock on the basis of the present worth of the expected flow of dividends for an almost indefinite period in the future. Actually, those who use this method make certain assumptions about the growth rate in dividends per share for a substantial number of years in the future, and further assume that the growth rate will gradually slow down over a subsequent period and finally level off.[3]

[3] One of the leading proponents of this school is Nicholas Molodovsky, Vice-President of White, Weld, and

## EXHIBIT 14 (III)

### LARGE MANUFACTURING COMPANY
### COMMON STOCK DATA

| Column | 1 | 2 | 3 | 4 | 5 |
|---|---|---|---|---|---|
| Year | Earnings Per Share[a] | Dividends Per Share | Dividend Payout Ratio | Market Price | Market Price-Earnings Ratio |
| 1966 | $3.89 | $1.80 | 46% | $117.00 | 30 |
| 1965 | 3.27 | 1.65 | 50 | 102.00 | 31 |
| 1964 | 2.88 | 1.50 | 52 | 83.06 | 29 |
| 1963 | 2.63 | 1.35 | 51 | 96.93 | 37 |
| 1962 | 2.40 | 1.20 | 50 | 79.50 | 33 |
| 1961 | 2.18 | 0.98 | 45 | 150.68 | 46 |

[a]Compound growth rate in earnings per share for 1961 to 1966 was about 11.8%.

This method is undoubtedly of value to some highly skilled analysts in estimating whether certain common stocks may be over- or under-priced. However, it would seem to be of limited value to the financial executive of a company who is trying to obtain an interpretation of how much return investors expect to receive in the future to justify their purchase of a stock. From the practical point of view, the average investor thinks about what he may receive in terms of dividends and market appreciation. This is the approach which was discussed above.

How do the methods based on growth rate help a company determine a common cost? They are just another tool that may be useful to arrive at an approximate return investors expect to receive. A company which has close contact with financial analysts may be able to

Co., Inc. See "Common Stock Valuation: Theory and Tables," by Nicholas Molodovsky, Catherine May, and Sherman Chattiner, *Financial Analysts Journal*, March–April 1965, Volume 21, Number 2.

obtain an idea of what they expect in growth in earnings per share and other factors necessary to apply the formulas.

## MEASUREMENTS REVIEWED

The types of measurements which we have suggested may be used to determine the common cost may be summarized as follows:

1. Earnings per share divided by market price, adjusted for financing costs, where no growth is expected.
2. The "lead and lag" approach—that is, later years' earnings per share figures divided by earlier years' market prices—adjusted for financing costs.
3. Earnings per share forecast by investors for a certain number of years ahead beyond which further growth is not expected, related to market prices adjusted for financing costs.
4. Growth rate approach, with yield added

to growth rate expected by investors, with adjustment for financing costs.

We were careful to point out the necessity of weighing any statistical approach in terms of the definition of common cost in order to be aware of the extent to which the statistics fail to conform to the definition.

## WHERE DO WE STAND?

In the first chapter of this book, we stated that every effort possible was exerted to make the book readable. After reading this chapter you may feel that you were somewhat misled. But we also said that you would have to put on your thinking cap. Undoubtedly you could now calculate the common cost for a company which represents a reasonably straightforward case. If you question your ability to determine the common cost for a complicated situation, that is to be expected. However, you will have acquired some ability to detect whether the experts are really expert. If you wish to become expert, you have the tools with which to work. You will certainly have made important strides toward a better handling of capital expenditures by having accomplished the following:

Become firmly convinced that common does have a cost.

Understood that cost size is affected by the risk of the business as viewed by investors, and by the amount of senior securities.

Obtained some general idea of the magnitude of common cost for high-grade common stocks and are aware that it must be increased substantially as the quality drops.

Covered some of the possible approaches that may be used in trying to measure common cost.

Appreciated the serious errors that may arise in determining the common cost if a person is not thoroughly familiar with the principles involved.

*CHAPTER IV*

# Senior Capital Cost

## AN APPROXIMATE RATE MAY SUFFICE

For a company like a finance company, which may have 75% or more of its capital structure in debt, the cost of senior capital is obviously important and careful attention will be required.

For most types of companies the amount of senior capital is relatively small and the cost of senior capital is less than one-half that of common. Therefore, generally, accuracy in determining the cost of senior capital is not critical in calculating the composite cost. As we have already suggested, it may be satisfactory to use an approximate interest rate based on judgment such as 4½%, 5%, 5½% or 6%, etc.

Two points, however, which you should not miss regarding senior capital are:

1. The period to use in determining the senior capital rate should represent average conditions under which the company could raise capital over a reasonable period of time, such as ten years. The same ideas apply to the period to use in determining the common cost. Periods you will generally avoid are historical, spot, or prospective. (This is explained fully in this chapter.)

2. Convertible securities should carry the common rate if there are any prospects for conversion.

Because senior capital cost is far less important than the common cost, this is one chapter with which you can rest on this brief summary. However, we hope your curiosity is sufficiently piqued to induce you to read at least the material under the heading, Period to Use.

## SENIOR SECURITIES: WHAT ARE THEY?

We have talked about two types of long-term capital: debt, and equity. We have commented that preferred stock is a form of equity. It is not a fixed obligation like a debt security which will put a company into bankruptcy. Furthermore, it provides protection for debt. It should be viewed as a form of equity in making a decision as to whether it is an appropriate type of security for a particular company.

There is another way to classify securities into two groups: senior securities, meaning all securities senior to common equity, and common equity. In this terminology, preferred is a senior security since it comes ahead of the common. It still should not be viewed as equivalent to debt.

There are many different senior securities, but the principal ones are as follows:

*Senior Securities*

DEBT
√ Leases capitalized
√ Mortgages
√ Mortgage bonds—bonds with a lien on
     property
√ Debenture bonds—unsecured bonds
Long-term notes—unsecured obligations
Subordinated debenture bonds—unsecured
     bonds in a junior position
Convertible debenture bonds
Income bonds—interest payments depen-
     dent on earnings

PREFERRED STOCKS
Preferred
Convertible preferred

If you are rusty on some of the ideas connected with debt cost, we have included in Appendix B some explanatory information to which you may wish to refer. Also included in Appendix B is back-up material for the exhibit in this chapter and some further information for making a refined calculation for senior capital cost. The method of determining the cost rates for leases is somewhat complicated. Since they represent a special situation they are covered separately in Appendix C.

## CONVERTIBLE RATE

In viewing convertible debentures and convertible preferreds for the purpose of security analysis, they must be included in the senior category. They are senior, until converted, because they rank ahead of the common. However, for Cost-of-Capital purposes, convertibles must be treated as common equity and carry the common cost. The reason for this is simple: their purpose is to provide more common equity through conversion. In order to achieve conversion, there must be enough earnings to enhance the value of the common stock so as to make conversion worthwhile. The senior capital rate is lower than the common rate. If the senior rate alone were applied to convertibles there would not be enough earnings to induce conversion. Applying the senior rate would defeat the purpose of convertibles. Furthermore, after they convert they fall completely into the common category.

If the conversion privilege has expired, then the security has lost its convertibility and the rate for the senior security would apply. There may be some other special circumstances in which it would be more appropriate to apply the senior rate: for example, when the price of the common stock is so far below the conversion price that there is no expectation of conversion. There must be a compelling reason to justify the use of the senior rate rather than the common rate.

## DEBT COST

The measurement of debt cost is relatively easy. The future interest is a known quantity; so is the final payment, since debt is repaid at 100% of principal amount. The debt cost is the yield to maturity based on—

the market or issue price, less financing costs, the future interest payments as expressed by the interest coupon; and the years to maturity, with payment at 100% of principal amount.

Yield to maturity spreads the premium above 100,[1] or the discount below, over the life of the issue. It is determined by reference to Bond Value Tables. The size of the rate depends on investors' assessment of risk. We can express the risk of a debt issue in terms of quality as reflected by bond ratings established by the three rating agencies: Fitch's Investors Service, Moody's Investors Service, and Standard and Poor's Corporation.

When a company sells a security, there are certain financing costs involved. We discussed this briefly in connection with the common cost. The company receives only the net amount, after the financing costs, to use for corporate purposes. In order to determine the cost to the company, the yield to maturity must be based on the net proceeds the company receives. We will illustrate this idea assuming a company sells a bond with a 25 year maturity and a 5% interest coupon to the public at a price of 103.

| Price to the public | | 103.00 |
|---|---|---|
| Less: Financing costs | | |
| Underwriter's commission | 1.00 | |
| Financing expenses (legal fees, printing costs for prospectus, accounting fees, etc.) | 1.00 | |
| | 2.00 | |
| Net proceeds to company | | 101.00 |

Now, we must refer to Bond Value Tables in order to calculate the yield to maturity. There are given below yields and prices taken from Bond Value Tables [2] for a bond with a 25 year maturity and a 5% interest rate.

| Yield | Price |
|---|---|
| 4.90% | 101.43 |
| | ←101.00 |
| 4.95 | 100.71 |
| 5.00 | 100.00 |

The net proceeds to the company of 101.00 falls between 101.43 and 100.71. By interpolating between these prices, the price of 101.00 produces a yield to maturity of about 4.93%. This is the cost rate for these bonds. The cost rate for notes, mortgages and other straight forms of debt are figured in a similar way.

## PREFERRED STOCK COST

The yield is easier to figure on a preferred stock than on a bond, since a preferred stock does not have a maturity. The yield without regard to maturity is referred to as a current yield. This yield is obtained by dividing the price directly into the dividend. For example, if a preferred stock sold for $102 and the dividend rate was $5 per annum, the yield would be 4.90%. To obtain the cost rate to the company, a deduction from the market price must be made for financing costs, including the underwriter's commission and the financing expenses. The two combined are generally higher for a preferred stock than for a bond. If financing costs were $3 for a preferred issue which was sold to the public at $102, the net proceeds to the company would be $99. With a $5 dividend rate the yield for Cost-of-Capital purposes would be $99 divided into $5 or 5.05%.

## PERIOD TO USE

There are four possible time periods that might be used to determine Cost-of-Capital. We touched on this problem when discussing the common cost. We will discuss each of them and eliminate all but one.

*Historical—No.*

Historical cost is the actual cost of each senior security that the company now has outstanding. A company cannot disregard the his-

---

[1] A bond may be in various denominations: $1,000, $5,000, etc. The price of a bond is expressed as a percent of principal amount. For example, if the price of a bond is 98%, this means that you would pay $980 for a $1,000 bond, $9,800 for a $10,000 bond, etc. The percent sign may be omitted after the price quotation.

[2] Financial Publishing Company, Boston, Massachusetts.

torical cost from a financial point of view because the rates on the existing securities are the ones that have to be paid. For example, if the company were fortunate enough to have sold bonds at a time of low interest rates, say with a 4% interest coupon, this is a financial advantage. On the other hand, if some of its existing bonds were sold during high interest rates, at say 6%, this is a financial disadvantage.

However, the historical cost of the existing securities, just like the historical cost of existing plants, is over the dam as far as determining pricing policy. For example, let us suppose that a company built a plant during a period of low construction costs for $5,000,000 whereas its competitor ran into strikes and other difficulties and built a similar one for $7,000,000. Neither of these historical costs in themselves would determine the prices at which the products would be sold. A similar type of situation would exist if one company built a very efficient plant and another slipped and built an inefficient one.

Costs, insofar as they affect prices through their effect on supply and demand, must be the costs of recent years. This is the last cost we will discuss below and the one which management must use in order to be in the swim in our competitive economic system.

*Spot—No.*

By spot cost is meant the cost rates at a moment in time, or during a short period such as a month, or one year. Rates for securities for a short period may be out of line with more representative figures taken over a longer period. Spot rates must be eliminated because they might give distorted and unrepresentative results.

*Prospective—No.*

What rates will a company have to pay for its senior securities in the future? If a company could guess, it might give some weight to such prospective rates in Cost-of-Capital. The fact is that it is difficult to forecast interest rates with any degree of accuracy. Therefore, for practical purposes, we must abandon the idea of prospective rates.[3]

*Average—Yes.*

We are left with one other period—average. This is sometimes referred to as "current," meaning a current span of years. On the basis of economic principles, we must accept the fact that prices of goods are determined by supply and demand. This tends to produce prices which will cover all costs, as costs affect the supply side of the equation. New supplies ultimately come on the market as a result of capital expenditures. Companies will make such expenditures when all costs are covered. This should include the Cost-of-Capital. We want a cost rate which will represent average conditions under which added supplies will come on the market. By average is meant a period covering a sufficient number of recent years to give a figure which represents the cost to raise capital under varying conditions of good years and bad, bull markets and bear—in other words, a complete cycle. This is what it takes to bring new supplies continuously on the market at the average costs associated therewith. You should use a similar average period to determine common cost.

What number of years to cover is a matter of judgment. It is necessary to include five years as a bare minimum in order to get away from "spot." A ten-year period might give more reasonable average results. Under some circumstances a longer period may be appropriate. Keep in mind that if the period does not include average conditions, it may be biased on the high or low side. Therefore, the final result for Cost-of-Capital will still have to be tempered with judgment.

[3] There is an exception in special circumstances for the regulated industries, such as the electric, gas, and telephone utilities. If regulatory authorities incorrectly force a company to use the historical cost approach for rate making purposes, some weight may be given to possible prospective rates when a company has an existing bond maturing in the near future with an interest rate much different from present day interest rates. The same type of situation exists where such a regulated company expects to do a large amount of financing and present day rates differ substantially from a company's historical rates.

## SOURCES OF DATA

*Yields Based on Net Proceeds
of New Issues*

What we want is the average yield, based on the net proceeds to the company, over an average period of from five to ten years. If the company sold senior securities each year during such a period and the nature of the company and its financial policy did not change during the period, we would have ideal figures to draw on.

This may sound as though we are using historical cost figures which we previously condemned. In this case, we are assuming that the company's experienced results give us a representative figure in each year. Of course, we cannot usually hope to find such good evidence. Generally, a company will have outstanding one, two, or three senior securities, which at best represent the cost to finance in a limited number of years. Existing financing might have been done many years ago.

Therefore, we may have to turn to sales of securities by similar companies in order to obtain a large enough sample. In using such figures, we must be careful that they are similar to the senior securities of our company in all principal respects. Such evidences are readily available for only a few industries. An example is included in Appendix B for electric utility companies.

*Yields Based on Outstanding Issues,
Adjusted*

The next best evidence is the yield to maturity based on the market price for outstanding issues. If, for example, a company has had a bond issue outstanding for many years for which there is an active market, this may be a source of evidence. The nature of the company must not have changed in the period. Erroneous results may be obtained if the maturity has become short in recent years due to the passage of time. Generally, short maturities have lower yields than long maturities.

The prices of outstanding bonds have to be reduced and the yields increased to allow for financing expenses, as discussed above, in order to obtain an estimate of cost rate based on the net proceeds to the company.

There is one further adjustment. Generally, outstanding bonds sell at lower yields than new issues with the same maturity coupon, terms, and quality. A higher yield is required on new issues as compared with similar outstanding bonds in order to induce investors to take up the large supply of the new bonds coming on the market. The market for outstanding issues represents prices for only a relatively small supply of bonds. The spread between the yield on new issues and that on similar outstanding bonds varies depending on conditions in the bond market. When the market is tight the spread tends to increase; when there is a seller's market the spread may disappear completely. The same idea applies to preferred stocks.

## SENIOR COST RATES BY QUALITY RATINGS

To give you some idea of the magnitude of the debt and preferred costs for large companies in recent years, there are shown in Exhibit 1 (IV) some average figures. They are based on outstanding issues with approximate adjustments for financing costs and the difference in yield between new issues and outstanding issues. The total adjustment in terms of yield will vary depending on such factors as market conditions, the maturity of a bond issue, the size of the interest or preferred dividend rate, etc.

We have included rates for the lower quality bonds. But, as will be explained later, it is almost impossible to figure the Cost-of-Capital for a company which is highly leveraged and has poor quality securities.

From the above discussion, it can be seen that for large companies for which it is possible to arrive at a quality bond rating, there are various sources of evidence to use in determining an approximate rate for the current cost of senior capital.

## EXHIBIT 1 (IV)

### INDEXES OF YIELDS FOR OUTSTANDING ISSUES OF SENIOR SECURITIES OF INDUSTRIAL COMPANIES, MOODY'S INVESTORS SERVICE, INC., WITH ADJUSTMENTS TO APPROXIMATE THE YIELDS BASED ON THE NET PROCEEDS FOR NEW ISSUES OF LARGE COMPANIES

| Column | | 1 | 2 | 3 | 4 |
|---|---|---|---|---|---|
| | | | | Bonds | |
| Line | | Aaa | Aa | A | Baa |
| 1<br>2<br>3 | Outstanding Issues Index<br>   5 Year Average<br>   1961 - 1965 | 4.26% | 4.37% | 4.46% | 4.95% |
| 4<br>5 | Adjustment to obtain yield<br>at net proceeds for new issue | 0.11% | 0.12% | 0.14% | 0.17% |
| 6 | Estimated new issue cost rate | 4.37% | 4.49% | 4.60% | 5.22% |
| 7<br>8<br>9 | Outstanding Issues Index<br>   10 Year Average<br>   1956 - 1965 | 4.05% | 4.16% | 4.28% | 4.80% |
| 10<br>11 | Adjustment to obtain yield<br>at net proceeds for new issue | 0.23% | 0.25% | 0.28% | 0.32% |
| 12 | Estimated new issue cost rate | 4.28% | 4.41% | 4.56% | 5.12% |

### Preferred Stocks

| | | High Grade | Medium Grade |
|---|---|---|---|
| 13<br>14<br>15 | Outstanding Issues Index<br>   5 Year Average<br>   1961 - 1965 | 4.15% | 4.49% |
| 16<br>17 | Adjustment to obtain yield<br>at net proceeds for new issue | 0.13% | 0.17% |
| 18 | Estimated new issue cost rate | 4.28% | 4.66% |
| 19<br>20<br>21 | Outstanding Issues Index<br>   10 Year Average<br>   1956 - 1965 | 4.22% | 4.60% |
| 22<br>23 | Adjustment to obtain yield<br>at net proceeds for new issue | 0.29% | 0.32% |
| 24 | Estimated new issue cost rate | 4.51% | 4.92% |

For small companies, there is not much published data; they generally have to pay higher rates. You must make a judgment based on your own experience, or ask a financial expert to make an estimate. In such a situation be sure to explain that you want a yield based on the net proceeds for new issues over an average period of five or ten years.

# CHAPTER V

# Capital Structure Components

We said that capital structure was the starting point of Cost-of-Capital because it gives the proportions of the different types of securities to which the cost rates are applied. Our excuse for postponing a discussion of it was to permit us to get right at the common cost.

We have already said the following:

There are two basic types of long-term capital—debt and equity—and equity includes preferred and common stock.

The term senior securities includes preferred stock, since preferred is ahead of the common equity.

For security analysis purposes, convertible securities should be treated as senior securities until converted. For Cost-of-Capital purposes the common cost should be applied to convertibles except in unusual circumstances.

## REPRESENTATIVE CAPITAL STRUCTURE

In measuring the over-all Cost-of-Capital, the important decision with regard to capital structure mainly involves what structure to use: the most recent, the prospective—that is, one giving effect to expected financing—or an average over a period of time?

The proportion which various securities represent of the total will vary from year to year through the sale of new securities, the retirement of existing securities either in total or partially through sinking fund, and through retained earnings or losses, etc. What we are trying to find is a capital structure which represents the company's financial policy as viewed by investors.

Generally, it is unwise to use spot figures—that is, figures from one particular time. For example, if a company sells debt one year and common the next year, the capital structure in either of the years alone would not give a true picture of policy. Investors will study a company's financial history over a period of years—five, ten and sometimes even longer—in order to decide what pattern may be representative. For this reason, an average figure based on a number of years may provide the best clue. This is not always true. If a company has changed its policy in recent years, a long-term average might be misleading and recent figures would give the best results.

One of the principal points to keep in mind is that the cost rates attached to the various securities must conform to the character of the capital structure finally chosen. For example, if the cost rates on a company's own securities are used as evidence to arrive at a Cost-of-Capital, the period from which they are drawn should conform to that from which the capital structure is taken. The same thought is pertinent if cost rates are derived from securities of other companies. It should be certain that there is similarity in financial policy between the two companies involved so that rates will relate to similar capital structures. Of course, there should also be a similarity in the nature of the companies so that business risk is roughly the same.

Sometimes the question is raised as to whether the capital structure ratios should be calculated with the market prices of the securities rather than book figures. Some financial analysts do calculate the ratios on this basis in addition to the book figures in determining the quality of securities. For purposes of Cost-of-Capital, book figures are the ones to use. The ratios based on market prices of securities will vary widely, depending on the level of security prices. Furthermore, the book figures more nearly represent the capital which a company has available on which to earn a profit and from which it must calculate the composite cost.

Generally, the figures at which senior securities are carried on the balance sheet are close enough to use in determining capital structure. Appendix B covers the details regarding the amounts at which to state senior securities.

The extent to which book figures represent true present values of assets can be easily challenged. The book figures may be under- or over-stated. It would be nice if all balance sheets were stated on the basis of true present values, but that would be expecting the impossible. In determining the quality of a company's securities, analysts will give some weight to such values where they may be known. For Cost-of-Capital purposes, the extent to which book figures vary from true present values should be kept in mind in deciding on the significance of capital structure ratios. Probably this is the best that can be done.

## LONG-TERM DEBT—
## WHAT IT INCLUDES

In the last chapter we listed some of the debt securities. Capital structure should include all long-term securities—that is, any item of permanent capital. By accounting definition, any debt is included with current liabilities if it has a maturity of one year or less, and with long-term debt if the maturity is longer than one year.

Debt with a maturity of only slightly over one year is not really permanent capital. Nevertheless, a dividing line has to be established and the choice of one year is to distinguish it from current liabilities, which include short-term borrowings on a seasonal basis and payables liquidated in the normal turnover of business. If a company relies too heavily on short-term debt, so that it becomes a permanent fixture, then such borrowings should be included in capital structure. For example, short-term bank loans and commercial paper which are regularly renewed and not cleaned up at any time during a year fall in this category.

Some capital, for most types of companies, is actually furnished through items in current liabilities, such as accounts payable, taxes payable, etc., but these have their counterparts in current assets. These liabilities are liquidated in the regular turnover of business. We will not be much concerned with them. If there are any interest payments connected with current liabilities, they are a part of the cost of doing business. Generally, they are small and can be disregarded. If they are significant, they should be included as part of operating expense in making a profit forecast. In figuring return on long-term capital, they should be separated from interest charges and deducted from income available for long-term capital.

If some items in current liabilities are shifted to long-term debt, care should be taken to note the effect this has on the assets which should be included for project analysis. We use our simplified balance sheets to explain the point in Exhibit 1 (V).

### EXHIBIT I (V)

### BALANCE SHEET

| Assets | | Liabilities | | |
|---|---|---|---|---|
| Current Assets | $100 | Current Liabilities | | $ 50 |
| Plant, Net | 50 | Long-Term Capital | | |
| | | Long-Term Securities | | 100 |
| Other Items | 0 | Other Items | | 0 |
| Total | $150 | Total | | $150 |

If current liabilities include $20 of short-term bank debt that is regularly renewed and consequently represents long-term debt rather than true current liabilities, the recast balance sheet would be as shown in Exhibit 2 (V).

Now, total long-term capital amounts to

### EXHIBIT 2 (V)

### BALANCE SHEET RECAST

| Assets | | Liabilities | | |
|---|---|---|---|---|
| Current Assets | $100 | Current Liabilities | | $ 30 |
| Plant, Net | 50 | Long-Term Capital | | |
| | | Long-Term Securities | $100 | |
| | | Short-Term Debt | | |
| | | Regularly Renewed | 20 | 120 |
| Other Items | 0 | Other Items | | 0 |
| Total | $150 | Total | | $150 |

$120 and for project analysis we would need to include assets as follows: Plant, Net $50 and Working Capital $70 (current assets less current liabilities) or a total of $120.

## LEASES—UNLESS CAPITALIZED PRODUCE A FALSE EFFECT

In order to determine a capital structure which is representative of a company's financial policy, leases which are a form of long-term financing should be capitalized. This may present problems if there is lack of information or if the leases are complicated in nature. Since approximations are perfectly satisfactory, it is generally possible to come up with a figure which will serve the purpose. The leased asset would then go on the asset side of the balance sheet. We can explain what happens if this is not done by using a simple example of the effect on return on capital.

Assume that we are dealing with a type of

company which can keep its securities high-grade with debt representing 50% of long-term capital. We have two plants, each costing $10,000,000 and each having a 10-year life. To start with, we finance one with bonds at 5% interest and the other with common stock. Assume that we have predetermined that the common cost is 10%. Then the composite Cost-of-Capital would be 7½%. Each plant should earn at least this rate. The simplified balance sheet, assuming current assets equalled current liabilities, and selected items from the income statement would be as shown in Exhibit 3 (V). Total return (interest $500,000

## EXHIBIT 3 (V)

## FINANCIAL STATEMENTS

### Balance Sheet

| Assets | | Liabilities | | |
|---|---|---|---|---|
| Current Assets | $ 5,000,000 | Current Liabilities | | $ 5,000,000 |
| | | Long-Term Capital | | |
| Plant A | $10,000,000 | Bonds | $10,000,000 | |
| | | Common | 10,000,000 | |
| Plant B | $10,000,000 | Total | | 20,000,000 |
| Other Items | 0 | Other Items | | 0 |
| Total | $25,000,000 | Total | | $25,000,000 |

### Income Statement Items

| | |
|---|---|
| Depreciation Plant A | $1,000,000 |
| Depreciation Plant B | $1,000,000 |
| Income Before Interest and Taxes | $2,500,000 |
| Interest | $ 500,000 |
| Income Taxes (50% rate) | $1,000,000 |
| Earnings for Common | $1,000,000 |

plus earnings for common $1,000,000) would represent 7½% on total long-term capital of $20,000,000.

Let us switch to financing Plant A with lease financing. We sell the plant for $10,000,-000 and lease it back. We use the proceeds from the financing to pay off the bonds. Now the balance sheet and selected items from the income statement would be as shown in Exhibit 4(V).

If we forgot Plant A, which has disappeared from the balance sheet, it looks as though the return on long-term capital has been increased to 10%, that is, $1,000,000 of income applicable to $10,000,000 of long-term capital.

## EXHIBIT 4 (V)

### FINANCIAL STATEMENTS RECAST

#### Balance Sheet

| Assets | | Liabilities | |
|---|---|---|---|
| Current Assets | $ 5,000,000 | Current Liabilities | $ 5,000,000 |
| Plant B | 10,000,000 | Long-Term Capital Common Equity | 10,000,000 |
| Other Items | 0 | Other Items | 0 |
| Total | $15,000,000 | Total | $15,000,000 |

#### Income Statement Items

| | |
|---|---|
| Depreciation Plant B | $1,000,000 |
| Income Before Taxes | $2,000,000 |
| Income Taxes (50% rate) | $1,000,000 |
| Earnings for Common | $1,000,000 |

Something is wrong! What happened to Plant A?

We do not own Plant A any longer since it was financed with a lease. Depreciation of $1,000,000 has dropped out of the income statement and also, since we paid off the $10,-000,000 of debt with the proceeds from the sale and lease back, the $500,000 of interest has dropped out.

But, what has been added and where? We have to make lease payments. Raising capital through the sale of property and then leasing it back is a form of debt financing. We saw above that the proceeds from the sale of the property were used to pay off the debt. If we leased Plant A in the first place, we would have been using lease financing as an alternative to financing the plant with debt and owning it.

The lessor generally expects to get back the principal which he put up to buy the property and also interest on the amount of the unpaid principal. Since the property owned by the lessor will be fully depreciated in 10 years on our assumption as above, the lessor would want to get back the equivalent of $1,000,000 of principal each year for 10 years. If we assume that the lessor would be satisfied with a 5% interest rate, he would expect to receive $500,000 in interest on his principal during the first year. Thus, the lease payments in the first year would total $1,500,000.[1]

In the first year, depreciation on Plant A and interest on the bonds are dropped from the

---

[1] Generally leases call for payments of varying amounts of principal and interest each year with the two combined being equal in amount each year. We have used the above assumptions to simplify the explanation.

income statement, as mentioned above. By selling and leasing back the plant, we add $1,500,000 in lease payments *above the line* in operating expenses. Selected items in the income statement would be as shown in Exhibit 5(V).

We have swapped the depreciation on Plant A and interest on the bonds for a like total of lease payments. On the basis of our assumptions, we would come out the same at the end of ten years whether we owned Plant A and

## EXHIBIT 5 (V)

### INCOME STATEMENT ITEMS

|  | With Plant A Owned | With Plant A Sold and Leased Back and Debt Paid Off |
|---|---|---|
| Depreciation Plant A | $1,000,000 | 0 |
| Depreciation Plant B | $1,000,000 | $1,000,000 |
| Lease Payments |  | $1,500,000 |
| Income Before Interest and Taxes | $2,500,000 | $2,000,000 |
| Interest | $ 500,000 | 0 |
| Income Taxes | $1,000,000 | $1,000,000 |
| Earnings for Common | $1,000,000 | $1,000,000 |

financed it with debt or leased it, except for two possible differences: One, under the lease we might have to pay some renewal rental charge if we wished to continue to use the property, and two, at the expiration of the lease, we would not own the fully depreciated plant; consequently, we might lose the residual value to the lessor.

But the picture looks a lot different on the surface. With the lease financing, we apparently have long-term capital consisting only of common equity, amounting to $10,000,000 showing a 10% return.

Right before your eyes something happened! But was it so dramatic? We merely swapped one form of debt for another. With lease financing we are in effect using $10,000,000 of a debt type of financing. Thus, the

common is leveraged to the extent of the lease financing and it should earn 10%.

In other words, without lease financing we earned 7½% on total capital of $20,000,000 with 10% on the common. With the lease financing, we substituted lease charges for a similar amount of charges on the debt. The common earnings come after the lease charges and the 10% return on the common is no better return than the 7½% over-all return without the lease.

We can make the two situations comparable by capitalizing the lease and putting Plant A back on the balance sheet with an equivalent amount of debt on the liability side as shown in Exhibit 6(V).

Now to figure the return we would take the interest part of the lease payment of $500,000

## EXHIBIT 6 (V)

## LEASES CAPITALIZED

### Balance Sheet

| Assets | | Liabilities | | |
|---|---|---|---|---|
| Current Assets | $ 5,000,000 | Current Liabilities | | $ 5,000,000 |
| Plant A leased | 10,000,000 | Long-Term Capital Lease Capitalized | $10,000,000 | |
| Plant B | 10,000,000 | Common Equity | 10,000,000 | |
| | | Total | | $20,000,000 |
| Other Items | 0 | Other Items | | 0 |
| Total | $25,000,000 | Total | | $25,000,000 |

and add it to the income for common of $1,-000,000 to get a total of $1,500,000. The long-term capital, with leases capitalized, would amount to $20,000,000. The return would be 7½%—the same as the return with Plant A owned.

Thus, if a company has used a large amount of lease financing, the return calculated on the long-term capital as shown on the balance sheet may be very misleading. A true picture of the return on total long-term capital can only be obtained by capitalizing leases and figuring the return so as to eliminate the leverage effect of the lease financing. A table for capitalizing leases is included in Appendix C along with additional information about leases.

## SHOULD ALL PARTS OF COMMON BE TREATED THE SAME?

One sometimes encounters complete misconceptions regarding the cost of earned surplus, even from supposedly financially sophisticated people. For example, a senior official in bank regulation talking about bank capital to a group of bankers said, "Earned surplus is your cheapest form of capital." Fortunately, the reaction of the group indicated that they were not impressed with the idea.

There is no distinction in the various parts of common equity as far as the common stockholders are concerned. It all represents part of their ownership. Surplus arising from retained earnings is equivalent to raising new common equity. In fact, as earnings are plowed back a company regularly raises new common equity every day. If management made a distinction regarding the rate to be earned on earned surplus, stockholders would be well advised to have the company pay out all its earnings in dividends and then raise new equity money by sale of stock. If you question this statement, consider a private company with one stockholder. Will he accept a lower return on money he *leaves* in than on money he *puts* in?[2] Stockholders of a publicly-owned company should not be treated differently by management.

[2] The owner of a privately-held company would weigh the effect of personal income taxes in determining the amount of earnings to retain. However, we pointed out in Chapter III, under the heading "Investors' Taxes," that taxes paid by investors do not come into play in calculating the Cost-of-Capital in the competitive capital market.

There is one possible difference between common stock sold to the public and earned surplus. A stock sale involves financing costs, including underwriter's commissions and financing expense; none of these is associated with retained earnings, which build up without financing costs. Therefore, it may be contended that a slightly lower rate should be applied to earned surplus to the extent of financing costs. There is a good argument against any difference: a company should earn enough on its common equity to be able to pay out all its earnings in dividends if it chooses to do so and still cover its Cost-of-Capital. In other words, dividend policy decisions should be made free from any pressure of capital requirements. As another argument, a company should not accept less profitable ventures than would be required to stand the test of the capital markets. This book treats all common equity the same.

Misconceptions regarding the cost of the earned surplus may lead managements to make unfortunate financial policy decisions. For example, for a publicly-owned company, one of the considerations in dividend policy should be to establish a cash dividend which will produce the best market price for the common stock in the long run. If management believed that earned surplus had no cost, it might also think incorrectly that the dividend payout should be held down in order to generate free capital. We are now getting far afield from the subject of this book; therefore, we will switch away from dividend policy. Some further remarks are made about the subject in Chapter XIII, Reducing the Cost-of-Capital.

In essence, the total common equity should represent the money that the company has invested in order to produce a profit. As stated above, analysts have to rely primarily on book figures, but will give weight to true present value if they know that there is a difference. If there are any fictitious items on the asset side of the balance sheet as a result of property write-ups, etc., which correspondingly inflate the common equity, they should be eliminated.

## DEFERRED TAXES

To the extent that taxes are deferred, the government provides capital without charge. The purpose of allowing for fast depreciation of assets which results in deferred taxes is to induce business to expand by making expansion more profitable.

In Chapter XV, it is explained how to calculate the profitability rate for a capital expenditure. The basis for the calculation is the cash flow after taxes actually paid. The deferrals will result in a greater cash flow at the beginning of the project and a smaller flow towards the end as the tax expense increases. Thus, for a particular project the tax deferral provides more immediate cash, which has a definite value. This is illustrated in Exhibit 7(V).

If a company normalizes its financial reports, the income statement for book purposes provides for taxes with depreciation on a straight line basis with the tax deferral making up the difference between taxes actually paid and taxes accrued. The liability side of the balance sheet includes the accruals. For example, a balance sheet with deferred taxes might look as shown in Exhibit 8(V).

Financial analysts will study the deferred taxes, but there does not seem to be any uniformity as to how they will treat them for capital structure purposes. For a growing industry, the argument may be made that the reserve will continue to grow and that it is a form of capital which protects the senior capital. This seems questionable, because it is a definite liability and not equity in any sense of the word: in liquidation accrued taxes are certainly a liability. In studying capital structure ratios, deferred tax accruals can either be shown separately as a part of total long-term capital or they can be left out and weight given to them separately on the basis of judgment. We prefer the latter treatment.

Similarly, for Cost-of-Capital calculations, we prefer to leave out deferred tax accruals and only consider the long-term capital provided

## EXHIBIT 7 (V)

### DEFERRED TAXES - INCOME STATEMENT ITEMS
### ASSUMING 50% TAX RATE

| Column | | 1 | 2 | 3 | 4 |
|---|---|---|---|---|---|
| | | Using Straight Line Depreciation for Books and Fast Depreciation for Taxes | | Using Straight Line Depreciation for Both | |
| Line | | Reported Book Figures | For Tax Purposes | Reported Book Figures | For Tax Purposes |
| 1 | Income before taxes and | | | | |
| 2 | depreciation | $26 | $26 | $26 | $26 |
| 3 | Depreciation | 6 | 8 | 6 | 6 |
| 4 | Net income before taxes | $20 | $18 | $20 | $20 |
| 5 | Taxes | 9 | 9 | 10 | 10 |
| 6 | Deferred taxes | 1 | | | |
| 7 | Income after taxes and | | | | |
| 8 | depreciation | $10 | $ 9 | $10 | $10 |
| | | | | | |
| 9 | Cash Flow | | | | |
| 10 | Depreciation | $ 6 | | $ 6 | |
| 11 | Deferred taxes | 1 | | | |
| 12 | Income after taxes | | | | |
| 13 | and depreciation | 10 | | 10 | |
| 14 | Total | $17 | | $16 | |

## EXHIBIT 8 (V)

### DEFERRED TAXES-BALANCE SHEET ITEMS

| Assets | | Liabilities | |
|---|---|---|---|
| Current Assets | $100 | Current Liabilities | $ 50 |
| Plant, Net | 55 | Deferred taxes | 5 |
| | | Long-Term Capital | |
| | |   Debt     $20 | |
| | |   Common | |
| | |   Equity   $80 | |
| | |   Total | 100 |
| Other Items | 0 | Other Items | 0 |
| Total | $155 | Total | $155 |

EXHIBIT 9 (V)

SECURITY COST RATES

---

Short-Term Debt
      Items in current liabilities        The interest cost should be
      carrying interest                   included as part of operating
                                       expense in making project
                                         analysis


Long-Term Capital
      Long-Term Debt
            Short-term debt such as bank      Interest cost should corre-
            loans regularly renewed and       spond to the quality of the
            reported in current liabilities    debt security.
            Leases capitalized
            Mortgages
            Mortgage bonds
            Debenture bonds
            Long-Term notes
            Subordinated debenture bonds
            Income bonds


Preferred Stocks                         Preferred cost


Convertibles
      Debenture bonds                 Common cost
      Preferred stocks


Common Equity
      Par value on stated value        Common cost
      Capital surplus
      Earned surplus
      Fictitious items eliminated

---

by investors. And also, in figuring the return on total long-term capital, we prefer to take the net income after normalized taxes and interest, add back interest on long-term debt, and then divide by total long-term capital, excluding deferred tax accruals.

In using assets as a base for calculating return on investment, allowance does have to be given to the deferred tax accruals. In the example above, Long-Term Capital $100 plus Deferred Taxes $5 provides a total of $105. The $105 provides Working Capital $50 (Current Assets $100 less Current Liabilities $50) and Plant, Net $55. In order to be consistent with the above comments, a 10% return on a $100 Long-Term Capital in the balance sheet above is equivalent to a 10% return on assets based on the following approach:

| Current assets | $100 |
| Less: Current liabilities | 50 |
| Working capital | 50 |
| Plant, Net | 55 |
| Total | $105 |
| Less: Deferred taxes | $ 5 |
| Assets provided by Long-Term Capital | $100 |

This gives effect to the fact that the deferred taxes do provide some of the assets.

If a company does not normalize its financial reports,[3] income will be increased to the extent that taxes are decreased. There will be no tax deferral item in the balance sheet. Consequently, the return on long-term capital will be distorted to the extent of the tax reduction.

## BALANCE SHEET LIABILITIES AND APPLICABLE RATES

As a stepping stone to the next chapter, there are given in tabular form in Exhibit 9(V) the various items which appear on the liability side of a balance sheet and the rates which we have suggested are applicable to each.

[3] Some regulated companies, either through preference or by regulatory order, show book figures on the basis of taxes actually paid. This tends to increase income and overstate the return on long-term capital.

# Composite Rate

We now have the three parts—capital structure, senior capital cost and common cost—to build a composite Cost-of-Capital. We repeat the simple example which we used in Chapter II. The composite Cost-of-Capital as shown in Exhibit 1(VI) is approximately 10%.

## EXHIBIT 1 (VI)

### COMPOSITE COST-OF-CAPITAL

|  | Amount | Rate | Cost |
|---|---|---|---|
| Long-Term Debt | 20% | 5% | 1.00 |
| Common Equity | 80% | 11% | 8.80 |
| Total | 100% |  | 9.80% |

## NOT SPECIFIC SECURITY RATE

In Chapter II, we pointed out that the interest rate alone is not the base on which to establish a Profit Goal. It is the composite rate which must be used for all capital expenditure decisions. We will review this idea to make certain that we do not leave any doubts.

If a $10,000,000 plant is financed with $10,000,000 of long-term bonds with an interest rate of 5%, why is not the capital rate for this plant 5%? If we made anything over 5% could we justify the construction of the plant? At first blush, this seems to make sense. In accounting terms we would show a bookkeeping profit, but this assumes that common equity has no cost. No matter how small, any earnings after interest and taxes are recorded as a profit.

This interest cost approach is so incorrect as

to cause serious error in decision-making.[1] A company cannot sell bonds unless it has some common stock. Bondholders require the protection of the stockholders' equity. The amount of common equity affects the interest rate on the bonds. The interest rate of 5% is actually made possible by the common stockholders' capital. Unless the project bears its proportionate share of the cost of the protection afforded by the common equity, it is not earning its way.

Suppose the same company went into another project for $10,000,000 and financed it with $10,000,000 of common stock. On the basis of the specific security cost approach this project would have to earn the full cost rate for common. It would not obtain any advantage from the fact that the company can finance part of its capital with lower cost bonds.

We should have as the basis for our goal a rate which reflects the security market appraisal of the risk of the enterprise and not the risk of the security which may be used to finance it. The composite Cost-of-Capital, based on all parts of long-term capital, gives us the over-all risk. We can use the composite cost rate for the company as a basis for a goal for a new project, providing the project has approximately the same risk as the company itself. Otherwise, we must make an adjustment for the difference in risk.

Even though the principle of composite cost is fully accepted, one form of financing may lead to the use of the incremental approach unknowingly, and that is lease financing. Sometimes we hear statements to the effect that a project may not be profitable if the plant is owned but will be profitable if the plant is leased. These statements are usually made by people who make other statements, such as: "We ought to lease the plant; we do not want to be in the real estate business; we want our capital invested in fast turnover assets."

This might be entitled: "How to fool yourself about your return on capital." It is going

to be increasingly difficult to fool others now that the accountants are requiring more information about leases.

In the previous chapter, we showed that when leasing is used as a medium of financing, the return, figured on the basis of the reported long-term capital and income, is increased due to the leverage. If you need some figures to visualize this idea, you may wish to turn back to the last chapter.

Actually the financing method, whether it be leasing, debt financing or equity financing, is an entirely separate question from whether to acquire the asset in the first place. The acquisition depends on the anticipated profitability in relation to the investment.

## TAX TREATMENT
## BEFORE OR AFTER TAXES

You have waited a long time for a discussion of the effect of tax-deductability of interest on Cost-of-Capital. Thus far, we have made our calculations on the basis of the rate required to attract capital, that is, the To Investor Rate. This is the rate paid to investors with adjustments for financing costs. Investors are not directly concerned with the income taxes that the company pays.

Now, we have to interpret this rate from the company's point of view and weigh the effect of interest on income taxes. We have already indicated that for the common equity the rate required by investors is identical, except for financing costs, to the cost of that capital to the corporation after corporate income taxes. In contrast, for debt capital the effective cost to the corporation is lower than the investor's rate because of tax savings arising from the income tax deductibility of interest.

In Chapter II, we talked about three rates: Cost-of-Capital, Return on Total Capital Target, and Profit Goal for Expansion. With regard to these rates, there are three ways to treat income taxes, as summarized below.

### To Investor Rate

This rate is based on the rates required by investors. It does include adjustments for

---

[1] Of course, the incremental cost approach is quite valid for certain other budgeting purposes.

financing costs, but it disregards any consideration of the effect of corporate income taxes.

This rate is the one we have already discussed as the starting point for figuring Cost-of-Capital. The Return on Total Capital Target is also calculated on this basis. It is directly comparable with the company's past experienced return. The company's experienced return is derived by adding the net income after taxes, before any dividends, to the interest charges on long-term debt and dividing the total by the total long-term capital.

This is the rate used for regulatory purposes for the regulated companies such as electric, gas and telephone companies. The actual reduction in taxes due to interest charges is taken into account in figuring cost in determining the sales prices for these services.

### Pre-Tax Rate

The nature of this rate is obvious; it gives the cost to the company before income taxes. Interest has to be charged at the full rate because it is before interest has any effect on tax savings. The common rate has to be increased sufficiently to allow for the amount of the income that will be absorbed by income taxes. The same treatment has to be given to the preferred stock rate and to the amount of allowance above Cost-of-Capital.

### After-Tax Equivalent Rate

An expansion project's profitability rate is generally figured on a fully taxed basis, but before interest or other securities charges. There is no adjustment made for the tax savings if the company has interest charges on long-term debt.

Therefore, to make the Cost-of-Capital comparable with the profitability rate calculated for a project, adjustment is made in the cost of debt for the related savings. The interest rate is reduced to the extent that the interest reduces taxes. The common cost is

the same as that used for the To Investor Rate. The allowance above Cost-of-Capital is treated in the same way as the common cost. In other words, this is an after-tax rate, adjusted for the tax savings resulting from interest charges. This is the rate generally compared with the forecast profitability of a project.

The three rates and how they are calculated are shown in Exhibit 2(VI). The rates for interest and common cost, as well as the allowance above Cost-of-Capital, are purely for illustrative purposes and not supposed to represent any company. The assumptions on which the calculations are based are shown at the top of the table. The allowance above Cost-of-Capital is shown as being 2% for the Return on Total Capital Target and 4% for the Expansion Profit Goal. As previously discussed, and as reviewed following the table, there generally should be a spread above Cost-of-Capital for the two other rates.

The table is filled in for all three rates for Cost-of-Capital. The other parts of the table are only filled in where those rates are generally used. The table can be completed readily for each of the three rates if desired.

The rates are carried out to the first decimal place in order to show how the calculations are made. In practice, for an industrial company, the totals would be rounded to a full percentage, because the results are not that precise and the purpose for which they are used does not call for any greater precision.

## ALLOWANCE ABOVE COST-OF-CAPITAL

We have already given reasons why the Return on Total Capital Target should be higher than Cost-of-Capital. Our main reason was that a company should earn something more than just its costs. Good managements do better than the Cost-of-Capital, poor ones do worse. We do not suggest any particular percentage allowance for an industrial company; this is a matter of judgment on the part of

# COMPOSITE RATE

## EXHIBIT 2 (VI)

### TAX EFFECT ON COMPOSITE RATES

---

## ASSUMPTIONS FOR CALCULATIONS

|  | Amount | To Investor Rates[a] |
|---|---|---|
| Debt | 20% | 5% |
| Common Equity | 80% | 11% |
| Total | 100% | |

Allowance above Cost-of-Capital for Return on Total Capital Target    2%

Allowance above Cost-of-Capital for Profit Goal for Expansion    4%

Income Tax Rate    50%

|  | COST-OF-CAPITAL | RETURN ON TOTAL CAPITAL TARGET | PROFIT GOAL FOR EXPANSION[b] |
|---|---|---|---|
| **TO INVESTOR RATE** | | | |
| Debt (20%) | ( 5%) 1.00 | ( 5%) 1.00 | |
| Common (80%) | (11%) 8.80 | (11%) 8.80 | |
| Total | 9.80 % | 9.80 % | |
| Allowance above Cost-of-Capital | | ( 2%) 2.00 % | |
| Total | | 11.80 % | |
| **PRE-TAX RATE** | | | |
| Debt (20%) | ( 5%) 1.00 | | |
| Common (80%) | (22%) 17.60 | | |
| Total | 18.60 % | | |
| **AFTER TAX EQUIVALENT RATE** | | | |
| Debt (20%) | (2 1/2%) 0.50 | | (2-1/2%) 0.50 |
| Common (80%) | (11%) 8.80 | | (11%) 8.80 |
| Total | 9.30 % | | 9.30 % |
| Allowance above Cost-of-Capital | | | (4%) 4.00 % |
| Total | | | 13.30 % |

---

[a] Rates are adjusted for financing costs so that they represent the cost to the company.

[b] This is also referred to throughout the book simply as the Profit Goal.

management. If a company earns more than the Cost-of-Capital, it is benefiting its stockholders. A company will, of course, strive to earn as much as possible in keeping with the competitive situation.

The Profit Goal should be higher than the Cost-of-Capital for three reasons:

1. A company will wish to achieve a Return on Total Capital Target for the entire company above Cost-of-Capital. In order to accomplish this result it must have a Profit Goal above Cost-of-Capital.

2. Some projects may have to be undertaken which provide no return, such as eating facilities for company employees. Some projects may have to be undertaken which do not completely cover Cost-of-Capital. These deficiencies below Cost-of-Capital must be made up by setting the Profit Goal on other projects above Cost-of-Capital.

3. Uncertainties in forecasting the results for a new project require an allowance above Cost-of-Capital. There may be lags in start-up time, disappointing sales, unforeseen expenses, additional investment, etc. If a company only achieved the Cost-of-Capital on some projects and, because of unexpected difficulties, failed to earn the Cost-of-Capital on others, the average result would be below Cost-of-Capital.

A distinction should be made between expansion and diversification. Diversification should generally require a higher standard because of unfamiliarity. Of course, we are talking not about immediate profits but about all future profits that are expected to accrue as a result of an investment.

How far a Profit Goal should be set above Cost-of-Capital for a particular project will have to be determined by management taking into account the above factors. No set rule can be formulated. Too high a goal may mean a pricing policy which will invite too much competition. Too low a Profit Goal will mean inadequate earnings. As previously reported, some manufacturing companies have used a Profit Goal as high as 20%.

It is interesting to note that the managements of companies which show good profits generally recognize the importance of setting high Profit Goals. On the other hand, some companies which show poor results argue that they cannot find projects which will provide high profits. They struggle with their consciences and in the end usually lower their Profit Goals. This can only lead to perpetuation of poor performance with all the unfortunate consequences of misdirecting capital.

## AN EXAMPLE—DOMESTIC INTEGRATED OIL COMPANY

As an example, we will estimate the Cost-of-Capital for a segment of the oil industry. This example is presented in condensed form and is primarily for the purpose of illustrating how to interpret the figures in terms of the principles and how to deal with some of the problems encountered.

No company is exactly like any other company, but we will use companies which the investing public thinks are reasonably like one another. Standard & Poor's Corporation classifies 20 companies[2] as domestic integrated oil companies. We will use the ten largest firms on the basis of sales. The results for these large firms may produce a lower Cost-of-Capital than for the smaller companies.

### Bond Cost

The ratings on the non-convertible debt of the ten companies by Moody's Investors Service, Inc. are as follows: one is rated Aaa, four Aa, three A, one Baa, and one is not rated. As

[2] Industry Surveys—Oil, April 14, 1966 (Section 3). Apco Oil Corp., Ashland Oil & Refining Co., Atlantic Richfield Co., Cities Service Co., Continental Oil Co., Kerr-McGee Oil Industries, Inc., Marathon Oil Co., Pennzoil Co., Phillips Petroleum Co., Quaker State Oil Co., Shell Oil Co., Shamrock Oil & Gas Corp., Sinclair Oil Corp., Skelly Oil Co., Standard Oil Co. (Indiana), Standard Oil Co. (Ohio), Sun Oil Co., Sunray DX Oil Co., Tidewater Oil Co., Union Oil Co. of California.

an approximation for the debt cost, we will start with the ten-year (1956–1965) average of Moody's Investors Service, Inc., indexes[3] of yields of outstanding industrial bonds of Aa and A grade.

Aa          4.16%
A           4.28
          ———
Average 4.22%

Two adjustments have to be made to convert average yields of outstanding bonds to the cost for new issues:

1. The prices of outstanding bonds have to be reduced and the yields increased to allow for financing costs in order to estimate the cost rate based on the net proceeds to the company.
2. Generally a higher yield is required on new bonds than the yield on outstanding bonds in order to induce investors to buy the large supply coming on the market.

We can approximate these two adjustments by adding 0.27%[4] to the average yield. Therefore, we will use a bond cost of 4.49%.

### Preferred Cost

To estimate the preferred cost, we will start with the ten-year (1956–1965) average of Moody's Investors Service, Inc., index of outstanding industrial preferred stock yields for high-grade low dividend issues. This average is 4.22%. The same adjustments that were made for the bond costs have to be made for the preferred costs and for this purpose we will use 0.29%.[5] Therefore, we will use a preferred cost of 4.51%.

### Convertible Securities

Some of the companies in our sample have either convertible preferred or convertible

debt outstanding. The common stocks are selling at prices above or near the level necessary to make conversion attractive. Consequently, we will apply the common cost to the convertible securities.

### Common Cost

In order to estimate the common cost, we must evaluate all possible evidence of investors' expectations of future earnings because they influence market prices of the stocks. Investors may expect earnings to remain stable, to grow, or even to decline. Our ten-company example is a good one, because it shows how various approaches may have to be used to arrive at a figure based on judgment.

To start with let us assume that investors in this industry expected no change in earnings. Then we can make an estimate by relating earnings per share to market prices over a ten-year period adjusted by 15% to allow for financing costs. Exhibit 3(VI) sets forth the average of these calculations for our sample:

The problem with these calculations is obvious. We have substantial evidence to indicate that investors did expect some growth in earnings per share over this period. Therefore, our average figure is too low as a common cost. Spot figures should not be used for Cost-of-Capital purposes. However, it is interesting to note that the earnings for 1966 for the ten companies as estimated by a leading statistical organization, divided into the average high-low market price for July 1966 and adjusted by 15% for financing costs, was 9.7%. This is too low as a cost rate for the same reason just mentioned.

As another estimate, let us assume that investors based their decisions on earnings estimates two years ahead and that their estimates were the same as those earnings actually realized. Exhibit 4(VI) shows these figures with market prices adjusted by 15% to allow for financing costs.

This approach has the following flaws:

1. It assumes that the earnings which investors estimated were the same as those

---

[3] See Appendix B for the yields by years.

[4] This adjustment is the average of the adjustments used in Chapter IV for Aa and A grade industrial bonds for the period 1956–1965.

[5] This is the adjustment used in Chapter IV for high grade industrial preferred stocks for the period 1956–1965.

## EXHIBIT 3 (VI)

## EARNINGS-PRICE RATIO, ADJUSTED
## BY 15% FOR FINANCING COSTS

|  | Average 1956-1965[a] |
|---|---|
| Atlantic Richfield | 11.0% |
| Cities Service | 10.6 |
| Continental Oil | 6.5 |
| Phillips Petroleum | 7.5 |
| Shell Oil | 7.4 |
| Sinclair Oil | 9.2 |
| Standard Oil (Indiana) | 9.7 |
| Sun Oil | 8.4 |
| Tidewater Oil | 10.5 |
| Union Oil of California | 9.5 |
| Average | 9.0% |

[a] Averages exclude Tidewater Oil Company for 1958. It reported a deficit in that year.

that the companies actually reported. Frequently, this is not so. Investors expect one level of earnings and may get something quite different.

2. Investors may base their decisions on estimates more or less than two years ahead. A comparable figure using one year's difference between price and earnings was 9.5% and using three years' difference was 10.8%.[6]

3. In any event, they would probably ex-

[6] Calculations of these percentages with figures for ten years results in averages based on nine periods for the earnings one year ahead, eight periods for two years ahead, and seven periods for three years ahead. Extending the figures back so that there are nine periods for each calculation produces results as follows: 10.1% for two years ahead and 10.7% for three years ahead.

pect some continued growth after the forecast year. Thus, using a limited number of years ahead for companies which have shown a growth pattern produces results which are too low.

Some investors think of future earnings in terms of an annual percentage growth and estimate their possible return in terms of yield plus growth in earnings per share. The following two assumptions, which are necessary to make this calculation work, were reasonably well satisfied by our data.

1. The price-earnings ratio at the end of the period is the same as at the beginning.[7]

[7] The average price-earnings ratio was 13.3 times at the end of the period and 13.9 at the beginning.

## EXHIBIT 4 (VI)

### MARKET PRICES DIVIDED INTO EARNINGS PER SHARE TWO YEARS AHEAD, ADJUSTED BY 15% FOR FINANCING COSTS

|  | Average 1956-1965[a] |
|---|---|
| Atlantic Richfield | 11.8% |
| Cities Service | 11.4 |
| Continental Oil | 7.3 |
| Phillips Petroleum | 7.9 |
| Shell Oil | 8.4 |
| Sinclair Oil | 9.0 |
| Standard Oil (Indiana) | 11.1 |
| Sun Oil | 9.3 |
| Tidewater Oil | 12.6 |
| Union Oil of California | 12.2 |
| Average | 10.1% |

[a] Since the market price in 1956 is related to earnings in 1958, etc., there are eight figures for each company.

2. The dividend payout ratio remains stable over the years.[8]

Exhibit 5 (VI) is based on yields and growth rates in earnings per share for the 1956–1965 period.

These data assume that the companies' earnings grew at the rate investors expected and this may not have been true for the 1956–1965 period. Using a compound growth rate in earnings over a period of years is supposed to eliminate short-run abnormalities and fluctuations in earnings. Actually, the most recent ten-year period begins during the Suez Crisis of 1956 when domestic oil companies fared very well. Growth rates based on a beginning period of abnormally high earnings will naturally be too low. The average earnings per share for these ten companies declined for the first two years and then showed a steady compound growth rate of 9.9% per year compared

with 5.3% for the full ten-year period. During the last eight years, the price-earnings ratio increased from 11.9 to 13.3. Thus, the data in the last eight years would produce a substantially higher result. However, we will not include it as part of the data to determine our final figure in order to be consistent with the period used for the other figures.

As a final test, we took a sample of five financial analysts who have followed the oil industry for many years to determine how rapidly they had expected earnings to grow in the period between 1956 and 1965. The average figure was 5.5%. Assuming that investors anticipated the same average yield of 3.2% that actually occurred, and adding it to this 5.5% expected earnings growth rate, produces a result of 8.7%, or 10.2% after adjusting for 15% for financing costs. In viewing this figure, we must have in mind the following questions: Were the financial analysts able to project themselves back to recall what their expectations were, or were they influenced by what actually happened? Does the small sample rea-

[8] The dividend payout naturally varied between companies and over the period to some extent with fluctuations in earnings, but the range between 42% and 58% was reasonably close to the average of 48%.

## EXHIBIT 5 (VI)

## YIELD PLUS ACTUAL GROWTH RATE IN EARNINGS
## PER SHARE ADJUSTED BY 15% FOR FINANCING COSTS

| Column | 1 | 2 | 3 | 4 |
|---|---|---|---|---|
| | Average Yield[a] 1956-1965 | Compound Rate of Growth in Earnings Per Share 1956-1965 | Yield Plus Growth Rate | Yield Plus Growth Rate Adjusted by 15% for Financing Costs |
| Atlantic Richfield | 4.5% | 2.8% | 7.3% | 8.6% |
| Cities Service | 4.3 | 4.2 | 8.5 | 10.0 |
| Continental Oil | 3.1 | 7.2 | 10.3 | 12.1 |
| Phillips Petroleum | 3.6 | 3.7 | 7.3 | 8.6 |
| Shell Oil | 2.8 | 6.1 | 8.9 | 10.5 |
| Sinclair Oil | 4.9 | 0.0[b] | 4.9 | 5.8 |
| Standard Oil (Indiana) | 3.2 | 5.0 | 8.2 | 9.6 |
| Sun Oil | 1.7 | 6.5 | 8.2 | 9.6 |
| Tidewater Oil | 0.0 | 6.0 | 6.0 | 7.1 |
| Union Oil of California | 3.4 | 11.5 | 14.9 | 17.5 |
| Average | 3.2% | 5.3% | 8.5% | 9.9% |

[a]In Chapter III, we describe this approach as the sum of the dividend yield when the stock is bought plus the compound annual growth rate in earnings per share. The yield shown in Column 1 is the average of the ten years.

[b]Sinclair Oil showed a decline in earnings. It is unlikely that investors would have accepted a 4.9% yield if they expected earnings to decline. Therefore, we have indicated the negative growth rate as zero.

sonably well represent the entire consensus of the market which caused the prices to be what they were? Was the dividend yield that occurred the same as was anticipated by investors during the period?

Summarized in Exhibit 6(VI) are the four calculations for the common stock for the ten years 1956–1965 (which provides a nine-year period) adjusted by 15% for financing costs.

This wide array of results and the questions which we raised with regard to each one illustrates the difficulty of estimating the common cost closely. However, it does appear that we have sufficient data to arrive at a reasonable

## EXHIBIT 6 (VI)

### COMMON RATES SUMMARIZED

| | |
|---|---|
| 1. Earnings - price ratio | 9.0% |
| 2. Market prices divided into earnings per share two years ahead | 10.1% |
| 3. Yield plus actual growth rate in earnings per share | 9.9% |
| 4. Yield plus growth rate in earnings per share as estimated by financial analysts | 10.2% |
| Average | 9.8% |

figure by applying judgment. The average assumes that the figures should be treated equally: this is not so. For the reasons already stated, we believe that the method of calculating 1, 2, and 3 produces unrealistically low results. We do not know whether 4 may be biased on the low or high side. In view of the fact that the figures are generally weighted on the low side, our judgment suggests a slightly higher figure than the average or at least 11%. The correct figure may be higher than this, but we have no basis on which to make such an estimate.

*Composite Cost-of-Capital*

Now that we have estimated a cost rate for each class of securities, we need a representative capital structure in order to estimate a

## EXHIBIT 7 (VI)

### COST-OF-CAPITAL

| Column | 1 Amount | To Investor Rate 2 Rate | 3 Total |
|---|---|---|---|
| Bonds | 19% | 4.49% | 0.85% |
| Preferred | 1 | 4.51 | 0.05 |
| Convertible securities | 4 | 11.00 | 0.44 |
| Common equity | 76 | 11.00 | 8.36 |
| Total | 100% | | 9.70% |

composite Cost-of-Capital. We will use the average capital structure[9] for the ten compa-

[9] No attempt was made to capitalize leases. This would add to the debt component of the capital structure.

nies over the ten-year period. In Exhibit 7(VI), a composite Cost-of-Capital is calculated with that capital structure on the To Investor Rate basis.

## EXHIBIT 8 (VI)

## COST-OF-CAPITAL

| Column | 1 | Pre-Tax Rate | | After Tax Equivalent Rate | |
| --- | --- | --- | --- | --- | --- |
| | | 2 | 3 | 4 | 5 |
| | Amount | Rate | Total | Rate | Total |
| Bonds | 19% | 4.49% | 0.85% | 2.25% | 0.43% |
| Preferred | 1 | 4.51 | 0.05 | 4.51 | 0.05 |
| Convertible securities | 4 | 22.00 | 0.88 | 11.00 | 0.44 |
| Common equity | 76 | 22.00 | 16.72 | 11.00 | 8.36 |
| Total | 100% | | 18.50% | | 9.28% |

The two other rates, assuming a 50% corporate income tax rate, would be as shown in Exhibit 8(VI).

We would round off these figures as follows:

| | Cost-of-Capital |
| --- | --- |
| To Investor Rate | 10% |
| Pre-Tax Rate | 19% |
| After-Tax Equivalent Rate | 9% |

Rates for the Return on Total Capital Target and Expansion Profit Goal should be higher.

A few comments may be in order. Cost-of-Capital depends on the nature of the business and the risks inherent in it. It is important to know if an industry changes over the years in such a way as to change the inherent risk. The integrated oil industry was certainly in a different position during the Suez Crisis than it has been before or since. This was not a period of normality for the industry and to that extent it is a source of error in our estimates. However, the disturbance to investor expectations probably extends beyond the actual crisis period and, therefore, we cannot solve the problem simply by eliminating that period from our calculations.

During the 1950's, oil financial analysts paid considerable attention to reserves in the ground. For this reason, some people might assert that reserves, in addition to earnings and dividend growth, were a major factor in determining market prices. A high level of reserves means high expectations of future earnings. Therefore, our figure may be somewhat too low. There is no way to make an allowance for this factor, but we feel that it is not a sufficient distortion to invalidate our results.

Unfortunately, accounting practices in the oil industry vary widely and, consequently, financial statements of the various companies in our sample are not strictly comparable. We hope that we have used enough companies to average out variations in accounting practices.

The companies in our sample showed an average return of 9% on their stated common equity in the ten-year period, and this is somewhat below our common cost. The return on the stated total long-term capital would similarly be below our composite Cost-of-Capital. Furthermore, the stated book figures are undoubtedly below the present value of the properties. On the other hand, the reported return may not correctly reflect the situation, because the oil reserves may represent a large part of the investment which will produce good profits in the future, but currently are not accounting for profits in proportion to their investment. Returns on the refining and marketing divisions of the business separately would be more meaningful. In fact, the risks in the three divisions—production, refining, and distribution—are sufficiently different so that a company should have different goals for each.

This chapter concludes the explanation of Cost-of-Capital and Profit Goals. In the remaining chapters we will discuss various related ideas which follow from the Cost-of-Capital concept.

# CHAPTER VII

# Capital Structure Effect

## EFFECT OF CAPITAL STRUCTURE MIX ON COST-OF-CAPITAL

One of the controversies about Cost-of-Capital revolves around the question of the effect of varying debt ratios. There are three schools of thought.

### Pure Theory—Capital Structure Has no Effect

Pure economic theory tells us that Cost-of-Capital is dependent on the risk of the enterprise and not on the way the capital structure pie is divided between debt and equity. Here we are talking about the To Investor Rate and not considering the effect of interest on tax savings.

This idea is based on the principle that as debt is increased, both the debt and the common equity become more risky and the rate on both must rise so that the two combined equal the same over-all cost.

For example, suppose one person owned all the company. Could he change the Cost-of-Capital by exchanging half of his stock for debt so that his investment would consist of 50% debt and 50% common? Obviously, it makes no difference to him how the pie is divided, the over-all risk is the same. Now, suppose the two different securities are owned by different investors. Would they take lower rates on each, or on either one so that over-all cost would be lower than with common only? Not on the basis of pure theory. And in our thinking about Cost-of-Capital, we should not lose sight of the fact that basically it is the risk of the enterprise that determines the rate.

However, this is not a very practical approach in view of the nature of our securities markets, and it does not take into account that interest does create a tax savings.

### Practical Approach—Proper Use of Senior Securities

We do have to allow for the fact that tax savings reduce the net cost of debt because interest reduces taxes. Furthermore, the markets for debt and common are not entirely overlapping. Debt may be used up to a certain point without substantially increasing the debt and common cost so that there will be a decrease in the over-all cost. Within a limited range of debt, so that the quality of the debt and common are maintained as high grade, there will be some increase in the cost of both, but not in the composite cost. At some point, as debt is further increased, risk is added to the enterprise as a result of an unbalanced capital structure. Then the rate on debt and common will rise to such an extent as to cause an increase in the composite Cost-of-Capital. The amount of debt which each company should carry will depend on a variety of circumstances.

This second school seems most sensible in that it follows sound principles of finance. It takes a long-range point of view within the realm of practicality.

### Short Range—High Leverage Unsound

There are those who erroneously believe that the Cost-of-Capital can be reduced by piling on all the debt the traffic will bear. They contend that debt, with the interest deductible for tax purposes, is cheap, and common is expensive; therefore, using all the debt possible will result in a decrease in the over-all Cost-of-Capital. The proponents of this third school tend to ridicule bond quality ratings and see no ill effects from having a company's bond rating fall to Baa and lower.[1] They fail to consider the greater risk to both the debt and the common stock and the fact that the rate on both debt and common will increase so as to cause an increase in the over-all cost.

In the short run, during a bull market when investors are not worrying about adverse developments, it may be possible to disregard temporarily the disadvantages and danger of too much debt. Of course, security holders who advocate this policy have in the back of their minds that they will sell their common before the company encounters adversity. Fine for them, but not for the stockholders in the long run.

Management that follows this policy may have in mind retiring before adversity hits, may be the high-pressure promoter type and throw sensible caution to the winds, or may be so naive as to believe that adversity will never be encountered.

From the long-range point of view of the

stockholders, the short-range approach must be assiduously avoided. The company does not have the mobility of a security holder who can sell out if he expects trouble. A company will have to consider the effect on Cost-of-Capital when adversity is encountered. There are many reasons why it is best for a company in the long run to keep its debt within the high-grade category. We discuss further the importance of a sound financial policy in Chapter XIII.

These three different schools of thought on the effect of capital structure mix on Cost-of-Capital are shown in the diagram in Exhibit 1(VII) as they might apply to a large, well-situated industrial company. The figures, bond ratings, etc., are for illustrative purposes alone and are not supposed to represent true numerical relationships.

What evidence can be advanced to prove the above conclusions? Because of the many factors which affect security prices, adequate statistical proof is not readily available to show the effect of differences in debt ratio on Cost-of-Capital. It is impossible to obtain adequate samples in which the effect of debt ratio is isolated from all the other factors which bear on security prices so as to determine its consequences alone. Those efforts at statistical proof which have been based on price-earnings ratios are wrong because they do not measure the common cost properly. We must look to logical reasoning on sound assumptions for a foundation for our conclusions.

### Hypothetical Example

Since adequate market evidence cannot be found which would screen out all other effects on Cost-of-Capital except differences of capital structure mix, you may obtain some idea of the magnitudes involved by setting up various hypothetical examples. There are shown in Exhibit 2(VII) three different capital structures as they might apply to an industrial company. Ratings are assigned to the different amounts of debt in order to help you visualize the quality of the securities.

These examples indicate the advantages of

---

[1] We refer to bond ratings throughout the book to describe debt quality. If you are not familiar with the ratings, they are explained in Appendix B.

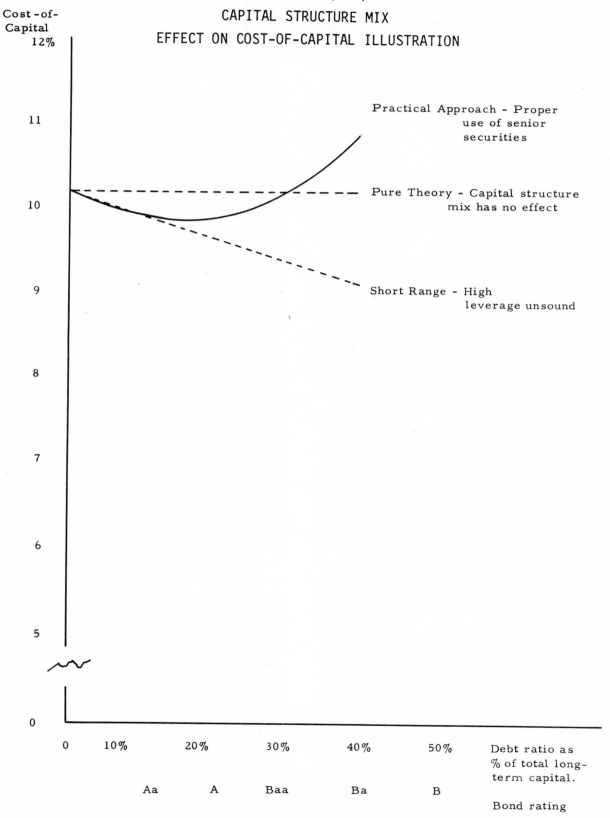

EXHIBIT 1 (VII)
CAPITAL STRUCTURE MIX
EFFECT ON COST-OF-CAPITAL ILLUSTRATION

Cost-of-Capital

12%

11

Practical Approach - Proper
use of senior
securities

10

Pure Theory - Capital structure
mix has no effect

9

Short Range - High
leverage unsound

8

7

6

5

0

0    10%    20%    30%    40%    50%    Debt ratio as
% of total long-
term capital.

Aa    A    Baa    Ba    B

Bond rating

## EXHIBIT 2 (VII)

### HYPOTHETICAL EXAMPLE OF EFFECT OF CAPITAL STRUCTURE MIX ON COST-OF-CAPITAL, ASSUMING A 50% CORPORATE INCOME TAX

| Column | 1 | 2 | 3 | 4 | 5 | 6 |
|---|---|---|---|---|---|---|
| | | | To Investor Rate Total Composite Rates the Same-10% | | After Tax Equivalent Rate Total Composite Rates the Same-9.663% | |
| Line | Bond Rating | Capital Structure | Rates | Composite Cost | Rates | Composite Cost |
| 1 | Aa | Debt 15% | 4.50% | 0.675 | 2.25% | 0.338 |
| 2 | | Common 85 | 10.97 | 9.325 | 10.97 | 9.325 |
| 3 | | Total 100% | | 10.000% | | 9.663% |
| 4 | Low A | Debt 30% | 5.00 | 1.50 | 2.50 | 0.750 |
| 5 | or | Common 70 | 12.14 | 8.50 | 12.73 | 8.913 |
| 6 | BBB | Total 100% | | 10.00% | | 9.663% |
| 7 | Very | Debt 60% | 6.00 | 3.60 | 3.00 | 1.800 |
| 8 | Low | Common 40 | 16.00 | 6.40 | 19.66 | 7.863 |
| 9 | Grade | Total 100% | | 10.00% | | 9.663% |

leverage and the fact that interest is deductible for tax purposes. However, when the quality of debt and common falls below good quality, it does not appear that the added return on common offsets the added financial risk with lack of financial flexibility, the disadvantages of a strained credit, possible effects on dividend payments, etc. Furthermore, it can be visualized that over the long run the composite cost might even be increased with excessive leverage.

For the To Investor Rate in Columns 3 and 4, we assign debt cost rates and calculate the common costs so as to make the composite come out the same 10% figure for the three capital structures. We note that the common rate is 10.97%, 12.14% and 16.00% respectively for the three capital structures. The two last percentages do not seem unreasonably high in view of the added risk due to leverage.

In the last two columns, we give effect to the tax savings from interest. We assume the same composite cost for the three capital struc-

tures, that is 9.663% and then note what this would do to the common cost. It went from 10.97% to 12.73% and 19.66% as the debt was increased. With that added leverage it is not unreasonable to expect that an even larger increase would be justified in view of the added risk. To help your thinking in this area you may wish to shadowbox with some capital structures of your own with various assumptions as to the cost rates.

## HIGHLY LEVERAGED CAPITAL STRUCTURE NO GOOD FOR CALCULATING COST-OF-CAPITAL

We stated above that no clear statistical evidence is available to show the effect of capital structure mix on Cost-of-Capital because it is impossible to obtain a uniform sample of companies similar in all respects except for differences in debt ratio. Likewise, broad data for Cost-of-Capital determination for highly leveraged companies is hard to come by. In order to make sure that the effect of leverage shows up in cost rates, we have to be certain to include periods in our study which fully test the disadvantages of leverage as well as the advantages. The disadvantages show up during periods of bad earnings and poor markets for securities. Market evidences for cost rates for the securities of a leveraged company during good times only are worthless for Cost-of-Capital purposes. Generally we will have to content ourselves with working with capital structures which have high-grade securities. This in no way should be considered a major stumbling block. It leaves us an adequate area in which to produce meaningful results which can be used as a basis for sound guides for management.

## BACKING INTO COST-OF-CAPITAL— EQUATING RISK THROUGH CAPITAL STRUCTURE

Under certain circumstances, it is possible to make a broad estimate of the Cost-of-Capital by an indirect approach.

The risk of an enterprise determines the Cost-of-Capital, if there is no financial risk added because of an unbalanced capital structure. With experience in finance, it is possible to make a judgment as to the amount of debt a company can carry and keep the debt in the good quality category. The common stock, representing the balance of the capital structure, would be high-grade if the enterprise is a type which investors do not consider a high risk.

We have seen that the Cost-of-Capital for a high-grade common stock of a large company may be in the neighborhood of 11%. If we estimate an approximate interest rate for the debt part of the capital structure, we have the ingredients needed to determine a composite rate.

Suppose after careful thought we decide that a company with the risk characteristics of a telephone company can have 35% of its capital structure in debt and be rated high-grade. Assuming an interest rate of 4%, we obtain a To Investor Rate, Cost-of-Capital as shown in Exhibit 3 (VII).

### EXHIBIT 3 (VII)

### COST-OF-CAPITAL

|  | Amount | Rate | To Investor Rate |
|---|---|---|---|
| Debt | 35% | 4% | 1.40 |
| Common | 65% | 10% | 6.50 |
| Total | 100% | | 7.90% |

As another example, suppose we are interested in obtaining the Cost-of-Capital for a large real estate development consisting of apartment houses. We know that debt financing on an apartment house may go higher than 70% of total capital but such a ratio would not mean highest quality. Providing the apartment house is well run and the occupancy rate is good, a debt ratio of 60% with an appropriate amortization would be conservative. The mortgage would be in the high-grade category and so would the common. Generally, mortgages on real estate developments carry somewhat higher rates than comparable corporate bonds; therefore, let us use 5% as an approximate interest rate, and 11% for the common. The picture would then be as shown in Exhibit 4 (VII).

## EXHIBIT 4 (VII)

### COST-OF-CAPITAL

|  | Amount | Rate | To Investor Rate |
|---|---|---|---|
| Debt | 60% | 5% | 3.00 |
| Common Equity | 40 | 11 | 4.40 |
| Total | 100% | | 7.40% |

This idea of backing into Cost-of-Capital works on the assumption that the common cost can be set at the high-grade rate by varying the debt ratio depending on the risk of the enterprise. It fails if an enterprise is very risky because of special circumstances, or if it is small and cannot carry any debt and have the common high-grade. In such a situation, the common cost would have to be increased to compensate for the added risk and we could not apply the idea of backing into Cost-of-Capital.

Even where applicable, this approach can only give a broad approximation, but it may be sufficiently close to be of value. It does require long experience in finance in order to come up with a capital structure which will meet the necessary objective of the common being very high grade.

This sounds rather simple, but in actuality it is very complex and it is fraught with danger! If a person does not have adequate experience in this field, there is a tendency to feel that a large amount of debt can be used and still have the debt and common high-grade. This, of course, will lead to serious error. In effect, leverage is added to the capital structure without an increase in the common cost to compensate for the risk. It has been explained how risk may be added with too much debt so that the composite Cost-of-Capital may be increased.

In the field of regulated industries some witnesses who oppose companies in rate case proceedings tend to use this erroneous approach. They use a high debt ratio and a low rate on the common which is entirely out of line with the high debt. Some regulatory authorities have even accepted it as the basis for their decisions.

# CHAPTER VIII

# Risk Differences

## RISK VARYING FROM PROJECT TO PROJECT

A company will first wish to determine the risk for the business as a whole through the Cost-of-Capital approach. However, the company may be involved in various businesses which have different risks, and it should establish different rates for the different parts of the business. It may be possible to find other companies similar to each separate business to use as a source of information on which to assess these different risks. More than likely, however, it will be necessary to rely on judgment.

If a company expands its existing business it can use the figure which has been developed for the company as a whole. However, if the expansion is in a different field it should use a figure based on the risk in that particular field.

For example, if a company has a Cost-of-Capital of 10% and it goes into a project which has a 12% risk, it should use the 12% figure as the basis for setting its goal rather than 10%. After the project is completed and it becomes a part of the company, the over-all risk of the company will change in proportion to the extent to which the new investment is related to the total investment of the company. Conversely, if the risk in the new proj-

ect is 8%, that figure should be used as the basis for a goal rather than the 10% company figure. After the project is completed and the earnings realized the total earning rate of the company will decrease, but so will the risk so that the investors will not be hurt.

A small company will generally be viewed by investors as having more risk than a large one, even though a moderate-sized company may be better able to compete in some businesses than a very large one. At what size the risk starts to increase from the investors' point of view will depend to some extent on the nature of the business. There is no clearly-defined dividing line. We suggest as a rough bench mark $100,000,000 of total assets or sales, whichever is larger.[1]

If a large company acquires a small one, it will have to consider the risk of the business

---

[1] National Credit Office ratings of companies are used by dealers in commercial paper. A company might find it difficult to sell commercial paper readily unless it was rated prime. The general definition of prime is as follows:

*prime*—Companies with a net worth or capital funds in excess of $25,000,000, nationally-known, sound earning records, strong balance sheets, and an excellent reputation.

Commercial paper is short term. This size test is somewhat smaller than we have suggested for long-term financing. An industrial company with $25,000,000 of net worth might have about $45,000,000 of total assets and $60,000,000 of sales.

being acquired. However, it may eliminate the risk element due to the small size because the company being acquired will receive the benefits of the larger size when it is merged.

## ALTERNATIVE OPPORTUNITY APPROACH

It is sometimes suggested that capital decision-making should be based on alternative opportunities. In other words, if there are four opportunities available with profitability prospects of 4%, 11%, 12% and 13%, the company should choose the one providing the highest return. Stated in this way the idea may be quite incorrect. Each prospective return must be evaluated in terms of the risk involved. This is consistent with the basic principles of investing in any form. For example, suppose the prospective returns and risks for these four opportunities are as shown in Exhibit 1 (VIII).

Alternatives 3 and 4 might produce losses in

## EXHIBIT 1 (VIII)

### ALTERNATIVE OPPORTUNITIES

| Alternatives | Prospective Return | Risk |
|---|---|---|
| 1. Government bonds | 4% | 4% |
| 2. Expansion in U.S. | 11 | 10 |
| 3. Diversification in U.S. | 12 | 13 |
| 4. Foreign expansion | 13 | 15 |

the long run. If they were the only ones available the company would be better off keeping the money in government bonds, where the return equals the risk, or returning the money to its investors. In our example alternative 2 is available and it is the only one which should be accepted in spite of the prospects of higher returns for 3 and 4.

Undoubtedly, managements will make mental assessments of the returns in relation to the risks in considering alternative opportunities, but the lure of the high returns can easily court disaster. A formal procedure should be used so as to avoid such a bias.

## FACTORS THAT AFFECT RISK

In assessing risk we must think in terms of how it is appraised by the investors who provide the capital. As we have stated previously, sometimes managements forget this idea and think only in terms of how they personally look at the risk. They are too close to the situation and often underestimate the risk. They have a tendency to think that a new project is a sure thing, while investors taking a broad view might feel quite differently. Furthermore, capital has to be obtained from investors and it is their appraisal which determines the cost rates for capital.

Risk is not susceptible to precise measurement. Some risks which affect the company as a whole are suggested below.

A new type of investment.

The size of the company—a small company is more vulnerable to adverse developments.

Sales to one customer—for example, an automobile parts manufacturer selling to one automobile company as compared to another selling to three different companies.

A company producing a product which is a fad, or a high-style business.

A company dependent on the skills of one or two individuals.

An industry in which there are many small operators who do not know their costs.

A company engaged in a field where entry by newcomers is relatively easy—where the capital costs and skills required are moderate and the return on investment at the particular time is inviting.

An industry in which government pressure or control may make it difficult to adjust prices when costs increase.

A company with a high wage factor.

A raw material which is a large element of cost of the final product and which may be subject to quick price increases causing a profit squeeze.

An extractive industry in which the source of supply of the product is uncertain.

A company which is dependent on government contracts, particularly those requiring large amounts of capital.

A company which has a large investment in fixed assets which cannot be liquidated readily or used for another purpose and for which there is a possibility of obsolescence, as compared with a company which has a relatively large amount of assets in current form, liquidatable at reasonable prices.

A company in an industry going through major changes in technology.

A company which is subject to major acts of Nature, such as a company which would be adversely affected by a hurricane.

A company requiring large and special research and development expenditures.

A company with important interests in foreign activities with unstable governments or soft currencies.

## FOREIGN INVESTMENT

Foreign investment may have strong appeal; the grass may look greener because the return seems higher than in this country. To the extent that the risk is correspondingly higher, there is no gain.

Foreign investment may carry three additional risks not present in this country:

### 1. Currency

Devaluation—loss in value of earnings and investment because of inflation and devaluation of the currency in terms of American dollars.

Inconvertibility—a dollar of earnings in this country is worth a dollar, but earnings abroad are worth dollars only if they can be turned into dollars.

### 2. Political

The attitude towards business in general and outside capital in particular, including the possibility of expropriation.

### 3. Operating Conditions

Including law and legal systems, government controls, taxes, labor, marketing methods, financing, accounting techniques, etc., which are unlike those in this country and with which management may have less experience.

These risks will vary widely in degree from country to country, but informed investors add substantially to their appraisal of risk for a company which has large foreign investment, depending on surrounding circumstances.

It is interesting to observe the thinking of some companies toward foreign investment. A company which has little foreign investment may anxiously seek more. On the other hand, a company with large foreign investments may strive to build more business in this country to offset the prejudices of investors against its large proportion of foreign investments.

These remarks merely suggest that management should weigh carefully the possible added earnings versus the greater risk as viewed by investors. Investors will take careful account of the nature, extent, and location of foreign investments. If the company does not produce sufficient earnings abroad to compensate for investors' appraisal of the additional risk, the prices of securities will suffer. A publicly-owned company cannot afford to use yard-sticks for foreign investments that vary too widely from those used in the securities market.

How do you assess the risk from country to country? This is a difficult question. If there were active markets in this country for a large number of bonds and stocks of foreign companies, we could appraise the risk by the Cost-of-Capital approach. Adequate data is not available. We must look for the answers primarily on the basis of judgment, since there is scant evidence to view.

The bulk of foreign securities in this country for which market quotations are available consists of government bonds payable in American dollars. Obviously, they do not represent the Cost-of-Capital for an industrial company, but they may help to direct our thinking. The figures may have some significance when compared to the yield on United States Government bonds.

Given in Exhibit 2 (VIII) are a few of the foreign government issues payable in American dollars which are listed on the New York Stock Exchange. Also included is a quotation on United States Government bonds and the percentage increase of the foreign bonds over those of the United States. They are not strictly comparable because of the difference

## EXHIBIT 2 (VIII)

### COMPARISON OF YIELDS ON U.S. GOVERNMENT BONDS WITH BONDS OF CERTAIN FOREIGN COUNTRIES[a]

| Column | 1<br>1965<br>Average<br>Price[b] | 2<br>Yield<br>to<br>Maturity | 3<br>Greater Yield<br>of Foreign Bonds<br>over U. S. Bonds |
|---|---|---|---|
| U.S. Government 4's of 1980 | 96-5/32 | 4.37% | |
| Canada 2-3/4's of 1974 | 85-5/16 | 5.00 | 14% |
| Australia 5's of 1983 | 97-3/8 | 5.24 | 20% |
| Norway 5-1/2's of 1977 | 99-1/4 | 5.59 | 28% |
| Japan Dev. 6's of 1978 | 98-5/16 | 6.20 | 42% |
| Finland 6's of 1976 | 96-5/8 | 6.46 | 48% |
| Mexico 6-1/2's of 1979 | 100-1/4 | 6.47 | 48% |
| Venezuela 6-1/4's of 1980[c] | 97-9/16 | 6.52 | 49% |

[a] This table was prepared with the assistance of George Henry, Carl Marks & Co., 20 Broad Street, which firm specializes in foreign securities.

[b] Quotations are based on American owned bonds and are not subject to interest equalization tax.

[c] Issued April 1965.

in maturity and coupon. They are spot figures for one year. If we were doing a thorough study we should use average figures over a number of years. However, they will be adequate for illustrative purposes.

This sample, which covers only debt securities, in no way shows the difference in risk for an industrial company for the following reasons:

The bonds are payable in American dollars, whereas earnings of an industrial company would be in terms of the local currency.

The bonds are government obligations and do not reflect the risks of domestic operations abroad that industrial companies would face.

However, even if these percentages alone were used to increase a Profit Goal established in this country, it shows that substantial increases would be necessary for use in foreign investment.

If you are interested in pursuing this approach for any particular country you will wish to review all possible sources of security information which might be available, including both industrial and government securities quoted in the United States. It may be of some interest to consider the returns that investors require in the foreign country itself, but of course this does not take into account the risk of American investors. As already stated, the amount of evidence is scarce at present.

A word of caution! Quotations of foreign securities are tricky to understand. They may not represent investors' true appraisal of risk involved for many reasons:

The market may be very thin

Special taxes may affect the yield

There may be a special demand for foreign exchange purposes, etc.

You would do well to consult an expert in foreign securities in order to avoid using misleading data.

To take an entirely different attack on the problem, a horseback way of looking at the return alone from a foreign investment might be as follows: A dollar of after-tax earnings in this country is worth a dollar, but the return from an investment in a foreign corporation only consists of the income received in this country. In other words, the transferable income from foreign investment might be considered as equivalent to earnings of a company in this country. On this basis, if a company in this country earned 10%, a foreign corporation paying out 50% of its earnings in dividends would have to earn 20% to be on an equivalent basis. Admittedly, this is rough figuring and leaves out the appreciation in principal and amount of earnings that could be transferred, but it is only for the purpose of broad thinking.

The value placed on foreign earnings of United States corporations by financial analysts will vary from time to time depending on developments in various countries which affect the risk. As stated above, we cannot obtain adequate data from this source to develop Cost-of-Capital figures, but any evidence of the analysts' long-range views should be considered. Following, the views of one analyst [2] are briefly summarized:

The attitude in this country towards foreign investments has gone through three post-war cycles: 1. Prior to 1956 there tended to be a low price/earnings multiple placed on all foreign earnings—either foreign earnings of domestic companies or foreign-based companies. 2. In the period 1956 to 1961 there was an improvement in attitude. A general squeeze on profit margins set in in the U.S., while abroad there was both less concern with this profit margin squeeze and what was thought to be a greater growth potential—Common Market expectations were very high. 3. Starting with the U.S. market break in May, 1962, there was a sharp fall in European share prices combined with a pause in European economic growth; price/earnings multiples accorded foreign earnings fell sharply and have never recovered.

To quote some specifics: Unilever (a

[2] Walter P. Stern, partner in charge of research, Burnham and Co., 60 Broad Street, New York City.

Dutch-based company) was accorded a price/earnings multiple of perhaps four times earnings in the early 50's, reached a peak of 14–16 times in 1960–1961; this multiple is now back to eight to nine times earnings. Philips Lamps (also Dutch-based) sold at five to seven times earnings in the early 50's, reaching a peak of 21 times in 1961 and is now back to eight to nine times earnings.

Foreign earnings of U.S. companies have similarly been looked at with varying degrees of pleasure or displeasure—unless they happen to be in a unique field which seems to offer extraordinary growth with little risk to any interruption of this growth. In these few cases (IBM, Xerox, Polaroid) the analyst has not placed any discount on foreign earnings and may, in fact, place a premium on it; these companies, however, are few and far between. The presence of foreign earnings in domestic companies tends to make analysis more difficult and tenuous and therefore the analyst more skeptical.

Analysts today want *a high degree of confidence* in earnings growth; this implies complete and full disclosure with no room for unpleasant surprises. There is a general feeling towards companies with foreign-based earnings that there is both a lack of full disclosure and an inability to follow what is going on, making the problem of obtaining and evaluating information more difficult. In addition, the differences in accounting treatment accorded foreign earnings—both in methods of consolidation and bringing (or not bringing) income, dividends received and/or taxes into the income statement—make analysis difficult.

In general Canadian earnings are treated the same as domestic earnings. Earnings derived from Europe and Japan tend to be given some discount, while earnings derived from Latin America and particularly Africa are generally accorded a substantial discount. More recently, the attention given possible devaluation in the U.K. has given rise to concern regarding handling of or protection against such devaluation. The desire of the analyst to have assurance of continuity of earnings growth and no unpleasant surprises implies that he will place some discount on all foreign-based earnings unless the company is particularly unique and operating in a very stable political and economic climate.

It should be appreciated that the reciprocal of the price-earnings ratios mentioned above cannot be used as a gauge for the common cost since they do not take account of earnings expected by investors. However, they do indicate the attitude of an analyst towards foreign investment.

Another approach to assessing risk in foreign investments is explained in several brief excerpts from an article by Millard H. Pryor, Director of Corporate Planning for the Singer Company: [3]

> Political risks are much greater abroad than in the United States. The danger that either war losses or expropriation will result in partial or complete loss of investment is far from remote. . . . To compensate for such risks, the return in any foreign country should be greater than the return in the United States by an amount at least equal to the cost of war risk and confiscation insurance.

> Loss of investment and earnings due to currency inflation represents a significant risk in many areas of the world.

> The costs of managing an international operation are usually greater than those in a corporate domestic business. . . .

> As a result of the potential risks in international operation, it is desirable to establish what can be called long-range "compensatory" financial goals for operations outside the United States. For example, if an appropriate long-range goal for activities in the United States is 12% return on invested capital, long-range compensatory goals for an international company's activities in three different countries could be established in the manner shown. . . .[4]

[3] "Planning in a Worldwide Business," *Harvard Business Review*, January–February 1965, Volume 43, Number 1.
[4] See Exhibit 3 (VIII).

## EXHIBIT 3 (VIII)

### HYPOTHETICAL INTERNATIONAL LONG-RANGE "COMPENSATORY" GOALS

(In terms of percentage return on investment)

| Column | 1 | 2 | 3 | 4 |
|---|---|---|---|---|
|  | U.S. Operations | Country A Operations | Country B Operations | Country C Operations |
| U.S. financial goal | 12% | 12% | 12% | 12% |
| Compensation for political risk | -- | -- | 2 | 5 |
| Compensation for currency risk | -- | 1 | 2 | 25 |
| Absentee management factor | -- | 1 | -- | 2 |
| Compensatory financial goal | 12% | 14% | 16% | 44% |

Information on profit results of the foreign investments of domestic corporations is limited and may not be strictly comparable. However, Business International [5] reports the following in its survey:

Riding the crest of the longest sustained boom in U.S. economic history, U.S. firms in 1965 made record earnings in the domestic market and reversed the traditional pattern of higher corporate profitability abroad. The over-all results of BI's fifth annual analysis of the financial reports of the 600 largest companies in the U.S. reveal that —for the 118 firms providing enough detailed information for meaningful comparative net earnings/net worth ratios for domestic and international operations— profitability was 12.8% abroad (against 14.1% in 1964) vs. 15.5% domestically (against 13.4% in 1964). Excluding the petroleum industry, domestic profits were higher than results abroad for the third consecutive year (17.5% vs. 13.1% abroad), and the 1964 spread (15.1% and 13.2%) was significantly widened.

Last year was the first in which overall domestic profitability exceeded foreign performance. The reasons for the turnabout include the unprecedented growth of the U.S. domestic market, fiercer competition, and slower growth in European markets, and continuing difficulties in Latin America. Foreign exchange losses were far smaller than the record write-offs in 1963 and 1964. . . .

Note that these returns are on net worth and not total capital. Some foreign investing is done on a highly leveraged basis through borrowing in the local country in order to reduce the amount of United States investment. It should be recognized that the high debt adds to the risk of the common and the return should be high because of this factor alone.

[5] *Weekly Report*—May 27, 1966, Business International Corporation, 757 Third Avenue, New York, New York 10017.

# Results of Corporate Earnings

For any one industry, maladjustment of supply may occur because of bad management or errors in forecasting demand so that sales prices do not produce a return sufficient to cover the Cost-of-Capital. With large fixed capital already sunk, an adverse situation may persist for an extended period. However, for industry as a whole supply should adjust to demand so as to produce prices which will cover all costs on the average, including Cost-of-Capital. At this point, let's see how industry has performed in comparison with the standards we have suggested.

## COMMENTS ON REPORTED EARNINGS

Before we look at corporate earnings, we make these observations:

There is obviously a wide range in profitability among companies: some are very profitable, some just plug along and some lose money—ours is a profit *and* loss system. Poor earnings serve a necessary function: they should be a warning to management not to waste[1] more capital in an area where the demand cannot support the supply; they may indicate the need for a change in management.

Some industries should earn somewhat more than others because of the difference in risk.

The average return for all manufacturing companies is in the Cost-of-Capital range.

Companies that continue to show good profits well above the Cost-of-Capital do so generally because superior management produces better goods and services. Consumers express their approval by choosing these products over those of competitors.

In some industries, there may be less opportunity to generate adequate profits because of the surrounding circumstances which may, in effect, increase the risk. Some examples of the type of problems that may cause trouble are as follows:

Some industries have small operators who do not know their costs.

Some family-owned companies tend to overlook the need for an adequate return on capital. They may think of anything

[1] A regulated industry such as the public utility industry may be forced by regulation to make capital expenditures in order to serve the public, even though the prospective return is inadequate. This adds to the risk for such a business.

over the interest rate as being a satisfactory profit.

Some major companies may be sales- rather than profit-oriented and may continue to commit capital at too low a rate.

In an industry requiring large capital investment, miscalculations in expansion programs by only a few companies can produce a serious over-supply situation. The imbalance may persist for a long time because of the problem of absorbing excess capacity.

Some industries may be subject to government pressure to hold down prices when costs increase.

Now we will look at some figures on profits for different types of business. Differences in accounting treatment, valuation of assets, etc., prevent the figures from being strictly comparable. A sophisticated study of corporate profits should take into account differences in such things as depreciation and tax treatment. Nevertheless, the figures do paint a broad picture of industry's record.

## RETURN BY TYPES OF BUSINESS

There are included in Exhibit 1 (IX) figures for the return on year-end [2] total long-term capital for the past ten years. The profit on year-end common equity is also shown.

Returns on total long-term capital are more meaningful than returns on common equity because the latter are affected by the leverage of the senior securities. The figures would be even more meaningful if long-term capital were adjusted to include leases capitalized, because in some businesses leases represent a large proportion of senior capital. This applies particularly to department stores.

Businesses which are less risky, such as finance companies and electric utilities, show a lower return on total long-term capital. The

[2] Returns on average of beginning and end of year capital would be somewhat higher. Such a figure may be more representative because it may approximate more closely the amount of capital a company has available for use during the year. The figures for the latest year based on average capital are shown in parenthesis in Exhibit 1 (IX).

returns on common equity for all types of business show some similarity, because the capital structures, with more senior securities for the less risky, tend to equate out risk for common stock. This was discussed in Chapter VII. These ideas can perhaps best be visualized by the figures shown in summary form in Exhibit 2 (IX). It gives returns on total year-end long-term capital and common equity for the ten-year averages with figures rounded to the nearest full percentage.

## RANGE OF PROFITABILITY

The range of returns on equity for the 500 largest companies in 1965 as reported by *Fortune* magazine is shown in Exhibit 3 (IX). The returns fall somewhat in a bell-shaped curve with the median being 11.8%. The same figure for 1964 was 10.5%. Some of the companies are relatively highly leveraged and therefore the returns are higher than they would be with a well-balanced capital structure. A company which is highly leveraged should not necessarily pat itself on the back for a high return on common. It should use the return on total long-term capital as the better performance test.

## HAVE CORPORATE EARNINGS BEEN INCREASING?—BAD REPORTING!

People may be led to believe that corporate earnings have been increasing. How else would they interpret the following often-observed newspaper headline?

> Corporate Earnings
> Show 5% Increase
> Over Last Year

An article following such a headline generally elaborates on the increase in earnings rather than explaining the significance of the figures. Earnings are only meaningful in terms of:

Capital invested
Purchasing power

# RESULTS OF CORPORATE EARNINGS

## EXHIBIT 1 (IX)

### EXAMPLES OF RETURN ON YEAR END TOTAL LONG-TERM CAPITAL[a] AND PROFIT ON YEAR END COMMON EQUITY[b] FOR VARIOUS TYPES OF BUSINESS

| Column | 1 | 2 | 3 | 4 | 5 | 6 |
|---|---|---|---|---|---|---|
| | Finance Cos.[c] | | Electric Utilities[d] | | Amer. Tel.&Tel. (Consol.)[e] | |
| | Return on Total Long-Term Capital | Profit on Common Equity | Return on Total Long-Term Capital | Profit on Common Equity | Return on Total Long-Term Capital | Profit on Common Equity |
| Year | | | | | | |
| 1966 | 5.9% (6.0%)[f] | 11.5% (12.0%)[f] | | | 7.6% (7.9%)[f] | 9.6% (9.9%)[f] |
| 1965 | 5.3 | 12.3 | 7.0% (7.2%)[f] | 12.3% (12.6%)[f] | 7.4 | 9.3 |
| 1964 | 5.3 | 11.9 | 6.8 | 11.9 | 7.3 | 9.1 |
| 1963 | 4.9 | 11.6 | 6.6 | 11.5 | 7.3 | 9.3 |
| 1962 | 4.8 | 11.4 | 6.5 | 11.3 | 7.1 | 9.1 |
| 1961 | 5.0 | 11.6 | 6.2 | 10.9 | 7.2 | 9.1 |
| 1960 | 5.4 | 12.0 | 6.1 | 11.0 | 7.4 | 9.6 |
| 1959 | 5.0 | 13.0 | 6.1 | 10.7 | 7.2 | 9.5 |
| 1958 | 5.1 | 13.4 | 5.9 | 10.7 | 6.7 | 8.6 |
| 1957 | 5.3 | 14.8 | 5.9 | 10.6 | 6.4 | 8.4 |
| 1956 | | | 6.1 | 10.8 | | |
| Average | 5.2% | 12.4% | 6.3% | 11.2% | 7.2% | 9.2% |

| Column | 7 | 8 | 9 | 10 |
|---|---|---|---|---|
| | Department Stores[g] | | Manufacturing Cos.[h] | |
| | Return on Total Long-Term Capital | Profit on Common Equity | Return on Total Long-Term Capital | Profit on Common Equity |
| Year | | | | |
| 1966 | | | 11.5% (12.1%)[f] | 13.1% (13.6%)[f] |
| 1965 | 10.2% (10.2%)[f] | 11.8% (12.2%)[f] | 11.3 | 12.6 |
| 1964 | 8.5 | 9.8 | 10.4 | 11.5 |
| 1963 | 8.1 | 9.0 | 9.4 | 10.2 |
| 1962 | 7.9 | 9.5 | 8.9 | 9.7 |
| 1961 | 7.5 | 9.2 | 8.2 | 8.8 |
| 1960 | 7.3 | 9.3 | 8.5 | 9.2 |
| 1959 | 6.4 | 8.4 | 9.5 | 10.4 |
| 1958 | 6.5 | 8.6 | 8.0 | 8.6 |
| 1957 | 7.0 | 9.2 | 10.0 | 10.9 |
| 1956 | N.A. | 8.9 | | |
| Average | 7.7% | 9.4% | 9.6% | 10.5% |

[a] Includes the year end stated book value of long-term debt, preferred stock and common equity, etc. Return is after taxes before interest on long-term debt estimated at 5% when not available.

[b] Profit available for common, after taxes, interest and preferred dividends.

[c] Combined figures for six major sales finance companies.

[d] Privately owned Class A and B electric utilities – Statistics of Electric Utilities in the United States - Federal Power Commission.

[e] American Telephone & Telegraph Company and subsidiaries consolidated.

[f] Figures in parentheses are based on average of beginning and year end capital.

[g] Combined figures for fifteen leading department stores for fiscal year ended January 31, compiled by Henry S. Kahn, Vice President, Harris Trust and Savings Bank, Chicago, Illinois.
Some department stores have large lease commitments. If the leases were capitalized in order to obtain a complete picture of total long-term capital and the return were calculated on that total, it would be lower than the figure shown in the table.

[h] For all manufacturing corporations except newspapers, Quarterly Financial Report for Manufacturing Corporations, Federal Trade Commission – Securities & Exchange Commission. Figures for preferred stock are included with common equity, but the amount of preferred is relatively small. Interest on long-term debt is estimated at 5%.

## EXHIBIT 2 (IX)

### INDUSTRY RETURNS ON CAPITAL
### 10 YEAR AVERAGE

|  | Return on Total Year End Long-Term Capital | Profit on Year End Common |
|---|:---:|:---:|
| Finance Companies | 5% | 12% |
| Electric Utilities[a] | 6 | 11 |
| American Telephone & Telegraph (Consol.)[a] | 7 | 9 |
| Department Stores | 8 | 9 |
| Manufacturing Companies | 10 | 11 |
| Average |  | 10% |

[a]It may be noted that the regulated utilities – electric and telephone – have been trying to improve their rate of return. This is shown in the previous exhibit by the trend in rate of return for these industries in the past ten years.

By the same token, union leaders would be justified in criticizing a newspaper story about wage increases which emphasized an increase in the total wages if the total increased only because labor worked longer hours and there was no increase in the rate of pay.

To look at it another way, suppose you buy a $1,000 bond and get $50 in interest, which represents a 5% return. Next year you continue to receive $50 in interest on your investment, but interest rates change and you buy another $1,000 bond and earn only $40 on your new investment so that your total interest is $90. Your wife might comment, "Aren't we fortunate—an increase in income from $50 to $90." You would probably blow your stack, and rightly so. You might then try to explain that the return on the savings should be related to the amount of capital invested and that it fell from 5% to 4½% ($90 in interest divided by $2,000 investment).

Both of these thoughts are analogous to the idea that a story about earnings for a company must be related to the capital invested; otherwise it is incomplete.

The capital of corporations increases from sale of securities and retention of earnings after dividends. The way in which retention of earnings increases capital and results in increased earnings per share is discussed in Chapter XI. Lack of information about the added investment may be responsible for making the public think that increases in earnings are unjustified.

There is another significant factor in interpreting increases in earnings. Labor is interested in receiving real wage increases. If prices go up more than wages, there is a decrease in labor's purchasing power. Likewise changes in corporate earnings should be interpreted in terms of the change in the value of the dollar. Perhaps we cannot expect newspapers to do this kind of reporting. Yet, it is a point that should be kept in mind in interpreting earnings when consumer prices rise.

Profits for manufacturing companies for the

EXHIBIT 3 (IX)

RANGE OF RETURN ON YEAR END EQUITY[a]
500 LARGEST COMPANIES IN FORTUNE[b] SURVEY
1965

| Return | Number of Companies |
|---|---|
| 20.0% and over | 41 |
| 18.0 to 19.9 | 27 |
| 16.0 to 17.9 | 37 |
| 14.0 to 15.9 | 58 |
| 12.0 to 13.9 | 81 |
| 10.0 to 11.9 (Median 11.8%) | 95 |
| 8.0 to 9.9 | 82 |
| 6.0 to 7.9 | 46 |
| 4.0 to 5.9 | 12 |
| 2.0 to 3.9 | 10 |
| 0.0 to 1.9 | 1 |
| -0.1 and below | 10 |
| | 500 |

[a]Referred to as invested capital by *Fortune Magazine.* Includes capital stock, surplus and retained earnings.

[b]Reprinted from the *Fortune Directory* by permission; © 1966 Time, Inc.

past ten years related to investment are shown in Exhibit 4 (IX).

The amount of profits for industrial companies has increased, as the first column shows. However, the rate of profit has not shown a corresponding upward trend because the amount of capital has grown.

Henry Ford II, Chairman of Ford Motor Company, gave an interesting talk about profits entitled "How High Is Up?"[3] He pointed out that the emphasis on all sides, from newspaper headlines, governmental economic advisors, and labor leaders, seems to be that profits are at a record high. He vividly contrasted the small growth in profits as compared

[3] Delivered at the 12th Annual Management Conference of the University of Chicago, Illinois, March 5, 1964.

## EXHIBIT 4 (IX)

### PROFITS FOR ALL MANUFACTURING CORPORATIONS EXCEPT NEWSPAPERS[a] RELATED TO INVESTMENT
#### (Billions)

| Column | 1 | 2 | 3 | 4 | 5 | 6 | 7 | 8 | 9 | 10 |
|---|---|---|---|---|---|---|---|---|---|---|
| | Profit for Common Equity[b] | | Common Equity[b] | | Long-Term Capital | | Return on | | | |
| | | | | | | | Long-Term Capital[c] | | Common Equity[b] | |
| Year | Amt. | Index[d] | Amt. | Index[d] | Amt. | Index[d] | Percent | Index[d] | Percent | Index[d] |
| 1966 | $31.0 | 201 | $236.8 | 167 | $293.1 | 175 | 11.5% | 115 | 13.1% | 120 |
| 1965 | 27.5 | 179 | 218.1 | 154 | 265.2 | 158 | 11.3 | 113 | 12.6 | 116 |
| 1964 | 23.2 | 151 | 201.4 | 142 | 242.0 | 144 | 10.4 | 104 | 11.5 | 106 |
| 1963 | 19.5 | 127 | 190.2 | 134 | 228.3 | 136 | 9.4 | 94 | 10.2 | 94 |
| 1962 | 17.7 | 115 | 181.9 | 128 | 217.9 | 130 | 8.9 | 89 | 9.7 | 89 |
| 1961 | 15.3 | 99 | 173.9 | 123 | 207.8 | 124 | 8.2 | 82 | 8.8 | 81 |
| 1960 | 15.2 | 99 | 165.6 | 117 | 196.9 | 117 | 8.5 | 85 | 9.2 | 84 |
| 1959 | 16.3 | 106 | 157.3 | 111 | 186.7 | 111 | 9.5 | 95 | 10.4 | 95 |
| 1958 | 12.7 | 82 | 147.1 | 104 | 175.5 | 105 | 8.0 | 80 | 8.6 | 79 |
| 1957 | 15.4 | 100 | 141.6 | 100 | 167.9 | 100 | 10.0 | 100 | 10.9 | 100 |
| Average | | | | | | | 9.6% | | 10.5% | |

[a] Same source of data as shown in Exhibit 1 (IX) in this chapter. See footnote (h) to that table.

[b] The figure for capital stock was not broken down into preferred and common stock, but the amount of preferred is relatively small.

[c] Includes stated book value of long-term debt, preferred stock and common equity, etc. Return is after taxes before interest on long-term debt estimated at 5%.

[d] Index with 1957 as the base year.

with many of our other economic indexes such as sales, gross national product and commodity prices.

One would think that corporate managements would point out that profit increases alone are misleading. Can you find an annual report that shows the relationship between increases in profits and capital investment? Perhaps this is being unfair to managements, because in annual reports they naturally wish to make the record look good to stockholders, who are interested in the raw increase in earnings per share.

At least, whenever the public is concerned, managements should emphasize the added investment which was risked in order to obtain the added profits. Our free press, the newspapers and magazines, which do so much to help preserve our democratic way of life by telling the public the facts, could help preserve our free enterprise system by telling a fuller story in reporting profits.

# CHAPTER X

# Interpreting Return on Total Long-Term Capital

In the last chapter, we looked at what industry earned in broad perspective. You are naturally more interested in how *your* company is doing. You can examine the profitability of a company by relating profits to various capital bases. In looking at the results from an investor's point of view, the best measure is return on total long-term capital. This is also a meaningful figure for management to follow. It can be compared directly with Cost-of-Capital. It is preferable to use the figures for total long-term capital rather than those for common equity, because the return on common equity is affected by leverage of senior securities, including significant financial leases. Return on common equity may be examined as a supplementary test.

Return on long-term capital and changes in return must be interpreted carefully. In this chapter we will discuss how to interpret the figures and some related ideas.

## CALCULATING THE RETURN ON TOTAL LONG-TERM CAPITAL

We have previously mentioned how the per cent return on total long-term capital is calculated, but if you need a review in detail here it is. The two components are as follows:

Income statement items to be totalled:
    Net income after taxes and interest, before dividends on preferred, convertible preferred, and common stock.
    Income applicable to minority interest.
    The annual interest part of significant financial lease payments.
    Interest on items in current liabilities

which should be included in long-term capital.

Interest on long-term debt and convertible debt.

Long-term capital items to be totalled:
Significant financial lease payments capitalized.

Items in current liabilities which should be included in long-term capital.

Long-term debt.

Convertible bonds.

Preferred stock.

Convertible preferred.

Minority interest.

Common equity, including common stock, capital surplus, and retained earnings.

This return is comparable to the Return on Total Capital Target calculated on the To Investor Rate basis. You will recall that in Chapter VI we gave a table which illustrated the different rates. To save you from turning back, we will repeat in Exhibit 1 (X) that part of the table which is applicable here.

EXHIBIT 1 (X)

RETURN ON TOTAL CAPITAL TARGET
TO INVESTOR RATE

|  | Capital | Rate |  |
|---|---|---|---|
| Debt | 20% | 5% | 1.00% |
| Common | 80% | 11% | 8.80% |
| Total | 100% |  | 9.80% |
| Allowance above Cost-of-Capital |  | 2% | 2.00% |
| Total |  |  | 11.80% |

You will note that the debt carries the full interest rate, without any reduction for the effect of taxes, since we are concerned with the rates that investors require in the competitive capital market. In the income statement items which were totalled above, we also use the full interest charges.

Deferred tax liabilities have been left out of the long-term capital. The reason for this was discussed in Chapter V.

*What Is Behind the Figures?*

Before the per cent return on long-term capital can be meaningful, you must know what is included in the income and capital. You will wish to know:

Whether the income statement represents true profits:
Are there any non-recurring items in the earnings?

Are the earnings under- or over-stated because of such factors as depreciation and maintenance charges?

Whether the long-term capital is correctly stated and what it represents:
Has there been reevaluation of assets which may have inflated the surplus accounts?

Are there obsolete plants which have not been properly depreciated?

Is there a large amount of assets which is not providing much income at present?

There is included in Appendix A a "List of Analytical Questions for Items in Balance Sheets and Income Statements," which gives a more complete list of critical questions which may be asked about the various items in the balance sheet and income statement.

We will now refer to two situations to indicate how the composition of the balance sheet may affect the return.

## A Company with a Large Amount of Assets Not Presently Productive

Let us assume that a company has generated a large amount of cash over the years and has not been able to find any satisfactory expansion projects. The company has put the cash in short-term government bonds returning 4%. Obviously, this will lower the company's return on total long-term capital since a large part of its assets will be in this low-income investment.

These remarks are not in criticism of such policy. A company might be far better off by following that procedure, or paying out surplus funds to its stockholders, than by spending the money on expansion below a sound Profit Goal. However, in order to obtain a picture of the return on total long-term capital without this distorting effect, the excess cash investments might be deducted from the total long-term capital and the applicable income deducted from total income, and then, the return calculated on the remaining capital. This would more correctly show how well the company was doing with the assets employed in production.

The return on long-term capital for a company with a large investment in assets such as oil and forestry reserves or real estate held for resale may be hard to interpret. If the reserves are just sufficient to maintain normal operations, the return on capital should be a meaningful figure and conform to the standards we have suggested. However, if the reserves are more than required the extra investment will tend to reduce the per cent return.

Whether such reserves represent a good investment must be based on a Time Value Profitability Rate analysis of the revenues that they may produce in the future. In such a calculation, the investment should be stated at its present market value. The Time Value Profitability Rate technique is explained in Chapter XV.

For a company which has natural resources and also manufacturing facilities, a return on the manufacturing facilities separately might be a more meaningful figure if it is possible to separate the applicable income.

## Pooling of Interests—Does It Avoid the Day of Reckoning?

If a company acquires another company by swapping stock and treats the acquisition as a pooling of interests,[1] the acquired company is included in the acquirer's balance sheet on the basis of its book value rather than at the acquisition price. The resulting return on capital is bound to be misleading. For example, suppose Company A acquires Company B on a share-for-share basis, as shown in Exhibit 2 (X).

The books will show an increase in the present return on total long-term capital from 10% to 10.18%. In actuality, there has been a decrease. The amount of capital invested by Company A in Company B is properly measured by the number of shares of stock Company A issued, that is 100,000 shares, multiplied by the market price of the stock of $100 at the time of the acquisition, or a total of $10,000,000. This figure is a correct measure of the cost of the acquisition.[2] Therefore, the return on the capital of the combined companies should be measured as follows:

Company A after acquiring Company B
   Total Long-Term Capital

| | |
|---|---|
| Common Equity (1,100,000 shares) | $60,000,000 |
| Net Income | $ 5,600,000 |
| Return on total Long-Term Capital | 9.33% |

[1] Accounting Research Bulletin No. 48, *Business Combinations*, defines a "pooling of interests" as contrasted with a "purchase." A "pooling of interests" occurs when a substantial part of the owners of two companies become the owners of a single company. The single company can be one of the original companies or a new company. A "purchase" of one company by another occurs when an important part of the ownership in the acquired company is eliminated.

[2] This leaves out any reduction in the cost of the acquisition for financing costs. Such a reduction may be justified on the basis that financing costs would have to have been deducted if the company had sold stock and acquired the company for cash. This is discussed in Chapter XII.

## EXHIBIT 2 (X)
## POOLING OF INTERESTS

Company A
  Total Long-Term Capital
     Debt                                      0

| | |
|---|---:|
| Company A | |
|   Total Long-Term Capital | |
|     Debt | 0 |
|     Common Equity (1,000,000 shares) | $50,000,000 |
|     Book Value Per Share | $ 50 |
|     Market Price Per Share | $ 100 |
|   Net Income | $ 5,000,000 |
|   Return on Total Long-Term Capital | 10% |
|   Earnings Per Share | $ 5 |
| | |
| Company B | |
|   Total Long-Term Capital | |
|     Debt | 0 |
|     Common Equity (100,000 shares) | $ 5,000,000 |
|     Book Value Per Share | $ 50 |
|     Market Price Per Share | $ 90 |
|   Net Income | $ 600,000 |
|   Return on Total Long-Term Capital | 12% |
|   Earnings Per Share | $ 6 |

With a pooling of interests, the total long-term capital and income after the acquisition would be as follows:

| | |
|---|---:|
| Company A after acquiring Company B | |
|   Total Long-Term Capital | |
|     Common Equity (1,100,000 shares) | $55,000,000 |
|     Book Value Per Share | $ 50 |
|   Net Income | $ 5,600,000 |
|   Return on Total Long-Term Capital | 10.18% |
|   Earnings Per Share | $ 5.09 |

The acquisition produced a decrease in present return on capital from 10% to 9.33%. The company was able to show an improved return on capital on the basis of book figures only because the true cost of the acquisition was lost sight of by the pooling-of-interest accounting treatment.

We are not suggesting that Company B should not have been acquired; that depends on future prospects for the company. We are here concerned only with the significance of the return on capital figure. It might be argued that it is preferable to write off the fictitious item of excess acquisition cost in order to keep the books clean. Perhaps so, but it would be more revealing if it were originally carried on the asset side of the balance sheet as "Excess of Price Paid for Acquisition over Asset Value" and on the liability side in segregated capital surplus as "Capital Surplus Arising from Excess Price Paid for Acquisition over Assets Value." Then the facts would be available for investors to use in their evaluation of the company's acquisition program.

Does pooling of interests and its consequent better showing of return on total long-term capital relieve the management of the day of reckoning as to the soundness of an acquisition? The answer is NO!

To permit a pooling of interests, common stock or voting preferred stock must be issued.[3] What will ultimately happen to the market price of the common will depend on the future earnings per share and the quality of the earnings. If future earnings per share, with those shares added due to the acquisition, do not come up to investors' expectations, the market price will ultimately suffer regardless of the immediate effect on return on total long-term capital and on present earnings per share. Exhibit 3 (X) illustrates this point.

While present earnings per share increased

## EXHIBIT 3 (X)

### EFFECT OF POOLING OF INTERESTS

| Column | 1 | 2 | 3 | 4 | 5 | 6 |
|---|---|---|---|---|---|---|
| | Cost-of-Capital | Number of Shares | Book Value Per Share | Present Earnings Per Share | Present Market Price | Ratio Present Market Price to Present Earnings Per Share |
| Company X Acquired | 10% | 1 | $100 | $10 | $200 | 20 |
| Company Y | 10 | 1 | 150 | 15 | 200 | 13.3 |
| Company X + Company Y | 10 | 2 | 125 | 12.50 | 200 | 16 |

| Column | 7 | 8 | 9 | 10 |
|---|---|---|---|---|
| | Expected Potential Earnings Per Share By Investors | Ratio Present Market Price to Potential Earnings Per Share By Investors | Forecast Potential Earnings Per Share By Companies | Future Market Price |
| Company X | $20 | 10 | $20 | |
| Acquired Company Y | 20 | 10 | 18 | |
| Company X + Company Y | 20 | 10 | 19 | $190 |

as a result of the acquisition, the price paid for Company Y in relation to its future earnings was too high. Consequently, if future earnings per share are realized as the companies forecast in Column 9, the earnings will be inadequate to maintain the market price. When the $19 per share is realized by the combined companies, investors will recognize the error in their forecast of $20 and will place a market price on the stock of $190.

The proper way to test the soundness of an acquisition is to relate the forecast return to the total long-term capital, priced at the acquisition cost, on a Time Value Profitability Rate basis.

[3] An acquisition is usually regarded as tax-free, that is, tax-free to the owners of the company being acquired, if the acquisition is accomplished through the issuance of new common stock or new voting preferred stock. Convertible debentures do not qualify. Treasury stock will not qualify, but if a company has treasury stock which it wishes to use for this purpose, the same result can be accomplished by canceling the treasury stock and issuing new stock.

## COMPARING ONE COMPANY WITH ANOTHER—THE EFFECT OF TAX SAVINGS FROM INTEREST

In comparing one company with another, the return on total long-term capital is preferable to the return on common equity because the return on total capital comparison tends to eliminate the effect of leverage. However, other things being equal, the company with the most debt will still show a greater return because of the tax reduction from the added interest charges. In order to eliminate this effect, it may be of interest to compare the return before taxes and interest on long-term capital. The three companies compared in Exhibit 4 (X) illustrate these ideas.

## CHANGES IN RETURN ON TOTAL LONG-TERM CAPITAL

Return on total long-term capital is interesting to view not only at one particular time, but also with regard to the changes that occur from time to time. Both must be interpreted in the light of all surrounding circumstances.

### Decrease on Existing Total Long-Term Capital

Generally, a downward trend in return on total long-term capital is not an attractive sign. Let us assume that a company has been very successful so that it has earned a return of 30% on total long-term capital. Under such circumstances, through no fault of the management, competition may drive the return downward and along with it earnings per share. If the return goes below the Return on Total Capital Target, the company has become unsuccessful. Here we are talking about reduction in earnings solely on existing investment.

### Decrease Due to Lower Return on New Investment

If a company is earning a return on existing total long-term capital well above Cost-of-

EXHIBIT 4 (X)

EFFECT OF TAX SAVINGS FROM INTEREST
ON RETURN ON CAPITAL

|  | Company A | Company B | Company C |
|---|---|---|---|
| Long-Term Capital | | | |
| Debt | $ 0.00 | $ 20.00 (Int. 5%) | $ 40.00 (Int. 6%) |
| Common | 100.00 | 80.00 | 60.00 |
| Total | $100.00 | $100.00 | $100.00 |
| Sales | $200.00 | $200.00 | $200.00 |
| Operating Expenses, including depreciation | 180.00 | 180.00 | 180.00 |
| Operating income | $ 20.00 | $ 20.00 | $ 20.00 |
| Interest | 0.00 | 1.00 | 2.40 |
| Income before taxes | $ 20.00 | $ 19.00 | $ 17.60 |
| Income taxes (50% rate) | 10.00 | 9.50 | 8.80 |
| Income for common | $ 10.00 | $ 9.50 | $ 8.80 |
| Operating Income to Long-Term Capital | 20% | 20% | 20% |
| Return on Long-Term Capital | 10% | 10.5% | 11.2% |
| Return on Common | 10% | 11.9% | 14.7% |

Capital, it may show a downward trend in return on total long-term capital after an expansion program and yet have the market price of the stock react favorably. This situation could occur if the return on the old investment held at the previous rate and the return on the new investment was below the return on the existing capital, but above the Cost-of-Capital. The figures used in the example in Chapter III (page 20) can be used to help you visualize how this could occur.

*Decrease Due to a*
*Defensive Move After a Mistake*

Another situation which would show a decrease in return on total long-term capital and yet would not mean that management was pursuing an unsound policy is as follows: A company has $100,000,000 invested in a division which has not been very profitable and earns only 8% whereas its Cost-of-Capital is 10%. There has been a past mistake, but now what does the management do? It has to reappraise the situation in the light of present circumstances. It finds that it can dispose of the division but only at a price of $60,000,000. The project is now earning $8,000,000 so the return on the present value of the division is 13⅓%, which is above the 10% Cost-of-Capital. Therefore, it should be retained unless of course there are other investments which would produce more than 13⅓% and the necessary capital cannot be obtained elsewhere.

However, on further analysis the management finds that in order to keep the division running, it will have to spend $10,000,000 for additional equipment, which will require that much long-term capital. There will be no additional profits. Therefore, the investment will be $60,000,000 plus $10,000,000 or a total of $70,000,000 and the total income will be $8,-000,000 as above. Now the effective return on capital is 11.43%. This is still above the Cost-of-Capital so the company should go ahead with the additional investment. However, on the basis of the balance sheet it will

have an investment of $110,000,000 and only $8,000,000 of income so that the reported return would be 7.27%. This is a decrease from the already reported poor return of 8%. It would look to an outsider as though the company were pursuing an unsound policy because of the downward trend in return on total long-term capital. Actually, this is the best that could be done with the alternatives available. The downward trend in this situation reveals a past mistake which has resulted in lost capital but does not signify whether the company's present decision is right.

A similar defensive move may arise where a company is compelled to acquire another company through exchange of stock. The move is due to the necessity to save or, perhaps more correctly, to improve some old investment. The figures on which the judgment is based must include at least a mental appraisal of the present value of existing assets and potential income before and after the acquisition. The same general ideas apply to a defensive merger consummated to save existing investment. Such calculations must be made by management, but investors would be unlikely to have sufficient figures to be able to tell whether sound policies were followed.

*Increase Is Not Necessarily*
*a Favorable Sign*

If a company is earning a very low return on its existing total long-term capital and earns a higher return on a new independent investment, which is still below the Cost-of-Capital, the return on total long-term capital after the expansion program will increase. However, since the new independent investment earned below the Cost-of-Capital, the expansion was unsound.

The above discussion on interpreting changes in return on total long-term capital is not intended to suggest that the concept is misleading and worthless. Quite the contrary, return on capital is a useful figure. However, you must have in mind all of the factors which may affect its size and cause it to change.

## RETURN ON TOTAL LONG-TERM CAPITAL VERSUS ASSETS VERSUS PLANT

We have already stressed the importance of understanding the relationship of the return on total long-term capital derived on the right-hand side of the balance sheet and the equivalent returns on various classes of assets. In order to leave no loose ends, we will now review this idea with the simplified balance sheet shown in Exhibit 5 (X).

Assume that the After-Tax Equivalent Rate for the Expansion Profit Goal is as shown in Exhibit 6 (X).

### EXHIBIT 5 (X)

### BALANCE SHEET

| Assets | | Liabilities | | |
|---|---|---|---|---|
| Current Assets | $100 | Current Liabilities | | $ 50 |
| Plant, Net | 50 | Long-Term Capital | | |
| | |   Debt | $20 | |
| | |   Common Equity | 80 | |
| | |     Total | | 100 |
| Other Items | 0 | Other Items | | 0 |
| Total | $150 | Total | | $150 |

If we wish to achieve 13% on total long-term capital of $100 for the After-Tax Equivalent Rate, then, switching to the asset side of the balance sheet, we only have to earn 8.67% on total assets of $150—$13 divided by $150. We have a different rate applied to a different base, but the result would produce our 13% on total long-term capital.

### EXHIBIT 6 (X)

### PROFIT GOAL
### AFTER-TAX EQUIVALENT RATE

| | Amount | Rate | Cost |
|---|---|---|---|
| Debt | $ 20 | 2.50%[a] | 0.50% |
| Common | 80 | 11% | 8.80 |
|   Total | $100 | | 9.30% |
| Allowance above Cost-of-Capital | | | 4.00 |
| Profit Goal | | | 13.30% - approximately 13% |

[a] Based on a 5% interest rate and a 50% income tax rate.

As another base, we might use plant, net $50. This would require a return of 26% in order to produce a rate of 13% on total long-term capital—$13 divided by $50.

Which base you use on the left-hand side of the balance sheet will depend on what you are trying to achieve and what best suits the management of the particular company. The application of return on investment by divisions as a management tool is discussed in Chapter XVI.

In the analysis of an expansion project by means of the Time Value Profitability Rate technique, you will generally use plant net plus working capital. The rate to be applied to this base approximates the rate of 13% on total long-term capital, because total long-term capital supplies $50 of plant net and $50 of working capital (current assets $100 less current liabilities $50) or a total of $100.

## RETURN ON SALES TIED TO INVESTMENT—THE SO-CALLED DU PONT FORMULA

On existing investment management is interested in increasing the return on capital employed. An increase in income or a reduction of the amount of investment will produce the desired result. Increasing income may be accomplished by improving sales or lowering expenses.

Two ratios are used to tie these factors together as a management tool. Combined, they are often referred to as the du Pont formula because the E. I. du Pont de Nemours Company is known to make use of them. They are:

$$\text{Earnings as a Per Cent of Sales} = \frac{\text{Earnings}}{\text{Sales}}$$

$$\text{Turnover} = \frac{\text{Sales}}{\text{Investment}}$$

Combined they produce return on investment.

$$\frac{\text{Earnings}}{\text{Sales}} \times \frac{\text{Sales}}{\text{Investment}} = \frac{\text{Return}}{\text{Investment}}$$

The formula as presented by du Pont is in much more detail; it is shown in Appendix D. These two simple ratios clearly emphasize the part which investment plays. If the management team can be trained to understand these relationships, they will help to point the way to better utilization of investment and consequently a better return.

### EXHIBIT 7 (X)

#### HYPOTHETICAL RANGE OF SALES PER DOLLAR OF CAPITAL, RETURN ON SALES AND RETURN ON TOTAL LONG-TERM CAPITAL

| Type of Business | Sales Per $ of Total Long-Term Capital | x | Return[a] on Sales | = | Return on Total Long-Term Capital |
|---|---|---|---|---|---|
| Very heavy industry and slow turnover | $0.50 | x | 20% | = | 10% |
| | 1.00 | x | 10 | = | 10 |
| | 1.50 | x | 6-2/3 | = | 10 |
| | 2.00 | x | 5 | = | 10 |
| Sales organizations with relatively little capital and fast turnover | 5.00 | x | 2 | = | 10 |

[a] Return available for stated book value of total long-term capital after taxes before interest on long-term debt.

*Examples of Return on Sales and Return on Total Long-Term Capital*

The per cent return on sales which is sufficient to provide an adequate return on capital depends on the amount of sales that can be generated with a certain amount of capital. This varies from industry to industry depending on the nature of the business. In broad terms, the idea is summarized in Exhibit 7(X). We have assumed a constant return on total long-term capital of 10%.

These figures show a range in capital turnover from once every two years to five times a year. Examples for a few types of businesses are shown in Exhibit 8 (X).

## BOOK VALUE PER SHARE OF COMMON STOCK AND MARKET PRICE RELATIONSHIP

In Chapter III, we discussed the question of the Cost-of-Capital being obtained from the

EXHIBIT 8 (X)

SALES PER DOLLAR OF CAPITAL, RETURN ON SALES
AND RETURN ON TOTAL YEAR END LONG-TERM CAPITAL FOR
CERTAIN TYPES OF BUSINESS[a]
1966

| | Sales Per $ of Total Year End Long-Term Capital | Return[a] on Sales | Return[a] on Total Year End Long-Term Capital |
|---|---|---|---|
| Electric Utility Companies[b] | $0.32 | 22.0% | 7.0% |
| Telephone American Telephone & Telegraph Company (Consol.) | 0.38 | 20.1 | 7.6 |
| All Manufacturing Companies[c] | 1.89 | 6.1 | 11.5 |
| Cement[d] Lone Star Cement Corporation | 0.81 | 9.4 | 7.6 |
| Building Materials and Equipment[d] Johns-Manville Corporation | 1.52 | 7.4 | 11.3 |
| Dairy Products[d] Borden Company | 2.12 | 4.1 | 8.6 |

[a] Income after taxes before interest on long-term debt divided by stated book value of total long-term capital.

[b] 1965. Privately owned Class A and B electric utilities – Statistics of Electric Utilities in the United States – Federal Power Commission.

[c] For complete figures see Appendix A.

[d] Company classifications and figures are as reported by Moody's Investors Service, Inc.

market price and its relationship to return on book value. We will now review the significance of the difference between market price and book value.

Book value per share represents the stockholders' investment. It can be calculated by totalling all the items included in common equity and dividing by the total number of outstanding shares. It shows how much was invested by the stockholders and how much was accumulated from retained earnings. It is only meaningful if the assets and liabilities are fairly stated on the balance sheet. To be completely meaningful, there should be an adjustment to show the present value of the assets. This would require considerable work, probably more than is justified by the value of the result. But at least its significance should be kept in mind in interpreting book value.

If the book value per share represents a fair value of the assets and it is possible to liquidate a company at such a value, stockholders will end up with the book value in final distri-

bution. This practically never occurs because most companies are not liquidated and in liquidation assets may have to be sold at distress prices. Generally, a stockholder gets his money back by sale of the stock in the market. For this reason, book value per share may appear academic. Nevertheless, it does represent the asset earning base for the stock and has some significance in security analysis. Furthermore, management should know what to expect in the relationship of market price to book value and what various relationships might signify.

Assume that a company's earnings are absolutely stable with no growth prospects and investors correctly appraise the situation. Theoretically, if the company just earns its Cost-of-Capital on an average, over good and bad markets, the market price will sell at a premium above book value so that, after allowing for financing costs, the company will receive the equivalent of the book value per share when it sells new stock. This is shown in Exhibit 9(X).

EXHIBIT 9 (X)

BOOK VALUE VERSUS MARKET PRICE

|  | Per Share |
|---|---|
| Book Value | $ 85 |
| Market Price | $100 |
| Earnings Per Share (no growth expected) | $ 10 |
| Price of new stock, net to company, after allowing 15% of market price for financing costs | $ 85 |
| Common Cost | $ 10 |
|  | $ 85 = 11.8% |

Under these theoretical conditions, if a company sells common stock to obtain money for expansion and earns the same rate on the new funds it will earn just enough so that it neither dilutes nor adds to the book value.[4] A com-

pany with absolutely stable earnings and which investors expect to be stable is an unlikely situation. If a company earns something over Cost-of-Capital, as it should if it is successful, the market price should be above book value.

[4] The above illustration is based on figures for the common equity alone. If we had started our example with a composite Cost-of-Capital, the above illustration would hold true only if the rates on the senior securities were at the current rates. Otherwise, the earnings for the common would be increased or decreased by the lower or higher charges on the senior securities.

If a company has a valuable pattern or franchise on which its earnings are dependent, and which does not show up on the balance sheet at its true worth, the market price of the stock may show no significant relationship to book value.

The relationship of book value and market price should not affect your expansion decisions. Regardless of the relationship, if you earn more than the Cost-of-Capital on new projects, the stock will benefit. We will illustrate this point with a simple example as shown in Exhibit 10(X), where the market price of the stock is well above book value and Cost-of-Capital is just being earned. To keep the picture simple, we will forget financing costs.

### EXHIBIT 10 (X)

### BOOK VALUE AND MARKET PRICE RELATIONSHIP IN EXPANSION

| | |
|---|---|
| Book Value Per Share | $100 |
| Present Earnings Per Share | $ 10 |
| Market Price Per Share | $200 |
| Expected Earnings Per Share by Investors | $ 20 |
| Common Cost | 10% |
| Market Price to Expected Earnings | 10 times |

Company sells one share at $200
Cost-of-Capital is earned immediately on the new investment

| | Old Share | New Share | Combined Per Share |
|---|---|---|---|
| Book Value | $100 | $200 | $150 |
| Present Earnings Per Share | $ 10 | $ 20 | $ 15 |
| Expected Earnings Per Share by Investors | $ 20 | $ 20 | $ 20 |
| Resulting Market Price Per Share | $200 | $200 | $200 |

We have assumed that investors expected the old share would earn $20 and that the Cost-of-Capital would be earned on the new investment; as a result the market price has been maintained. If more than the Cost-of-Capital were earned on the new investment the market price would benefit.

These observations about book value per share versus market value can be summarized as follows:

When market value is below book value, the prospects for earnings are below the Cost-of-Capital on the stated book value. This may be due to inadequate earnings, or it may be an admission that some of the old investment has been lost. It has no bearing on a company's decision on new projects.

When investors have expectations of high growth in earnings, the market price will be substantially above book value.

A successful company should exhibit a growth in earnings per share due to plowback of earnings per share and it should earn more than the Cost-of-Capital. Under these circumstances you should expect market price to be well above book value.

### Book Value's Significance in Acquisitions

It is prospects of future earnings which determine the price you can afford to pay for an acquisition. However, it is wise to consider whether the relationship of price to book value may give some clue as to the reasonableness of the price.

If you are paying a premium over book value of common equity, the premium may be termed good will, but it might be viewed as some form of expenditure such as for research and development, a patent, an exclusive franchise, a start-up cost for a new business, etc. If you are certain that the book value represents a sound present value of the assets, you might ask yourself these seven questions regarding the premium:

1. Is the premium a reasonable amount to pay for research and development, a patent, an exclusive franchise, a start-up cost for a new business, or whatever definition is most appropriate to apply?
2. If instead of the acquisition, you had started the business from scratch and had spent the same amount of money for assets as well as the premium, would you consider that it had been a good investment for your company in view of future prospects for earnings?
3. As an alternative, could you start the business from scratch, spend the money for assets and something less than the premium over book value in start-up

costs, advertising, etc. and have as good earning prospects as acquiring the company at the asking price?
4. Is the return so high on the book value of the assets as to create vulnerability from competition?
5. Is it reasonable to expect that you could earn a satisfactory percentage return on the purchase price of the acquisition, including the premium over book, under competitive conditions in which your competitors would only be seeking to earn a satisfactory return on their investment in assets?
6. What would be the return on the book assets necessary for you to earn adequately on the total purchase price?
7. What dollar amount of added profits will be required as a result of the acquisition to produce an adequate return on the premium over book value?

In an acquisition in which stock is acquired some managements seem to change their entire standards for capital investment. An evaluation of the acquisition in relation to premium over book value, as suggested in the above questions, may help to bring management back to reality. Also, it may be of some significance in estimating the extent of potential losses that might occur if the acquisition turned out to be a turkey and had to be liquidated.

## CHAPTER XI

# Increasing Earnings Per Share—
# The Significance

We have just discussed how to interpret the reported return on long-term capital. Since managements are singularly sensitive to common stock earnings per share, we will devote this chapter to a discussion of this test of success and the various ways in which earnings per share can be increased. There are seven ways: generally, the converse of these seven ways will decrease earnings per share. Managements should be able to see their relationship to the return on total long-term capital.

### INCREASE IN RETURN ON TOTAL LONG-TERM CAPITAL

If a company increases its earnings on its total long-term capital, earnings per share will increase while the capital remains the same. This may be a very sound way of increasing earnings per share. Since the quality of the stock remains the same as regards its proportion in the capital structure, stockholders benefit correspondingly.

It is possible for a company to show an increase in earnings per share due to a higher re-

turn on total long-term capital and still be following unsound expansion policies. This was discussed previously. For example, it can happen when a company uses treasury cash and invests it in a new project below the rate which the project should carry to compensate for the risk.

### PLOW-BACK OF EARNINGS
### INCREASE DUE TO MORE CAPITAL

When earnings per share increase, managements tend to pat themselves on the back. Actually, unless a company pays out all its earnings in dividends, earnings per share *should* increase. The part of the earnings which is retained represents new capital. If the return on the old capital remains the same and some return is earned on the new capital, earnings per share will have to increase.

The rate of compound growth in earnings per share as a result of plow-back of earnings is a function of the earnings retained and the return on the common. It is obtained by multiplying the per cent of the earnings retained, which is 100% less the per cent paid out in dividends, by the rate earned on the common equity book value.

For example, suppose that a company has one share of stock with a book value of $100, and it earns 10% on the book value and pays out 50% of the earnings in dividends. The compound growth rate would be (100% − 50%) × 10% = 5%. This is illustrated in Exhibit 1(XI).

Given in Exhibit 2(XI) are the growth rates

## EXHIBIT 1 (XI)

### COMPOUND GROWTH RATE IN EARNINGS PER SHARE FROM PLOW-BACK
### 10% RETURN ON BOOK VALUE - 50% DIVIDEND PAYOUT RATIO - 5% COMPOUND GROWTH RATE

| Column | 1 | 2 | 3 | 4 | 5 | 6 | 7 |
|---|---|---|---|---|---|---|---|
| Year | Common Shares | Book Value | Return on Book Value | Earnings Per Share | Dividend Payout Ratio | Dividends Per Share | Retained Earnings |
| 1 | 1 | $100.00 | 10% | $10.000 | 50% | $5.0000 | $5.0000 |
| 2 | 1 | 105.00 | 10% | 10.500 | 50% | 5.2500 | 5.2500 |
| 3 | 1 | 110.25 | 10% | 11.025 | 50% | 5.5125 | 5.5125 |

for two different returns and payouts. A similar table can readily be developed for any range of rates of return and dividend payouts.

An increase in earnings per share due to plow-back alone does not necessarily mean any greater percentage return on capital. In fact,

## EXHIBIT 2 (XI)

### SOME COMPOUND GROWTH RATES IN EARNINGS PER SHARE FROM PLOW BACK

| Column | 1 | 2 | 3 | 4 |
|---|---|---|---|---|
| Return on Common Book Value | 10% | | 15% | |
| Divided Payout Ratio | 50% | 75% | 50% | 75% |
| Compound Growth Rate in Earnings Per Share | 5% | 2.5% | 7.5% | 3.75% |

a company may show an increase in earnings per share and a decrease in return on total capital. This can occur when the earnings rate on the new investment resulting from plow-back is less than the return on the old capital. If a company earns less on the retained earnings than the common cost rate, the stockholders are hurt even though earnings per share increase.

## SALE OF STOCK ABOVE BOOK VALUE

We have discussed the relationship of book value per share to market price in Chapter X.

Here we will cover only the effect on earnings per share.

Managements generally are reluctant to sell common stock because they dislike the fact that the additional shares immediately reduce present earnings per share. Naturally, other sources of capital, such as treasury cash or the proceeds from the sale of debt securities, seem more attractive because they avoid this dilution.

However, it is incorrect for management to assume that sale of common stock will necessarily reduce earnings per share, except in the short run before the money has been put to work and earnings are realized on the new capital. In fact, if stock is sold above the book value and the return realized on the new capital is the same as on the book value of the outstanding stock, earnings per share will increase. This can be seen from the figures in Exhibit 3(XI).

There has been an increase in earnings per

## EXHIBIT 3 (XI)

### SALE OF STOCK ABOVE BOOK VALUE - EFFECT ON EARNINGS PER SHARE

| Column | 1 | 2 | 3 | 4 | 5 | 6 | 7 | 8 |
|---|---|---|---|---|---|---|---|---|
| | Common Shares | Book Value Total | Per Share | Return on Book Value | Earnings Total | Per Share | Price-Earnings Ratio | Market Price |
| Outstanding | 1 | $100 | $100 | 10% | $10 | $10 | 12 | $120 |
| New | 1 | 120 | 120 | 10% | 12 | 12 | | |
| | 2 | $220 | $110 | 10% | $22 | $11 | 12 | $132 |

share and market price. The reverse would occur if the stock were sold below book value and the same return earned on the new capital as on the outstanding stock. The ultimate effect on earnings per share depends on the extent to which the stock is sold above book value and the rate of return earned on the new investment.

The above remarks should not be interpreted as suggesting that a company should never sell stock below book value. One sometimes hears statements to this effect. Obviously this should be avoided because of its adverse effect on earnings per share. A company will always wish to sell stock under favorable market conditions. However, a company which needs capital and cannot obtain it except through the sale of common equity may be making the correct decision to raise more common stock capital if it can earn a return above the Cost-of-Capital on the new investment.

This would be true even though the new stock has to be sold below book value.

## ACQUISITION OF COMPANY WITH LOW P/E RATIO BY COMPANY WITH HIGH P/E RATIO

If a company's stock sells at a high price-earnings ratio and it acquires another company which sells at a lower price-earnings ratio on an exchange of stock based on market prices, the earnings per share of the acquiring company will automatically be increased. This can be seen from the figures in Exhibit 4(XI).

Company A sells at 20 times earnings because investors have high expectations. As a result of the acquisition, earnings per share increased from $10 to $15 per share. The market price would still be $200 if investors used a price-earnings ratio of 13⅓ times, which is a weighted average of the figures for the two

## EXHIBIT 4 (XI)

### HIGH PRICE-EARNINGS COMPANY ACQUIRING LOW PRICE-EARNINGS COMPANY INCREASES EARNINGS PER SHARE

| Column | 1 | 2 | 3 | 4 | 5 | 6 | 7 | 8 |
|---|---|---|---|---|---|---|---|---|
| | | Book Value | | Return | Earnings | | Price- | |
| | Common | Total | Per Share | on Book Value | Total | Per Share | Earnings Ratio | Market Price |
| | Shares | | | | | | | |
| Acquiring Co. A | 1 | $100 | $100 | 10% | $10 | $10 | 20 | $200 |
| Acquired Co. B | 1 | $200 | $200 | 10% | $20 | $20 | 10 | $200 |
| Co. A + Co. B | 2 | $300 | $150 | 10% | $30 | $15 | 13-1/3 | $200 |

companies separately, that is 20 times and 10 times.

The effect of such an acquisition can be visualized more readily if we think in terms of the reciprocal of the price-earnings ratio, that is, the earnings-price ratio. Since the acquisition is based on market prices of the companies' stocks, the company acquired will have a higher earnings-price ratio and consequently will immediately increase the earnings of the acquiring company.

The real market price kick in such an acquisition occurs when a glamour company buys a lower price-earnings ratio stock. The market then values the increased earnings at the same price-earnings ratio as the glamour company. For example, if Company A were a glamour company and after the acquisition the new earnings per share of $15 were valued at 20 times earnings, the price would jump from $200 to $300. Such a situation occurs when investors expect that the glamour company will be able to work magic with the acquired company and boost its earning power substantially.

An acquisition program based on this approach has great appeal for the promotional type of management and for the speculative investor. Ultimately, however, the market price will be sustained only if management can produce the results expected by investors.

## INCREASE IN LEVERAGE

If a company's over-all return on total long-term capital remains the same but the proportion of senior capital increases, the earnings per share on the common stock will increase, providing the rate of interest on the new debt is lower than the rate earned on the total capital. This is illustrated by the figures in Exhibit 5(XI).

In the second capital structure, we increased the leverage by doubling the proportion of debt, with the same over-all return. We increased the rate on the new debt because the quality decreased. Earnings per share increased from $3.00 to $3.83, but the quality of the common stock declined.

When return on total long-term capital increases, leverage causes a greater increase in earnings per share. However, when there is a decrease in return on total long-term capital, earnings per share fall at a faster rate. Ultimately, a point could be reached at which the earnings per share for the higher leveraged situation are smaller in dollar amount than for the less leveraged one. For example, using the figures above, if the return fell to 4% on total long-term capital, the earnings per share would be $1.00 with 25% debt and $0.83 with 50% debt. Furthermore, the break-even point be-

EXHIBIT 5 (XI)

INCREASE IN EARNINGS PER SHARE
DUE TO LEVERAGE

```
Long-Term Capital (Debt 25% - Common Equity 75%)
        Debt                        $ 25 - Interest rate 4%
        Common Equity - 3 shares    $ 75
        Total                       $100   Return on total capital 10%

        Total return                $10.00
        Less Interest ($25 x 4%)     1.00
        Total income for common     $ 9.00 Per share $3.00

Long-Term Capital (Debt 50% - Common Equity 50%)
        Debt                        $ 25 - Interest rate 4%
        New debt                      50 - Interest rate 5%
        Common Equity - 3 shares      75
        Total                       $150   Return on total capital 10%

        Total return                         $15.00
        Less Interest ($25 x 4% + $50 x 5%)   3.50
        Available for Common                 $11.50 Per Share $3.83
```

tween profit and loss is higher for the more highly leveraged situation.

The effect of leverage and a change in the capital structure mix on Cost-of-Capital was discussed in Chapter VII. How much debt to use is a matter of financial policy. This book does not attempt to cover this subject, but it is commented on briefly in Chapter XIII.

## DECREASE IN CHARGES ON SENIOR CAPITAL

Earnings per share will increase if the overall rate of return on total long-term capital remains the same and the charges on the senior capital, such as long-term debt and preferred stock, are reduced. For example, if the amount of bonds or preferred stock is reduced or they are refunded at a lower interest and dividend rate, there will be more earnings for the common stock. This is too obvious to discuss further.

## RETIREMENT OF COMMON STOCK—USE OF EXCESS CASH

If a company has excess cash for which it has no foreseeable need, such as for expansion or acquisitions, there are various ways in which it might be used.

The first step that should be considered is the advisability of strengthening the capital structure by retiring senior securities, if they are too heavy. This will increase the quality of the company's credit and place it in a better position to do financing in the future if it should ultimately need capital. As just noted, such a reduction in the amount of senior securities produces some increase in earnings per share.

Assuming that a company has good credit and the proper regular dividend policy and has some excess cash, the next step might be payment of an extra dividend. The advisability of this policy depends on the nature of the stockholders, their income tax bracket, etc. As an alternative to the payment of an extra dividend, thought may be given to the purchase of the company's own common stock in the market. This will generally increase earnings per share[1] if the purchase results in permanent retirement of the stock.

There are various reasons why a company may wish to acquire its own stock: to have stock available for stock option plans, for employee stock-purchase plans, or for acquiring other companies. When used for acquiring other companies, it has the same ultimate effect on earnings per share as though the acquisitions were made with cash. In other words, cash is used to purchase the company's own stock, which in turn is given to the stockholders of the company being acquired rather than giving them cash directly.

A company may acquire its own stock in order to reduce permanently the amount of outstanding common. In such a situation, the question arises as to what the company should pay. There is a price at which it is foolish to purchase stock. When a company has to make such a decision it will probably not be too concerned with theory, but here again, to be perfectly correct we have to refer to the principles of Cost-of-Capital. The decision requires an appraisal by management of the relationship of market price to the company's estimate of future earning power and the market's appraisal of risk. Stated another way, if investors' expectations of future earning power is less than the company's estimate, the remaining stockholders will be benefited by a reduction in the amount of common stock. This means that the stock is underpriced on the basis of investors' appraisal of risk and the company's estimated potential earning power. We will not give you figures to illustrate the point because the decision arises so seldom. But if you want a teaser you can have some fun building your own example.

A company with poor credit should not try to improve the market price for its common stock by buying it in. Such a company needs more common rather than less and probably better earnings. In fact, a company should never purchase its own stock merely because it thinks the market price is too low and wishes to support the price: this borders on manipulation.

The novice in finance who suddenly discovers what can be done to earnings per share by a company's purchase of its own stock may inadvertently fall into unsound financial policies. Suggestions have been made urging managements to follow a so-called policy of dynamic capital structure: build up earnings per share by selling debt and retiring common. All this amounts to is imparting leverage to the capital structure. Usually, such suggestions avoid the important question as to what is a proper debt ratio for a particular company. They fail to recognize the importance of borrowing reserve, the inflexibility of capital structure when a company has too much debt, and other important financial policy factors.

If there are sound reasons why a company should purchase its own stock, stockholders should be fully informed about the program. The procedure for purchase of common should be carefully spelled out in a legal document so that the stockholders will be safeguarded from insiders' taking advantage of the situation. In fact, as part of the procedure, directors and officers should not be allowed to buy or sell stock during the period. Laws,[2] the

---

[1] Earnings per share would *not* be increased if the proceeds used for purchasing common came from the sale of temporary investments which had an earnings rate

equal to or higher than the earnings-market price relationship for the common.

[2] Among the laws covering these problems is the Securities Exchange Act of 1934—Section 9 "Prohibition Against Manipulation of Security Prices" and Section 10 "Regulation of the Use of Manipulative and Deceptive Devices."

Rule 10(b)(5) adopted in 1942 under Section 10 of the Securities Exchange Act of 1934 has been invoked most frequently and is the basis of a good deal of litigation. It is summarized as follows:

It shall be unlawful for any person, directly or indirectly, by the use of any means or instrumentality of company's charter, and bond indentures should be examined to determine whether there are any restrictions against such purchase.

Purchase of a company's own stock—except for such corporate purposes as employee stock purchase, stock options, or stock for acquisition purposes—is a process of corporate liquidation. We are not recommending corporate liquidation. However, such a procedure is far better than management using treasury cash for expansion or acquisitions which will return less than the Cost-of-Capital. It is unfortunate that some managements would prefer to grow larger by expanding below the Cost-of-Capital and ultimately hurting their stockholders because the alternative—sound liquidation—would mean a smaller empire for them to control.

We conclude this chapter by acknowledging that all corporate financial moves should be tested for their effect on present earnings per share because of the immediate market reaction. However, an understanding of the various ways in which earnings per share can be increased may prevent managements from being misled into temporary expedients which are basically unsound in principle and fail to provide an adequate return in the future on total long-term capital. The latter is the primary guide for management to follow.

---

interstate commerce, or of the mails, or of any facility of any national securities exchange,

1. to employ any device, scheme, or artifice to defraud,
2. to make any untrue statement of a material fact or to omit to state a material fact necessary in order to make the statements made, in the light of the circumstances under which they were made, not misleading, or
3. to engage in any act, practice, or course of business which operates or would operate as a fraud or deceit upon any person, in connection with the purchase or sale of any security.

# CHAPTER XII

# Some Applications of Principles— Acquisition Standards?

We have about finished the material necessary for a complete understanding of Profit Goals. We will now discuss three related questions, often raised by management, to which there is no simple answer. They apply particularly to acquisitions. We have alluded to the answers, but a fuller discussion will provide an opportunity for you to appreciate your understanding of Cost-of-Capital. Insofar as possible, we will use simple figures in order to facilitate the mental gymnastics.

## THE ACQUISITION FEVER

We are in an interesting period with regard to acquisitions. Looking back on corporate history, acquisitions were in style in the 1920's, culminating in the 1929 boom. Then in the depression of the 1930's our industrial empire was strewn with the wrecks of some companies which had grown large by this means. As a result, people became aware that putting companies together did not necessarily solve problems, but might in fact aggravate them. As we went into the business and stock market boom after World War II, the past became dimmer and dimmer until we have arrived at a stage of almost drunken acquisition fever.

Financial manuals are dog-eared by researchers looking for acquisition candidates. Large companies have acquisition experts. Some financial middlemen, in hopes of earning a commission, beseech companies to make acquisitions. Some managements feel that if they do not have an acquisition to report to their stockholders each year they will fall behind the parade. They use almost any approach to justify the asking price. Some business magazines tend to herald almost any acquisition as a corporate milestone regardless of its price.

The acquisition fever has pushed prices of companies so high that it is difficult to find an attractively-priced candidate. Actually, at today's prices acquisitions may not be justified unless there is a substantial improvement in earnings as a result of the acquisition. However, this does not seem to have abated the fever.

The stockholders and professional financial analysts cannot obtain adequate information about an acquisition to make an immediate judgment as to whether it is beneficial. If they could, it is possible that some managements might not appear in a favorable light. Unfortunately, the financial consequences are so subtle that errors may escape detection for a long time.

It appears that some managements have lost sight of the fact that new ideas generated through research and development may prove more profitable than acquisitions at excessive prices.

A nice question to try on an over-zealous acquisition executive is: "Are you trying to buy companies or are you trying to buy profits?" Dollars to doughnuts the question will stop him. He will not be sure whether you are pulling his leg. Undoubtedly, he has been trying to buy companies and justifying the price on various bases so that he can make the acquisitions.

It is amusing to talk with some managements who are hell-bent on an acquisition program. They may concede that return on capital is a test; but then they will try to avoid the subject, or by emphasizing that it is only one test, act as though they hoped it would disappear. Their comments range from some of the other important tests to such far-out comments as:

To help the company's image.

Because of the psychological effect.

The need to diversify.

Of course, return on capital is not the only test; many factors have to be evaluated. However, if the return on capital test is not met,

taking into account all elements of possible future return, all the other tests are worthless —and we say that emphatically!

## INCREASING PRESENT EARNINGS PER SHARE, A POOR GOAL FOR ACQUISITIONS

Here is a simple example which illustrates why concentrating on the effect on present earnings per share in an acquisition may be disastrous. In the illustration, the potential future annual earning power will be represented by a single figure rather than a stream of future earnings. Further, we will assume that a Profit Goal is the same as Cost-of-Capital, whereas it should be higher.

We will designate Company A as the one which will do the acquiring. We will assume that the risk in the business is 10% on the basis of Cost-of-Capital. Its long-term capital consists of 10 shares of stock. Its stock is selling at a high price in relation to present earnings, but it is properly priced on the basis of the risk of the business in relation to its substantially higher potential future earning power. The figures for Company A are shown in Exhibit 1 (XII).

It decides to acquire Company B, which has a similar risk factor. Its long-term capital also consists of 10 shares of stock. The market price of Company A is the same as that of Company

EXHIBIT 1 (XII)

COMPANY A

| Column | 1 | 2 | 3 | 4 | 5 |
|---|---|---|---|---|---|
| | Shares | Total Annual Earnings | Annual Earnings Per Share | Price-Earnings Ratio | Market Price |
| Present Year | 10 | $ 50 | $ 5 | 20 | $100 |
| Potential future earning power | | $100 | $10 | | |

B, so it is agreed that Company A will issue 10 of its shares for 10 shares of Company B. Company B is selling at a lower present price-earnings ratio than Company A, but Company B is over-priced in relation to the risk factor be-cause its investors believe that its earnings have growth prospects although actually they have none. Company A is aware of the actual outlook for Company B. The figures for Company B are shown in Exhibit 2(XII).

## EXHIBIT 2 (XII)

### COMPANY B

| Column | 1<br>Shares | 2<br>Total<br>Annual<br>Earnings | 3<br>Annual<br>Earnings<br>Per Share | 4<br>Price-<br>Earnings<br>Ratio | 5<br>Market<br>Price |
|---|---|---|---|---|---|
| Present Year | 10 | $80 | $8 | 12-1/2 | $100 |
| Potential future earning power | | $80 | $8 | | |

In making its decision, Company A disregards its Profit Goal criteria and decides to go ahead with the acquisition because its present earnings per share will be benefited. We will assume that there are no other benefits or savings expected from the acquisition.

After the acquisition present earnings per share of Company A will be increased 30% as shown in Exhibit 3(XII).

However, when the future potential earning power of the combined companies is realized, investors will ultimately appraise the

## EXHIBIT 3 (XII)

### COMPANY A AFTER ACQUISITION OF COMPANY B

| | Shares | Annual Earnings | |
|---|---|---|---|
| | | Total | Per Share |
| Present Year | 20 | $130 | $6.50 |

stock realistically in relation to the assumed 10% risk. This will mean that the stock will sell at 10 times earnings. The picture will then be as shown in Exhibit 4 (XII).

If the acquisition had not been made, Company A's potential future earning power of $10 per share would have supported a price of $100 based on the same price-earnings ratio.

If Company A had properly appraised the acquisition on the basis of potential future earning power and 10% Cost-of-Capital, it would have seen that it could have paid only $80 per share for Company B. Thus, it would have turned down the acquisition at the $100 price.

At a price of $80 per share for Company B, the market price would have been just maintained after the acquisition based on potential future earning power. Company A would have issued only 8 shares for the 10 shares of Com-

## EXHIBIT 4 (XII)

### COMPANY A AFTER ACQUISITION OF COMPANY B

| Column | 1 | 2 | 3 | 4 | 5 |
|---|---|---|---|---|---|
| | Total Shares | Annual Earnings | | Price-Earnings Ratio | Market Price |
| | | Total | Per Share | | |
| Potential future earning power | 20 | $180 | $9 | 10 | $90 |

pany B, and the ultimate effect would have been as shown in Exhibit 5 (XII)

*Maintenance of Growth Rate in Earnings Per Share*

An acquisition specialist suggested that an acquisition could be justified if the acquiring company maintained or improved present earnings per share *and* the forecast growth rate in earnings per share. This test alone does not meet the principles of Cost-of-Capital. The following added criteria must be present in order for it to do so:

1. The current earnings per share and the forecast growth rate in earnings per share of the acquired company must bear the

## EXHIBIT 5 (XII)

### COMPANY A AFTER ACQUISITION OF COMPANY B

| Column | 1 | 2 | 3 | 4 | 5 |
|---|---|---|---|---|---|
| | Shares | Annual Earnings | | Price-Earnings Ratio | Market Price |
| | | Total | Per Share | | |
| Potential future earning power | 18 | $180 | $10 | 10 | $100 |

same relationship to the price paid [1] as the current earnings and *growth rate expected by investors* for the acquiring company bear to the market price of the acquiring company.
2. The risk of the company acquired must be the same as or less than that of the acquiring company.
3. The capital structure of the company

being acquired must not have more leverage from senior securities than that of the acquiring company.

Under these circumstances, if present earnings per share and the growth rate expected by investors are just maintained, the Cost-of-Capital is just met. They should be improved so that there will be an amount above Cost-of-Capital for a proper Profit Goal.

In the previous chapter, there were explained the various ways in which earnings per share can be increased. A goal based on growth

[1] The price paid is measured by the market price of the acquiring company's stock times the number of shares given up in the acquisition.

can be readily translated into a composite rate on total long-term capital, where the growth in earnings per share is due to plow-back of earnings alone. For example, a certain company had as its goal to increase earnings per share at a compound rate of 10% annually. The company had a dividend payout policy of 50%. As explained in the previous chapter, growth in earnings per share at a 10% rate due to plow-back in earnings, with a 50% dividend payout policy, would require a 20% return on common. The company had a capital structure policy of 25% debt. Using an interest rate of 4% for the debt, the picture would be as shown in Exhibit 6 (XII).

## EXHIBIT 6 (XII)

## TO INVESTOR RATE

|        | Amount | Rate | Cost  |
|--------|--------|------|-------|
| Debt   | 25%    | 4%   | 1.00  |
| Common | 75     | 20   | 15.00 |
| Total  | 100%   |      | 16.00% |

Thus, in this situation a return of 16% for the To Investor Rate on total long-term capital is equivalent to a 10% compound growth rate in earnings per share.

## DOES GOAL RATE CHANGE WITH SOURCE OF FUNDS?

In Chapter VI, we pointed out that the rate for a particular project should be based on the composite rate and not on the particular security used to finance the project. Let's examine this a little further. Suppose a company has the following possible sources of funds for an expansion program:

1. Cash.
2. Short term government bonds with a 4% interest rate, producing the equivalent of a 2% after-tax income with a 50% income tax rate.
3. Proceeds from the sale of bonds at a 5% annual interest rate, the equivalent of an after-tax cost of 2.50% with a 50% income tax rate.
4. Proceeds from the sale of convertible securities, which provide a low rate until conversion takes place.
5. Proceeds from the sale of common stock, or exchange of stock.

It might appear that a different rate could be applied as a goal for each of the sources of funds because of the different effect on earnings per share of common stock. The use of cash would increase earnings per share the most, because there would be no loss of income and no charge to the income statement. The other sources would have a decreasing beneficial effect on earnings per share in the order shown. Thus management would prefer to use them in descending order. However, this does not justify the proposition that the goal should be different for each source.

To illustrate the reasoning behind this statement, we will use as an example a company with one share of stock which has all its assets represented by $100 of cash. We invest the $100 of cash in a project with a 10% risk, and the earnings resulting therefrom are $10. Assuming that the market settles down and correctly appraises the change in risk, this will maintain the future market value of the company's stock at $100. Thus no one will be hurt. If the return is above $10, say $12, the company's stock will appreciate in market value. On the other hand, if the project shows a return below the Cost-of-Capital, say 8% or $8, the ultimate effect will be that earnings will only support a market value of $80, and there will be a $20 loss of capital. This is in spite of the immediate effect of an increase in present earnings per share.

The same reasoning applies to each of the sources of funds, regardless of the immediate effect on present earnings per share. If funds are invested below the Cost-of-Capital, the ultimate result will be a loss to investors; if the project provides a return greater than the Cost-of-Capital, investors will be benefited. A company should only be interested in a return greater than the risk of the project in which it is investing; the source of funds does not affect this risk.

As already stated, management would prefer to show the greatest possible increase in present earnings per share. This will make investors happy. They tend to view such an increase as an indication of brighter future prospects, and temporarily the market price will probably react favorably. Investors do not have the data available to evaluate correctly the ultimate effect.

A company with a large amount of cash might be faced with the necessity of acquiring another company with a swap of stock because the company to be acquired makes this a prerequisite. As we mentioned previously, in such a situation the acquiring company can achieve the same effect on earnings per share as in a cash deal by buying its own stock in the market and then using stock for the acquisition.

If the stock used for an acquisition is treasury stock, the market price of the stock at the time the stock was repurchased is academic. The company has to consider the value of the stock in terms of the price it could now get if it were sold on the market.[2] The company has the alternative of selling stock for cash and investing the proceeds.

In an acquisition which is consummated with stock, it may be maintained that the cost of the acquisition should be figured on the

basis of the present market price of the acquiring company's stock discounted for financing costs. The reasoning behind this argument is as follows: A company has the alternative of selling the stock in the market and using the proceeds for expansion. If the stock were sold, financing costs would reduce the amount that the company would receive in net proceeds. In Chapter III, in which we discussed the common cost, we suggested 10% to 15% for total financing costs for common stock for various types of large companies. Since we increase our common cost in the Cost-of-Capital determination to allow for financing costs, this argument has logic.

## DANGER OF FOCUSING ON RETURN ON COMMON IN AN ACQUISITION

A word of caution should be noted for acquisitions where stock is acquired rather than assets. If the company to be acquired has a capital structure consisting solely of common stock, the risk factor involved is the risk of the business as a whole. However, if the company to be acquired has some senior securities outstanding, then the earnings applicable to the common are affected by the leverage. Thus, the common earnings rate would have to be higher in order to compensate for the leverage. In making an analysis of such an acquisition, it is preferable to analyze the forecast return on total capital rather than on the common alone, with the common stated at the price the acquiring company expects to pay.

In such a situation, it should further be recognized that a company with a large amount of debt will have a reduction in income taxes due to the large interest charges. A simple example is shown in Exhibit 7 (XII).

The return on total long-term capital is 12.50% ($10 + $2.50 divided by $50 + $50) and on common it is 20% ($10 divided by $50).

For the risk of the business, we will assume that 50% is too much debt, and that on the

---

[2] In an acquisition, a company issued 100,000 shares of convertible preferred stock with a $4 dividend in exchange for the common stock of the company which was acquired. The preferred stock was convertible into one share of common stock. The market price of the common stock of the acquiring company was $80 per share. The company erroneously believed that the price it paid was $8,000,000 based on the present market price of the common, that is $80 per share, multiplied by the number of shares of common which would exist after the conversion of the preferred occurred, that is 100,000 shares. The correct measure of the cost of the acquisition was the price at which the convertible preferred could have been sold in the market at the time of the acquisition, less financing costs. It was estimated that such a convertible preferred stock could have been sold in the market for a net price of $100 per share. Therefore, the cost of the acquisition was $10,000,000. The company gave up in value the worth of the convertible preferred at the time the deal was consummated.

## EXHIBIT 7 (XII)

### COMPANY TO BE ACQUIRED
### BALANCE SHEET

| Liabilities | | Assets | |
|---|---|---|---|
| Current Assets | $100 | Current Liabilities | $ 50 |
| Plant, Net | 50 | Long-Term Capital | |
| | | Debt $50 | |
| | | Common 50 | |
| | | | 100 |
| Other items | 0 | Other items | 0 |
| Total | $150 | | $150 |

### Income Items

| | |
|---|---|
| Income before interest and taxes | $22.50 |
| Interest (@5%) | 2.50 |
| Income Taxes (@50%) | 10.00 |
| Net income for common | 10.00 |

basis of sound financial policy it should only have 20%, or $20 of debt. This would require a restatement of the income items as shown in Exhibit 8 (XII).

The change in the debt ratio reduced interest charges but increased taxes. Now the return on total long-term capital is 11.70% ($10.80 + $0.90 divided by $20 + $80), and

## EXHIBIT 8 (XII)

### INCOME ITEMS RESTATED

| | |
|---|---|
| Income before interest and taxes | $22.50 |
| Interest (using 4-1/2% because of the better credit) | 0.90 |
| Income taxes (@50%) | 10.80 |
| Net income for common | 10.80 |

on common it is 13.50% ($10.80 divided by $80).

If the acquiring company, either for cash or through swapping stock, paid twice the stated book value of the stock as shown in

Exhibit 7 (XII), the adjusted return on total long-term capital, assuming a 20% debt ratio, would be 7.8% ($10.80 + $0.90 divided by $20 + $80 + $50) and on common equity 8.3% ($10.80 divided by $80 + $50). This is a far cry from what the original book figures showed.

## THE CHINESE MONEY QUESTION

If a company's stock is selling at a relatively high price, does that necessarily mean that it can pay a higher price for another company through an exchange of stock?

This question is often referred to as the Chinese Money Question, the idea being that over-valued stock is like Chinese money and has a false value.

In Exhibit 9 (XII) each company has a Cost-of-Capital based on the risk of the business of 10%. Neither one actually has any growth prospects and present earnings represent their future earning power. Investors, however, expect growth, and they have bid up the stocks excessively so that they are both equally over valued.

Company A acquires Company B on a 1 for

### EXHIBIT 9 (XII)

### CHINESE MONEY ILLUSTRATION

| Column | 1 | 2 | 3 | 4 |
|---|---|---|---|---|
| | Shares | Present Earnings Per Share | Present Price-Earnings Ratio | Present Market Price |
| Co. A | 1 | $4 | 25 | $100 |
| Co. B | 1 | $4 | 25 | $100 |

1 basis. Then the results would be as shown in Exhibit 10 (XII).

Ultimately investors will come to realize that they made a mistake in expecting growth,

and the market price will collapse to $40 per share on the basis of a price-earnings ratio of 10 times. This is in line with the 10% risk based on Cost-of-Capital.

### EXHIBIT 10 (XII)

### CHINESE MONEY ILLUSTRATION, CONTINUED

| Column | 1 | 2 | 3 | 4 | 5 |
|---|---|---|---|---|---|
| | Shares | Total | Present Earnings Per Share | Present Price-Earnings Ratio | Present Market Price |
| Co. A + B | 2 | $8 | $4 | 25 | $100 |

If Company A had not acquired Company B, the stock of Company A would likewise ultimately have collapsed to $40 per share when investors realized their mistake. Thus, as a result of the merger, Company A issued more shares but it gained nothing. We will demonstrate that there was an alternative available which would have been preferable.

The point we make is that any time a company has capital, or raises capital, no matter what the security medium or its price, it should never expand or make an acquisition below the Cost-of-Capital commensurate with the risk. In this case, the company issued one share of stock which could have been sold in the market for $100. It is this amount of capital which Company A actually invested in Company B. It should not have done so unless the return on the $100 was equivalent to the risk of the business. Actually, the return was only 4% since the earning power of Company B was only $4 per share; it should have been $10 or 10%.

If Company A had sold the share of stock in the market and retained the cash until it found a similar investment which would provide a 10% return commensurate with the risk, it would have obtained additional earnings of $10. This $10 combined with Company A's $4 would produce total earnings of $14 or $7 per share.

After investors' false hopes had vanished, the stock would sell at 10 times earnings or $70 per share. Thus, the stockholder in Company A would have his stock fall from $100 per share to $70 rather than to $40 as happened when Company B was acquired. The only depreciation in value that the stockholder would suffer would be due to his own mistake of over-valuing the stock of Company A. There would be no additional loss due to the fact that Company A improperly invested the proceeds from the issuance of the new share of stock below the rate commensurate with the estimated risk.

If Company A cannot find any place to invest the proceeds from the sale of a share of stock at $100, it always has the alternative of putting the money in high-grade short-term bonds. We will assume that it invests in tax-free bonds which provide a return of 4% or $4.00. This return is on the high side, but it helps simplify our example and it does not destroy the principle we are illustrating. This return would be in line with the risk of those securities—or in line with the lack of risk. Exhibit 11 (XII) shows what would have happened if Company A had followed that policy.

EXHIBIT 11(XII)

CHINESE MONEY ILLUSTRATION, CONTINUED

| | Shares | Present Earnings Total | Per Share |
|---|---|---|---|
| Co. A-old share | 1 | $4 | $4.00 |
| Co. A-new share | 1 | $4 | $4.00 |
| Total | 2 | $8 | $4.00 |

Now Company A's earnings are still $4.00 per share, but note that the over-all risk factor has changed from 10% to a combination of 10% and 4%. This would represent a weighted average risk of 5.71%[3] and a price-earnings ratio of 17½ times. Thus, ultimately the price of the stock would be $4.00 × 17½ or $70.

To recapitulate, in the above example, we

[3] Total earnings of $8 divided by total market value of $140 sustained by these earnings.

started with two companies which had stocks equally over-valued. Then after the acquisition, when the market woke up to the true picture of earnings in the future and when the air went out of the balloons, investors suffered a loss because of their foolishness in over-valuing Company A's stock. There was a similar loss due to the acquisition of Company B, because Company A acquired Company B at such an inflated value. We pointed out that if it had invested the money in short-term bonds until it found a chance to make an investment above the Cost-of-Capital, it would have prevented that part of the loss which resulted from the acquisition. A company always has this alternative.

If the acquiring company is more over-priced than the company to be acquired, when the day of reckoning arrives and the market reflects the true value commensurate with the risk the deflation will be less drastic for the acquiring company. The deflation will be lessened by the better position of the company being acquired. In any situation, the extent of the ultimate deflation depends on the extent to which the stocks are over-priced both absolutely and relatively.

The ideas which we have just expressed might be viewed in another way as follows. If an investor owns a stock which is too high and sells it, he should not reinvest the cash in another stock if he thinks other stocks are over-priced. He should put the money in government bonds. The two situations are analogous, and the whole idea is just as simple as that.

Managements which at least understand the importance of obtaining an adequate return on capital in an expansion program where money is invested directly in plant seem to change their standards of valuation when there is an acquisition or merger through stock-swapping. As an example, a certain company wished to acquire another company through a stock-swap. The fair book value of the common stock of the company to be acquired was $1,300,000, the estimated earning power was $200,000, and the risk of the business appeared to be about 10%. The acquiring company observed that similar stocks sold at 15 times earnings, and therefore felt it could afford to give enough of its shares on the basis of market value to pay $3,000,000—*until* the following was suggested: "Suppose you had owned the assets of this company from its beginning and invested $1,300,000 in the plant and another $1,700,000 for start-up costs to get the plant operating efficiently so that it would earn $200,000. The total investment would be $3,-

000,000. Then the return on your total outlay would have only been 6⅔%. Would you have considered this a good project?" The answer was: "Absolutely not!" The fact that the acquisition was going to be made with stock clouded the management's thinking. The acquisition could have been justified only on the basis of forecast profits which would produce a substantially higher rate.

Some managements may react to the ideas suggested above as follows: "The stock of my company is very high-priced. In fact, I am sure it is over-valued. Should I just do nothing and not take advantage of the high price?"

The answer is that if a company is sure it needs more common stock money, and if the market price is high, it should obviously sell common stock. The company owes it to its existing stockholders to sell stock under favorable circumstances if it is possible to do so.

However, the facts of life are such that the management of a company is a very poor judge of the market value of its own stock. Even if it is correct in its appraisal of the market price, management cannot just raise money and let it sit idle. Stockholders expect a company to put money to work.

There is a sound rule of thumb in finance that management should not try to outguess the securities market. It should only do financing when funds are needed for some specific purpose. It should accept the market conditions as they are and raise the capital. For a company which finances regularly, it will thus obtain an average of market rates. For a company which finances only occasionally, this is a more difficult problem. It should try to avoid chaotic market conditions by using short-term bank loans and it may be able to vary the type of security sold, depending on the conditions of the market. But this is quite different from trying regularly to outguess the market.

You may feel that we have given too little weight to the realities of the securities market in this chapter. We used one example in which earnings per share decreased when the proceeds from the sale of stock were invested in government bonds. Although the market price for the stock might show an immediate decline due to the reported decrease in earnings per share, ultimately the price of the stock should hold up because the risk in the earnings decreased proportionately.

The picture might be summarized as follows: Management should avoid acquisitions, mergers and expansion programs which will have an adverse effect on the company's long-range earning power, in spite of the fact that temporarily it might improve earnings. A project which will benefit long-range earnings must also be studied for the short-range effect. It is possible that the severity of the adverse effect in the short run might be such as to make the project undesirable even though its long-range effect were beneficial. This calls for keen judgment.

Once you accept the principle that all capital has a cost and that you should use the composite Cost-of-Capital commensurate with the risk of the contemplated investment, you will have no difficulty in seeing that investing capital below cost will ultimately result in a loss. As we suggested in Chapter II, this truth would be clearly evident if all capital consisted of debt. Then, if the expected return on any investment were below the interest rate investors required, commensurate with risk, default would follow. Equally serious results follow no matter what the source of capital; the only difference is that management errors do not become immediately apparent and investors are currently led to misinterpret the picture.

Because investors are influenced by the reported earnings per share figure, management has them at its mercy. Maneuvers which produce temporary earnings improvement provide an opportunity for management which wishes to jazz up the common stock for a few years for stock option purposes, to make a good showing before retiring, or to justify becoming a bigger company.

An amusing incident occurred at a management meeting of a company which had acquired a number of other companies. The presidents of the acquired companies were now presidents of divisions. The purpose of the meeting was to set goals for return on investment. In one of the discussions, a division president spoke up and said:

> I certainly can meet your goal on the asset value of my company, but you can't expect me to meet it on the price you paid.

That thought is a good finale for this chapter.

# Reducing the Cost-of-Capital

Since managements naturally strive to reduce all costs, you undoubtedly have been thinking about how Cost-of-Capital can be reduced. We have emphasized that Cost-of-Capital depends largely on the risk of the enterprise as viewed by investors. It follows that this cost can be reduced by improving their view. This encompasses all phases of a company's operations which affect risk. We will comment on those elements which apply to finance. Since this is not a book on financial policy [1] we will not go into specifics but only indicate the general direction which your thinking should take.

## JUDICIOUS USE OF SENIOR SECURITIES—WELL-REASONED CAPITAL STRUCTURE POLICY

When the question of reducing the Cost-of-Capital arises, the means which *appears* most enticing is to use a large amount of cheap debt and minimize the amount of high-cost common stock. We have emphasized that this may work in the short run, but that it is unsound and in the long run may cause financial dif-

[1] For a discussion of financial policies for corporations, see *Long-Term Financing* by John F. Childs, Prentice-Hall, Inc., 1961.

ficulties, add to the financial risk, and increase the Cost-of-Capital.

Many companies are able to provide funds for expansion purposes from internally generated cash. The compound growth rate of the common equity is a function of the rate earned on the common equity and the per cent of earnings retained. This was reviewed in Chapter XI. For example, if a company earns 10% on the book investment and pays out 50% of its earnings in dividends, the compound growth rate in common equity book value will be 5%. This will permit a 5% compound growth in senior securities and maintain the same ratio of senior securities to total long-term capital. However, a company may need to draw on outside funds not only for expansion, but also for repayment of maturing obligations. How does it prepare itself to be able to do so on a satisfactory basis?

If a company could dictate the conditions under which it might have to finance, everything would be clear sailing. Unfortunately, it cannot do so, nor can it foresee what the conditions may be. Unforeseen adversities may be experienced in four areas:

The Company
The Industry

General Business Conditions

Security Markets

A company must be in a position to finance on a satisfactory basis when difficulties are encountered so that it can take advantage of opportunities for profitable investment. Generally, common stock cannot be sold under such circumstances. Therefore, a company must be able to sell debt securities at a reasonable rate and terms without straining its credit. This dictates that a company should keep its debt within reasonable bounds when it is prosperous.

This idea is hard to sell to some managements, particularly new managements in an industry which has experienced a rapid boom with skyrocketing stock prices. Such managements are imbued with the idea of borrowing money and further increasing earnings per share through leverage.

Experience in finance teaches that it is a tedious task to straighten out a company that has damaged its credit. Furthermore, it takes even longer to convince investors that improvement has taken place. Once the bloom of investor interest leaves a company or an industry it is a long dreary period before that interest materializes again. Then a company is a cripple that has relied so much on debt in the past that it is blocked from further financing.

Keeping a reserve of credit during good times for adverse conditions is known as maintaining a "borrowing reserve." How much debt a company can carry and still have "borrowing reserve" depends on the circumstances surrounding the company. It is not the purpose of this book to establish bench marks for debt policy: that is a major field of corporate finance. Suffice it to say that the approach must be made through an understanding of the quality of securities. The quality of a security determines whether it can be sold and the rate and terms that have to be paid. A simple expression of the quality for debt securities for large companies can be found in the bond ratings established by Fitch Investors

Service, Moody's Investors Service and Standard & Poor's Corporation. The first step is to decide what quality rating will provide adequate financial strength and borrowing reserve. The second step is to decide how much debt a company can carry and achieve the desired rating; this is done through the application of security analysis techniques.

For small companies it may not be possible to use bond ratings as a guide. Small companies are automatically graded down in rating because of the added risk due to their small size. However, the same general type of reasoning can be applied in terms of credit—high-grade, medium-grade, and low-grade.

Privately-owned companies may be more flexible, because they are not subject to the whims of the stock market in raising new common. The private owners can add new common based on their intimate knowledge of prospects for the company, regardless of its present poor showing. This greater flexibility assumes, of course, that the owners have more cash available to put up if it is needed.

In the above discussion, the main point stressed is the danger of being unable to raise capital if debt is used excessively in good times. There are other damaging results:

It may mean a wider fluctuation of stock prices with bad dips during adverse circumstances—a Yo-Yo stock.

It may necessitate a dividend cut with the consequent damaging effect on the common stock market price.

Terms may be imposed when financing is done which will restrict a company's freedom of action.

The ultimate possibility of bankruptcy.

A company is never made great merely by the use of debt. A management can go into debt without having the slightest financial ability when a company is experiencing good earnings. Throughout this book we have championed the idea that the ability to earn a satisfactory rate on total long-term capital is what makes for a company's success, as well as having the gumption to keep it financially sound in the face of strong pressures in the other direction from many members of the financial community.

The attitude of some managements toward lease financing would be amusing if it were not so sad. Presumably, management works for its stockholders. And yet you can find some managements which contend that lease financing has an advantage in that it is a means of hiding debt from stockholders. Their reasoning goes along these lines: stockholders are unaware of the lease form of debt financing since it is off the balance sheet; therefore, they will pay more for the stock. We ask, "What kind of sense does it make to fool the people you are working for?" Unfortunately as far as stockholders are concerned, there may be some managements who do not care to understand their obligation to their stockholders. A decision on lease financing should be based on a cost comparison with the alternative of debt financing.

We have not meant to discourage the use of senior securities. On the contrary, senior securities used in proper balance with common equity may reduce the Cost-of-Capital. Furthermore, when the market for a company's common stock is unattractive, the only source of capital is through the sale of debt securities. And when a new company is started excessive reliance on debt may be the only way that sufficient capital can be raised. In such situations, where a company has had to deviate from a well-balanced financial policy, the important thing is for management to know what the correct financial goal should be and gradually try to get there as earnings and capital requirements permit. Generally, it is impractical for a company to move too fast in rectifying a bad financial picture. It might hurt common stock earnings and temporarily increase the Cost-of-Capital.

Management cannot plan financially unless it has a well-reasoned policy regarding the best type of capital structure for the company. If it does not have such a goal, each piece of financing will be a matter of momentary expediency. This will lead in the right direction only by chance. Furthermore, in appraising a company's securities, investors will wish to know what capital structure policies the company has in mind. It is a legitimate question. A weak statement will raise doubts in investors' minds as to the management's ability.

Simplicity in financing will tend to reduce investors' appraisal of risk. A complicated financial structure with many types of securities adds to the difficulty in analysis. The bright newcomers to finance have a tendency to try to distinguish themselves by the use of complicated types of securities for which they can make intriguing stories as to the advantages thereof—particularly convertibles, warrants, leases, and the like. Before long the capital structure is a total mess. The more sophisticated in finance strive for simplicity.

## DIVIDEND POLICY TO PRODUCE BEST MARKET PRICE IN THE LONG RUN

Stockholders receive only two things—cash dividends and appreciation in market price. A company should establish the dividend policy which will produce the best market price for the company's stock *over the long run* so that dividend income and market appreciation combined will be maximized.

Dividend policy may affect the price of a stock and to the extent that it does it will affect the common cost. This is not to suggest that a high payout will necessarily result in a high price. The effect of dividends on price depends on the nature of the company and its stockholders. For some new speculative companies no dividends may be the best policy. The stockholders of such companies may be in a high income tax bracket and would be seeking capital gains. On the other hand, a mature, stable company which attracts income-conscious stockholders may do best with a relatively high payout.

The rate a company earns on its common equity, which affects growth through plowback of earnings, is an important consideration in the payout ratio. The higher the return, the greater the justification for a lower pay-out—if the company can reinvest the money at the same or a better rate. If a company is weak financially it may have to forego dividend payments in order to avoid hurting its credit standing. Providing a company has no such problems, it should not let cash requirements for expansion restrict its dividend payments. Dividend policy should be decided upon first. Then if there is not enough cash available for expansion, the needed funds should be raised through financing. It would be an understatement to say that some managements determine this policy on the basis of the cart before the horse.

Historical dividend pattern is important in its effect on the market price of a stock. A company should follow financial policies so that it can maintain an attractive pattern. It should show courage during adversity and, within the bounds of sound credit, it should avoid cutting a dividend. If a company decides it has too high a payout policy, it is preferable to correct the situation by holding the payments level and letting the payout ratio drop as earnings increase.

It has been amply demonstrated that stock dividends affect the market price of a stock for a very brief period of time.[2] A company should not duck the question of the proper cash payment by substituting a stock dividend which is ineffective and is expensive to issue, an expense which is not tax deductable.

## FINANCIAL POLICIES IN GENERAL

There are many facets of financial policy other than those already mentioned which af-

fect the stockholders. We will illustrate with one example.

When a company sells common stock it may have the choice of selling directly to the public or through rights to the stockholders. Some companies tend to favor a direct offering and would use a rights offering only under special circumstances. Which method to use will depend on all the conditions at the particular time.

A good case can be made for the proposition that stockholders are generally benefited more with a rights offering. We will not try to settle this argument here. It is merely used to illustrate the type of financial policy questions which management should decide on the basis of the long-range benefit to stockholders. To the extent that rights offerings do benefit stockholders, the stock will sell at a better level and the Cost-of-Capital will be reduced.

## INVESTOR RELATIONS

Lack of knowledge about a company's operations will lead investors to increase their appraisal of risk. A publicly-owned company should have a well-planned and directed program to keep investors fully informed about its operations *both favorable and unfavorable*. This is known as investor relations. It involves primarily the cultivation of financial analysts, since they have the greatest impact on the market price. The size of the program will depend on the size of the company, the extent of investor interest and the nature of the business. In the long run, a well-planned program will result in a company's securities' selling at better prices because investors prefer to buy securities about which they know all the facts. It will also facilitate raising capital on the best possible basis.

Furthermore, the management of a publicly owned company has an obligation to give out continuously all the pertinent facts. The securities of publicly-owned companies are bought and sold every day and they are ana-

[2] See articles by C. Austin Barker (Partner, Hornblower & Weeks—Hemphill, Noyes) such as *Harvard Business Review*, "Evaluation of Stock Dividends," July–August, 1958, pp. 99–114; *The Analysts Journal*, "Are Accounting Requirements for Stock Dividends Obsolete?", November, 1958, pp. 69–72; *Investment Dealers' Digest*, "Utility Stock Dividends—Their Problems and Benefits," Section II, Public Utility Survey Issue of April 6, 1959, pp. 27–28; and *The Journal of Finance*, "Price Changes of Stock-Dividend Shares at Ex-Dividend Dates," September, 1959, pp. 373–378.

lyzed every day. Investors have a right to buy and sell a security at a fair price. The price will be fair only if those who are able to use the data are given the necessary facts on which to base their judgment.

The point we wish to stress is the importance of having a program carried out on a regular basis. Some companies seem to feel that they should talk before groups of financial analysts only when they have some new developments to explain, or when operating results are favorable. Some companies shy away from financial analysts when their picture is so complicated that it would be hard to explain. A business recession can almost be charted by cancellations of appearances of companies before analysts' societies. A company may have been scheduled to appear many months in advance. When the time to appear arrives, the company's earnings may be on the decline and management may not wish to talk about the bad news. Such an approach is totally unsound. The financial analysts need to know the bad news as well as the good. Once they sense that a management withholds the bad news, they will be hesitant to recommend a company's securities—and so they should!

The most crucial time in an investor relations program is when a company takes its first step. For example, a new company which has been highly successful becomes publicly-owned and the management is bursting with pride to tell its story to the financial community. It talks about its glowing future. Later on the picture does not glow, but the management has misunderstood the true purpose of an investor relations program and the fact that it must carry on the program just the same with bad earnings. It is unprepared for this situation and withdraws into its shell.

Before a company ever starts on a program, the top management should become thoroughly knowledgeable as to its real purpose. Only then will the program be conceived in such a way that it can be kept on a continuous basis without any embarrassment to management when bad times occur.

## PROPER PROFIT GOALS

Since the entire subject of this book is Profit Goals, there is little need to remind you of their importance. If the management of a company sidesteps sound Profit Goals and their application, investors should shy away from such a company. The following comment is not uncommon in the financial community.

The Management is sales- and size-happy.

If investors get a clue that a company lacks knowledge in this field they are bound to increase their risk appraisal. The company's securities will react accordingly and so will the Cost-of-Capital.

## THE DIRECTORS

We end this chapter on financial policies affecting the Cost-of-Capital with a few words about those on the management team who specifically represent the stockholders' interest. Financial experts weigh the make-up of the board when they evaluate a security. They are bound to appraise a company more favorably if they feel that the board is highly qualified.

Directors should be:

Well-regarded in their own respective fields and experienced so that they can determine whether management is doing a good job.

Able to spend time studying the company so that they will be fully informed.

Devoid of any taint of self-interest in dealings with the company regarding their own person or the company they may represent, or in the use of inside information for trading in the company's securities.

Above all, not a rubber stamp for management.

A primary function of directors is to elect competent management and, if the occasion should arise, to remove incompetent management. Do the directors truly represent the stockholders in this function? Are they beholden to management for their appointment? Did they take the appointment primarily to enhance their own standing in the business world?

For a long time the science of management has been applied to many phases of a company's operations, but it seems that in some respects the directors may have been slighted.[3]

[3] The New York Stock Exchange has published (November, 1965) an interesting booklet on the subject of directors, *The Corporate Director and the Investing Public*. It also comments on disclosure of corporate news.

At least, stockholders should be assured of an active board by means of a resolution which will call for retirement of directors at a certain age if they become ill, if they leave the position which they occupied when they became a director, or if they leave the area so that they cannot regularly attend directors' meetings. With regard to Profit Goals, they should be sufficiently knowledgeable to be able to review management's policies on major capital expenditures and acquisitions.

# CHAPTER XIV

# Brief Review of Profit Goals

Now that you have completed the part of the book dealing with Profit Goals, perhaps a brief statement of some of the ideas we covered will help you review your thinking on the subject. We will do that in this short chapter.

We gradually led up to the proposition that Cost-of-Capital should be the basis for establishing a Profit Goal and that Cost-of-Capital depends on the risk of the enterprise. The risk must be viewed in terms of those who supply the capital—the investors—and not on some subjective appraisal of risk in the management's mind.

The Cost-of-Capital for a company is determined in the competitive market for long-term capital. The common equity part has a cost just as much as the senior securities, but it is hard to understand: for this reason we took part of a chapter to explain what it means. We did not hedge in any way about the principles of common cost: they are like scientific principles. The common cost must be based on investors' expectations. Because of the difficulty of measuring investors' expectations, we did not hesitate to admit that calculating the common cost is an art and a hard one to boot. We cautioned that serious errors may result unless meticulous care is taken to see that each step in the calculations adheres to the definition.

Some additional ideas in determining Cost-of-Capital were:

The final result should be figured over a period of years in order to obtain an average figure under favorable and unfavorable conditions.

A highly leveraged capital structure is no good for determining Cost-of-Capital.

In the very beginning of the book we mentioned that if capital expenditures are made below the Cost-of-Capital, the company's stockholders are hurt and the industry is blighted. But even more important, capital is misdirected and wasted; this will have an adverse effect on our standard of living.

We explained that a company should earn more than the Cost-of-Capital to be successful and, when it expands, it should have its Profit Goal even higher above Cost-of-Capital.

We suggested some bench marks: the less risky regulated industries, electric and telephone, on which much work has been done. We included a composite figure [1] of 6¾% to 7% for the electric utilities and 8% for telephone. We pointed out that if our competitive economic system worked well, then all industry should earn the Cost-of-Capital on the average. We showed that in the years 1956–1965 all manufacturing companies showed a return on year end Total Long-Term Capital of 9.5% and on Common Equity of 10.4%. Based on an average of beginning and year-end capital, these figures would be about 10% and 11% respectively.

We outlined the three different effects of taxes on the three different composite rates and set this up in a table:

[1] Return on Total Capital Target—To Investor Rate.

|  | Cost-of-Capital | Return on Total Capital Target | Profit Goal for Expansion |
|---|---|---|---|
| To Investor Rate |  |  |  |
| Pre-Tax Rate |  |  |  |
| After Tax Equivalent Rate |  |  |  |

There is a serious error in applying the cost rate applicable to a particular security to an expansion project, even though the project is financed with that security. For any capital expenditure the composite rate should be used. Leases present a case in point, and in judging a capital expenditure financed with a lease care must be taken not to be deluded into thinking that the lease financing method can make successful a project which would not be successful with ownership.

It is interesting to note that industries tend to equate their differences in risks for the common by the use of different amounts of senior securities. However, drums were beaten to emphasize the fallacy of thinking that the composite Cost-of-Capital could be reduced in the long run by excessive debt.

The management of a company should become thoroughly knowledgeable about an approximate Cost-of-Capital for its entire operation. If the company includes different risks, then the company figure should be broken down by divisions, but only if there is a significant difference in risk of at least 1% or more. The calculations cannot be more precise nor do they need to be.

The added risk of foreign investments is the area of gravest danger—increased earnings abroad do not necessarily mean a true increase in profit; this will depend on the risk.

We hope we knocked into a cocked hat such fallacies as:

The goal changes with the source of funds.

Increasing present earnings per share is a good goal in itself.

A high-priced stock permits a company to pay a high price for acquisitions.

Because earnings per share are followed so closely by management, we spent an entire chapter talking about this subject. Current earnings per share cannot be disregarded by any means, but your thinking should be focused primarily on the long run rather than the short run so that permanent benefits to the stockholders will be maximized. We hope we convinced you that capital management can only be handled successfully if the principles behind Cost-of-Capital are well understood and conscientiously applied. Otherwise, you will have to rely heavily on Lady Luck to bail you out.

The last chapter gave suggestions of a few ways to reduce the Cost-of-Capital.

Now that we have completed our discussion of Profit Goals, we turn to the methods for determining the per cent profit rate a capital expenditure or acquisition will produce.

# Profitability Rate[1]

As part of the process of deciding on new investments and liquidations of existing property, a correct profitability rate for the proposed investment must be figured. It is this profitability rate with which a Profit Goal is compared. Use of the wrong measure may lead to making substantial, unsound capital commitments. About two out of three companies still rank capital investment projects solely by "payback" or "accounting return on investment" methods—and neither of these methods gives a true picture.

Profitability rate cannot be calculated without a forecast. This book does not cover that subject, but a few words about the significance of forecasting is a necessary introduction to the subject of profitability rate.

[1] This chapter was contributed by Dr. Victor H. Brown, Partner, Touche, Ross, Bailey & Smart, 80 Pine Street, New York City. Some of the material appeared in his article, "Rate of Return: Some Comments on Its Applicability in Capital Budgeting," *Accounting Review*, Volume XXXVI, No. 1, January, 1961.

## FORECASTING

It should be unnecessary to present arguments in favor of forecasting. However, some people seem to have little faith in the idea of forecasting and feel the same way about a profitability rate based thereon. Believe it or not, the management of one company stated that since they had never made a correct forecast they had decided not to make any more. The quick answer to that statement is that the stockholders needed new management to save them from reliance on pure luck.

Those who try to shun forecasts may argue that a company spends millions on pure research without explicitly forecasting the profits resulting from these expenditures. Companies must at least evaluate the over-all results of pure research. Because of the nature of the expenditure, the evaluation may have to be on a post-audit basis. However, the limitation of forecasts for research expenditures in no way argues against profit forecasts which can be used as the basis for judgment in deciding on other types of capital expenditures.

Each capital decision in fact involves a forecast—the forecasting process is employed even though a forecast is not put down on paper. In effect, if no written forecast is made, the management is saying that it expects, or mentally forecasts, that profits on the proposal will be satisfactory. The purpose of a written forecast is to provide a background on which to base judgment and aid management in its mental processes. It is the best kind of mental discipline to force thinking about all the elements which will affect profits. It provides a basis for post-audit appraisal.

A financial forecast is an attempt to describe future events in numerical terms. Its accuracy is limited proportionately with our ability to see into the future—like a man peering into a haze, the farther we try to see, the less certain we are about what is out there. This is no argument for abandoning forecasts. All the tools at your disposal must be used in order to improve the vision; even a hazy picture of the future is better than no picture at all.

However, it is important to know how much weight to give to your forecast in making a decision. What are the chances that the forecast is seriously wrong? One way to try to answer this question is to bracket your forecast with two others—one if everything goes right and another if all the problems you are worrying about in fact occur. These bracketing forecasts give some idea of what happens if the central forecast is wrong. If certain items which are key to the success of a project are hard to foretell, various forecasts might be made with the key items varied within a realistic range in order to show possible effects. In addition, there are more sophisticated techniques that can be used to test the reliability of forecasts and to show how important each assumption is to the final outcome. For the technician they may be helpful, but they would be of little value for presentation to top management; the raw forecast figures would mean more.

When forecasting is mentioned, someone may ask "For how many years should the forecast be made?" If ten years is suggested, there may be some cynical comment such as: "I defy anyone to show me someone who has made a correct forecast in my industry for more than three years." This, of course, is no answer and only indicates that the person has missed the point. Even if definite figures cannot be established, projections can be made on the basis of reasonableness, or should we say within the range of possibility. If these figures are translated into a profitability rate which can be compared with a Profit Goal, they can be the basis of a reasoned decision of go or no go.

No definite figure can be given as to how many years the forecast should be extended. This will depend upon the circumstances. In cases where, for example, an entire company is acquired, the forecast may be projected for as long as 20 years based on possible percentage growth rates. At the end of the forecast period it will be necessary to estimate a terminal value if there will be valuable assets at the end of the period. This is illustrated in Appendix E in the example showing how to calculate the profitability rate.

As will be explained, the forecast should give cash flows. These cash flows can be picked out of the forecast income statements and balance sheets.

Each part of the capital decision-making process should be perfected as far as possible so as to arrive at correct decisions. Granted that forecasting is the key to the whole investment decision and that it may include errors, we see no reason why the profitability rate itself should compound the errors by being calculated incorrectly. This is the reason for this chapter.

## COMMON MEASURES

Let's consider several ways of determining a profitability rate for Project A, shown in Exhibit 1(XV). This project will require a $100,000 initial investment and is expected to increase annual corporate profits, after depre-

## EXHIBIT 1 (XV)

## PROJECT A

| Column | 1 | 2 | 3 | 4 |
|---|---|---|---|---|
| Year | Investment | Profit After Tax | Depreciation | Cash Flow |
| 0 | $100,000 | - | - | - |
| 1 | | $10,000 | $ 25,000 | $ 35,000 |
| 2 | | 10,000 | 25,000 | 35,000 |
| 3 | | 10,000 | 25,000 | 35,000 |
| 4 | | 10,000 | 25,000 | 35,000 |
| Total | $100,000 | $40,000 | $100,000 | $140,000 |

### Commonly Employed Investment Measures

$$\text{Payback Period} = \frac{\text{Total Investment}}{\text{Annual Cash Flow}} = \frac{\$100,000}{\$ 35,000} = 2.9 \text{ years}$$

Accounting Methods:

$$\text{Return on Total Investment} = \frac{\text{Annual Profit After Taxes}}{\text{Total Investment}} = \frac{\$ 10,000}{\$100,000} = 10\%$$

$$\text{Return on Average Investment} = \frac{\text{Annual Profit After Taxes}}{\text{Average Investment}} = \frac{\$10,000}{\$50,000} = 20\%$$

---

ciation and income taxes, by $10,000 during its estimated four-year economic life. The proposed $100,000 investment involves the purchase of machinery which will be depreciated on a straight-line basis at $25,000 annually; the machinery is expected to have no salvage value at the end of its four-year life.

Exhibit 1(XV) includes three commonly employed measures to appraise the profitability of this investment.

The first measure—the payback period— shows that it will take about 2.9 years to recover the $100,000 initial investment from the $10,000 annual profit and the $25,000 annual depreciation. The second—the return on total investment—simply divides the expected $10,-000 in annual earnings by the $100,000 total investment. The third—the return on average investment—relates the expected $10,000 in annual earnings to the average investment outstanding over the life of the project. In the case of Project A, with straight line depreciation, the average investment is $50,000, that is, the $100,000 initial investment plus the $0 ending investment, divided by two to get the average.

Each of these three measures is widely used in industry today. Which is a valid profitability rate? Which can be compared with a Profit Goal to determine whether the investment is worthwhile? Unfortunately, to use any of them may lead to unsound investment choices.

The correct profitability rate is actually 15%. It can be determined by discounted cash flow procedures to be described later.

## WHY COMMON MEASURES ARE INADEQUATE

Because the three profitability measures discussed above—payback period and both accounting methods—are so widely employed, it is worthwhile to point out just why they may produce unreliable profitability rates. First, we must admit that both the payback period and accounting methods are easy to compute and easy to understand.

### Payback Method

The method which industry uses most often to rank capital investment proposals is payback —the number of years it takes a project to pay back its initial capital outlay from cash flows[2] produced by profits and depreciation. As a measure of risk, it actually is useful. It is easy to see that the faster your initial capital outlay is recovered, the less time your capital is at risk. However, payback does not measure profitability. A payback evaluation ignores all of the cash flows expected after the payback

period; these post-recovery cash flows can be of vital importance to a project's profitability.

For example, suppose we are considering two projects, each of which requires a $100,-000 initial capital outlay. Each will generate $50,000 cash each year for the first two years. Both projects will obviously have an equal payback period—two years. But suppose the cash flows from Project One cease after those first two years, while Project Two continues to produce cash flows at the rate of $50,000 annually for another two years. In this extreme example it is easy to see that the payback method offers the decision-maker no assistance at all in evaluating the post-recovery income.

Another major objection to payback is that it fails to consider the time value of money. Suppose we add Project Three to the example above and assume that it also requires an initial $100,000 capital outlay. Its cash flows, however, will be $75,000 the first year, $25,000 the second year and then $50,000 for the next two years. The cash flows of these three projects are shown in Exhibit 2 (XV).

Payback will indicate that Project Three has the same two-year capital recovery period as the other two projects; it thus seems equally desirable. However, it is actually more desirable than Project Two, since the extra $25,-000 return in the first year can be put to work earning more income in the second year.

Despite these two major objections we do not recommend dropping payback computations completely, but we do suggest that payback is helpful only in measuring risk by showing how soon we will get our money back. It is certainly not a valid profitability rate.

### Accounting Methods

Neither of the so-called accounting return on investment methods provides a valid profitability rate. In the capital investment process, they are useful only as very quick and crude profitability indicators for preliminary evaluations. For some proposals they may come fairly close to a true profitability rate, but for others they may be very misleading. The basic

[2] If the cash flows are not constant, as in our example, deduct the net cash flow each year from the initial investment until the remaining initial investment is less than one year's cash flow. Then determine the proportion of that year's cash flow required to complete the repayment of the initial investment. The cash flows should be net after any additional investment. If there are negative net cash flows in any year, due to losses or investments greater than cash flow incomes during the year, they should be deducted from the positive cash flows in calculating the payback period.

### EXHIBIT 2 (XV)

#### CASH FLOWS - PROFIT, AFTER TAX, PLUS DEPRECIATION

| Year | Project One | Project Two | Project Three |
|---|---|---|---|
| 0 | | | |
| 1 | $50,000 | $50,000 | $75,000 |
| 2 | 50,000 | 50,000 | 25,000 |
| 3 | | 50,000 | 50,000 |
| 4 | | 50,000 | 50,000 |

faults of the accounting methods are two: one, they focus upon accounting income figures rather than upon cash flows; and two, they fail to consider the time value of money.

*Cash Flows*

Why is it important to look at cash flows rather than at expected income in evaluating capital investments? Very simply because it is not until we actually spend cash that we have incurred any monetary sacrifice; conversely, it is only when we receive cash—not income as accounting measures it—that we have received something which can be put back to work to earn more money.

For correct decision-making in the case of Project A, shown in Exhibit 1(XV), the profitability measure should focus upon the $35,000 annual cash receipts that we expect— not on the $10,000 annual accounting income figures. It is these $35,000 cash flows that can be put back to work earning more money. The accounting return on investment methods focus upon the $10,000 expected income, not upon the $35,000 cash flows which are more significant for decision-making purposes. This may sound as though we are interested in the return *of* capital rather than the return *on* capital. Actually, the cash flows include both the return of capital and the return on capital. The return of the capital reduces the investment base on which the earnings are figured to produce a true profitability rate on capital. We will explain this idea shortly.

### TIME VALUE OF MONEY

The concept of time value of money is central to the whole approach of determining a correct profitability rate. Both the payback and accounting methods fail to consider properly the time value of money.

Just what do we mean when we say money has a time value? It means that a dollar due in the future is worth less than a dollar we have in hand today. Why? Because today's dollar can be put to work to earn more money between now and that future date. Put another way, if someone owes you $1 and offers to pay either $1 today or $1 a year from now, which would you choose? Normally you would choose today even if you do not need the money right away, because you could put it into a savings account or some other investment. A year later, that dollar would have grown to $1.04 if the savings account paid interest at an annual rate of 4%. In its most basic form, then, this is the meaning of time value of money—a dollar today is worth more than a dollar received at a future date; how much more depends on how much we should earn[3] with today's dollar between now and that future date.

Our aim, then, is to develop a method of measuring the profitability rate of a proposed project in a way that correctly handles the time

---

[3] Even without considering risk, the time value of money is a valid concept. If you are absolutely sure of receiving that $1 a year from now, it is still less valuable than $1 in hand. The question of risk was explained in the previous part of the book on Cost-of-Capital.

value of money. The projects we are considering will almost always extend over more than one year; if an investment does not affect more than one year, it is probably more of an operating decision than a capital budgeting decision.

*Compounding*

This leads us into the effects of compounding. In case it has been a number of years since you thought about compound interest, here is a one-sentence refresher: Compound interest means that each year we compute interest earned on that year's invested principal and then add the interest earned to the principal amount; this compound sum, that is, interest plus principal, then becomes the new principal for computing the interest earned the next year.[4] In other words, in the second year you earn interest on the initial principal, plus interest on earnings of the first year. A simple illustration may help.

Suppose you put $10,000 in a savings bank that offers annual interest of 4%. If you left it there for two years, you should be quite unhappy if it had earned only $400 the first year and $400 the second year. The second year your deposit should have earned $416—4% on the initial $10,000 plus 4% on the $400 earned the first year. At the end of the second year, then, your $10,000 has grown to $10,-816.

Instead of going through these several multiplications each time, it is much simpler to consult tables which show the amount to which $1 will grow; multiplying that amount by the actual dollars invested will give us the

same answer much more rapidly. Exhibit 3(XV) shows a sample of such a table. To illustrate: the figure of 1.082, which is shown in the 4% column for period 2, multiplied by the $10,000 initial investment in the example above, indicates that you will have a sum of approximately $10,820 at the end of two years if you invested $10,000 at an interest rate of 4% compounded annually. Tables carried to more decimal places are available which will give the more precise $10,816 result we obtained in the previous paragraph. Three or four decimal places are usually adequate for capital budgeting purposes.

*Discounting or Present Value—
the Other Side of the Coin*

Now let us just turn the compounding approach around. This will produce discount or present value factors. In compounding, we derived the amount to which $1 will grow at compound interest. Discount factors answer the question "What amount do I have to invest today, in order to have $1 at the end of 'n' years, assuming 'i' interest rate 'compounded'?" Another way of saying it is that the discount factors give the present value of a sum due at a future date at a certain rate of interest. Exhibit 4(XV) is a sample table of discount or present value factors.

To illustrate the use of Exhibit 4(XV) suppose we want to know what amount will grow to $1 by the end of two years, if we invest at 4% compound interest. The table shows $0.925 would be the answer. The proof of this is as follows: First year, adding investment of $0.925 to interest of $0.037 results in $0.962 at the first year end which will earn $0.038 during the second year, for a total of $1.00. A discount factor is the reciprocal of the corresponding compound interest factor. For example, the compound interest factor for 4% for two years is 1.082. The discount factor for 4% for two years is 1/1.082 or 0.925.[5]

The amounts in Exhibit 4(XV) can be mul-

[4] Throughout this book we use annual compounding because it is easy to use in explaining principles. In actual practice, of course, interest can be compounded more than once a year, once a quarter, monthly, or for whatever period you choose.

It is certainly not practical to assume that all your corporation's income will come on the last day of each year. Even so, annual compounding will give reasonably accurate results. If further refinement is necessary, the details of more frequent compounding into monthly or even continuous compounding rates can be left to your financial analysis group. For references, see tables in footnote to Exhibit 3 (XV); Sample Table of Compound Interest Factors.

[5] These figures are rounded to three decimal places; carried out further they are 1.081,600,000 and 0.924,556,213 respectively.

## EXHIBIT 3 (XV)

### SAMPLE OF COMPOUND INTEREST FACTORS[a]

(The future worth of $1 invested today, at compound interest; or amounts to which $1, invested today, will grow in the future, at compound interest)

| i \\ n | 4% | 6% | 8% | 10% | 15% |
|---|---|---|---|---|---|
| 1 | 1.040 | 1.060 | 1.080 | 1.100 | 1.150 |
| 2 | 1.082 | 1.124 | 1.166 | 1.210 | 1.323 |
| 3 | 1.125 | 1.191 | 1.260 | 1.331 | 1.521 |
| 4 | 1.170 | 1.262 | 1.360 | 1.464 | 1.749 |

FORMULA:  $f = (1+i)^n$

f = Compound interest factor

n = Number of compounding periods

i = Interest rate per period

[a]One of the most complete set of tables is the *Financial Compound Interest and Annuity Tables,* Third Edition. Publication No. 276 (1961) of the Financial Publishing Company, Boston (Price $15). This book contains almost 1,000 pages of tables. The tables cover rates of interest ranging from 1/12% to 100%, with different compounding periods. Each table contains factors to 10 decimal places compounding and discounting and four other types of value computations. The book also contains some auxiliary tables and many examples of applications.

Also for continuous compounding see tables available in *Principles of Engineering Economy,* Fourth Edition, revised by Eugene L. Grant and W. Grant Ireson, Ronald Press, 1964, Appendix 4 (Price $9.50).

tiplied by amounts other than $1 to determine the present value of such other amounts. For example: What would need to be invested at 10% compound interest to have $10,000 at the end of two years? From the exhibit, in the column for 10% on the line for 2 periods, we read the factor 0.826; multiplying $10,000 times 0.826 gives us $8,260—the amount which we would have to invest now in order to have $10,000 two years hence.

The time value of money is a key concept in all correct capital budgeting techniques, because it enables us to convert all the cash flows pertaining to a proposed project into their equivalent values at a single point in time.

The single point in time is referred to as the "zero point" in time. This permits us to make a correct comparison between the investment and the expected return. There are various techniques which take into effect the time value of money. Let us look at the technique which we recommend for capital budgeting— the "Time Value Profitability Rate"[6] technique.

[6] You may see this technique, in other authors' writings, called "Internal Rate of Return," the "Investors' Method," or the "Discounted Cash Flow" technique. "Discounted Cash Flow" is probably the most widely-used term, but it is somewhat misleading; all three of the correct capi-

## EXHIBIT 4 (XV)

### SAMPLE TABLE OF DISCOUNT OR PRESENT VALUE FACTORS

(The present worth of $1 due in the future at compound interest; or amounts which will grow to $1 in the future, at compound interest)

| i<br>n | 4% | 6% | 8% | 10% | 15% |
|---|---|---|---|---|---|
| 1 | 0.962 | 0.943 | 0.926 | 0.909 | 0.870 |
| 2 | 0.925 | 0.890 | 0.857 | 0.826 | 0.756 |
| 3 | 0.889 | 0.840 | 0.794 | 0.751 | 0.658 |
| 4 | 0.855 | 0.792 | 0.735 | 0.683 | 0.572 |

FORMULA: $f = \dfrac{1}{(1+i)^n}$

f = Discount or present value factor

i = Interest rate per period

n = Number of compounding periods

By comparing this rate to your profit goals, you have a way of evaluating how desirable the project is expected to be. For Project A, which we used as an example at the beginning of this chapter, we stated that the correct profitability rate, by which we meant the Time Value Profitability Rate, was 15%, whereas the two accounting methods showed 10% and 20%—quite a difference.

## TIME VALUE PROFITABILITY RATE TECHNIQUE

To determine the Time Value Profitability Rate for a project, the technique finds, by trial and error, the rate which makes the pres-

ent value of the future cash flows, at the "zero point" in time, equal to the value of the initial investment. Basically, the Time Value Profitability Rate technique employs what Operations Research people call an "Iterative" approach. This high-flown title merely means "trial and error." In other words, this technique starts out with some trial rate. If this first rate does not provide the answer, another higher or lower second rate, depending on the results of the first rate, is chosen and the computations performed again. This process continues until the correct rate is found.

As an example, to make that statement clearer, we will use Project One referred to in the first part of this chapter. Project One called for an investment of $100,000 and had an expected economic life of four years. For simplicity, we assumed that the investment is fully depreciable and will be depreciated on a straight-line basis; this resulted in an annual

tal budgeting techniques actually use the principle of discounting cash flows, so to entitle just one as the "Discounted Cash Flow" technique is confusing. Therefore, we suggest the title "Time Value Profitability Rate" as the best descriptive term.

## EXHIBIT 5 (XV)

### ILLUSTRATION OF TIME VALUE PROFITABILITY RATE TECHNIQUE

#### Project A

| Column | 1 | 2 | 3 | 4 (1+2+3) | 5 | 6 (4x5) | 7 | 8 (4x7) |
|---|---|---|---|---|---|---|---|---|
| | | Expected Cash Flows | | | Expected Cash Flows Discounted | | | |
| | | | | | Discounted at 10% | | Discounted at 15% | |
| Year | Investment | Profit After Depreciation and Taxes | Depreciation Add-Back | Net Cash Flow | Factor | Amount | Factor | Amount |
| 0 | $(100,000) | | | $(100,000) | 1.000 | $(100,000) | 1.000 | $(100,000) |
| 1 | -- | $10,000 | 25,000 | $ 35,000 | .909 | $ 31,820 | .870 | $ 30,040 |
| 2 | -- | 10,000 | 25,000 | 35,000 | .826 | 28,910 | .756 | 26,460 |
| 3 | -- | 10,000 | 25,000 | 35,000 | .751 | 26,290 | .658 | 23,030 |
| 4 | -- | 10,000 | 25,000 | 35,000 | .683 | 23,910 | .572 | 20,020 |
| Total | -- | $40,000 | $100,000 | $ 140,000 | | $ 110,930 | | $ 99,960 |

depreciation charge of $25,000. The forecast showed a profit after tax of $10,000 annually. The first four columns of Exhibit 5(XV) show this assumed information. Suppose we select a trial rate of 10% for Project One. In Column 5 of the exhibit, we write the present value factors for 10% taken from the table in the previous exhibit. Each year's Net Cash Flow in Column 4 is then multiplied by that year's factor, and the multiplication results are written down in Column 6. Column 6 is totaled, for the four years, excluding the initial $100,000 investment. This total is $110,930; it means that if Project One required a $110,930 initial investment and we expected to receive four annual cash flows of $35,000 we would be earning 10% on our investment. But the proposal we are evaluating does not require an initial investment of $110,930; it requires only $100,000. Because the $110,930 exceeds the required $100,000 capital outlay, the proposal's correct profitability rate must exceed 10%.

We therefore select a second trial rate—say 15%—and repeat the process. Column 7 sets forth the present value factors for 15%. Now each year's $35,000 net cash flow is multiplied by the 15% present value factor for that year, and the results are shown in Column 8. The resulting total in column 8 is $99,960 which is nearly $100,000, the amount of the proposal's initially required capital outlay. Therefore, the project's Time Value Profitability Rate is approximately 15%.

All very well, but just what does this 15% Time Value Profitability Rate mean? Actually, it is the rate of profit which is expected to be earned each year on the unrecovered capital investment in the project. This is illustrated in Exhibit 6(XV). At the beginning of the first year, $100,000 is invested. Part of the first

## EXHIBIT 6 (XV)

## MEANING OF TIME VALUE PROFITABILITY RATE
### Project A

| Column<br><br><br><br>Year | 1<br>Unrecovered<br>Investment<br>(at Beginning<br>of the Year) | 2<br><br>Total<br>Cash-<br>Flow | 3<br>Where Cash Flow Goes<br>Annual Earnings<br>(15% of Unrecovered<br>Investment) | 4<br><br>Reduction of<br>Investment<br>(2-3) |
|---|---|---|---|---|
| 1 | $100,000 | $ 35,000 | $15,000 | $ 20,000 |
| 2 | 80,000 | 35,000 | 12,000 | 23,000 |
| 3 | 56,000 | 35,000 | 8,550 | 26,450 |
| 4 | 30,550 | 35,000 | 4,450[a] | 30,550 |
| 5 | -0- | | | |
| Total | | $140,000 | $40,000 | $100,000 |

[a]Rounded because rate is not exactly 15%.

year's $35,000 cash flow is first applied to the $15,000 earnings expected ($100,000 by 15%); the $20,000 balance of the cash flow ($35,-000 — $15,000) then goes to reduce the investment to $80,000 at the beginning of the second year. In the second year the earnings on the $80,000 unrecovered investment are $12,000 ($80,000 by 15%) and the balance of the

$35,000, or $23,000, goes to reduce the investment. The same steps occur in the third and fourth years; the fourth year's reduction of investment reduces the unrecovered investment to zero.

The exhibit shows that the principle of the Time Value Profitability Rate is this: Each year part of the net cash flow is first applied to annual earnings at the applicable rate on the unrecovered investment; then the balance of the cash flow represents a recovery of the capital originally invested in the project.[7] On the earlier inflows, more goes for earnings, but in later years larger proportions of each payment are applied to reducing the principal of the investment.

In other words, the Time Value Profitability Rate method assumes that the initial investment will be recovered. In addition, it answers the question, "What return will be earned on the unrecovered investment each year?"

## IS THE TIME VALUE PROFITABILITY RATE TECHNIQUE REALLY COMPLEX?

A question that often arises in discussing the Time Value Profitability Rate technique is whether the increase in accuracy obtained by this technique is really worth all that complexity. At first, it appears to be complicated and hard to understand. While the underlying concepts of compound interest and of the present value of money are familiar ones to bankers, their use in capital budgeting decisions was close to nil until perhaps ten years ago.

There are two answers to this accusation of complexity. First of all, part of the problem is that its use is unfamiliar and therefore seems much more confusing than it really is. Close scrutiny will show that it is actually only the computations which are really different—the basic forecasts are already essential to proper capital budgeting, even if one of the inadequate methods such as payback is used.

So it is only the computations that bear the

brunt of the complexity allegation. But are they very complex? Not really. In some cases the Time Value Profitability Rate can be read from graphs, tables, or computed with templates,[8] with sufficient accuracy for practical purposes. When computations are required, they are readily reduced to routine. In fact, some companies now utilize computer programs which will perform the mechanics of trial and error to derive the rate for the longer-term analyses required.

The second answer to the complexity question is that the amount of time and effort required, except for the smallest investment decisions, is more than counterbalanced by the importance of capital budgeting. Given the fact that capital investment decisions often have more impact on the company's future than many of management's other decisions, it seems logical to present management with as reliable a guide as possible. This is particularly appropriate when, using the Time Value Profitability Rate technique, necessary computations can be performed by clerical or computer time, thus affording a better rationing of top management's time and effort.

## IS THE TIME VALUE PROFITABILITY RATE TECHNIQUE ALWAYS WORTHWHILE?

The spectrum of capital projects to which the Time Value Profitability Rate technique can be applied is quite broad. This is not to say, however, that it is worthwhile for every project.

If the financial outcome is exceedingly uncertain, a rate of return analysis may be of very little practical value. We have already suggested as an example corporate expenditures on fundamental research. Although financial forecasts of the possible benefits from these expenditures may be worthwhile, risk considerations and experienced management judgment are probably more important to the

---

[7] If there is inadequate cash flow to provide income in any year, the process allocates income to that year by adding the amount of this income to the investment to be recovered in subsequent years.

[8] Discounted Cash Flow Templates, developed by the Treasurer's Department, Standard Oil Company of New Jersey, 30 Rockefeller Plaza, New York, New York, 10020. Order forms can be obtained by writing to this company.

decision than are detailed profitability rate analyses.

Other proposals may be so clearly attractive or unattractive that no analysis is necessary. Clearly undesirable projects can be rejected without detailed analysis. Others may be so obviously desirable that detailed profitability calculations are superfluous—for example, expenditures for emergency repairs to assembly line facilities to assure a continued production flow.

Still other capital investments may be so small that the work involved in making detailed analyses is unwarranted. To provide a suitable segregation of such proposals, management may set a level of investment below which the analysts need not make detailed supporting analyses.

The answer to the question, then, is that the Time Value Profitability Rate technique is not always worthwhile, but it can be very valuable for a great majority of capital investments. It is a straightforward analytical tool which considers all of the relevant facts included in the forecast.

In Appendix E there are examples to show how to use the Time Value Profitability Rate for those who wish to put it to work. Even if you are not a technician it may be worthwhile for you to glance over the examples to see how it is applied and how the results compare with the accounting methods.

## DISADVANTAGES OF TIME VALUE PROFITABILITY RATE—OTHER CORRECT TECHNIQUES

Technicians in the field of project analysis have strong feelings about the particular method they favor. If theirs is other than the Time Value Profitability Rate, they may couch their criticisms of the Time Value Profitability Rate in technical terms which are not easily understood, but which sound devastating. This is not helpful. Granted, there are some drawbacks. They may arise when it is necessary to decide which of two or more projects to select, each of which shows Time Value Profitability Rates in excess of the Profit

Goal. The problem which arises in such a situation is due to the "implied reinvestment assumption." [9] Further complications may occur when a project's expected net cash flows change from positive to negative. These problems should be examined in order to have a thorough understanding of the subject. They are fully discussed in Appendix E. However, they are not of such importance as to eliminate the Time Value Profitability Rate as a sound tool. Their existence merely means that the Time Value Profitability Rate, like any other analytic tool, must be used with understanding.

When criticisms are leveled at the Time Value Profitability Rate, it may be made to appear that they are strictly limited to that rate.

Actually, they generally apply to any percentage rate on whatever basis it is calculated.[10] A percentage rate tells just so much and that is all, but at least, the Time Value Profitability Rate produces a true rate. If properly calculated, it gives a correct answer when comparing any project's rate with the cutoff rate, that is, the Profit Goal. In other words, if a company has a number of projects under consideration and wishes to accept all that are above the Profit Goal, the Time Value Profitability Rate gives the correct answers as to which ones to adopt.

Those who criticize the Time Value Profitability Rate suggest other correct techniques which combine the principles of forecasting cash flows and considering the time value of money, such as Excess Present Value or Annual Excess Value. We have no major objection to them and some people may find them more readily adapted to their particular purpose. In Appendix E these techniques are explained along with a discussion of their merits.

[9] In some writings on the subject, the term "implicit" rate is used for the reinvestment rate assumption if no other rate is specifically applied. If some other rate is applied for the reinvestment, it is referred to as the "explicit" reinvestment rate.

[10] As an example, some of the criticisms are similarly applicable to the rates based on the accounting methods. However, it should be realized that the accounting methods are wrong in the first place.

# CHAPTER XVI

# Profit Performance Standards [1]

In Chapter XV we talked at length about using a profitability rate to compare against our company's Profit Goal. This profitability rate measures the expected earning power of a particular capital investment. In this chapter we will discuss an earnings rate as a measure of the earning power of the total organization and its components. There are at least three uses to which top corporate management can put the concepts which we will now discuss. They are:

As an analytic tool to improve corporate profits.
As a divisional profit performance standard.
As a long-range planning device.

## RETURN ON INVESTMENT AS AN ANALYTIC TOOL

The first use of return on investment is to assist management in fully comprehending the factors which make for successful profit per-

formance. For this use the "du Pont" formula, which was mentioned in Chapter X and is included in Appendix D, is quite helpful. It is expressed as follows:

$$\text{Return on Investment} = \frac{\text{Earnings}}{\text{Sales}} \times \text{Turnover}$$

or

$$\text{Return on Assets Employed} = \frac{\text{Earnings}}{\text{Sales}} \times \frac{\text{Sales}}{\text{Assets Employed}}$$

The essence of this formula is to separate return on investment into its two components: profit margins and asset turnover. The arithmetic involved is quite simple and there is no mystery attached to the analysis. However, it is often quite helpful to focus on the two components bearing on the production of a satisfactory return on assets employed. Thus, comparisons among companies are possible and guides may be obtained concerning whether profit problems relate to profit margins' being too low or to turnover's not being at a satisfactory level. Further, breaking the analysis into two pieces facilitates an understanding of the factors going to make up return on assets employed.

[1] This chapter was contributed by Dr. Victor H. Brown, Partner, Touche, Ross, Bailey & Smart, 80 Pine Street, New York City.

Indeed, some companies have found it helpful to analyze their returns on investment in more detail than is set forth by the "du Pont" formula. In Exhibit 1 (XVI) is shown a schematic which several companies have found helpful in assessing ways of improving on return on assets employed. Set forth in the Exhibit are the returns actually experienced in one fiscal year for the company, showing the individual assets and income statement elements going to make up the return. Also shown is the company's proposed profit plan for the succeeding year broken down in a similar fashion. To the extent that the proposed profit plan yields an unsatisfactory return on investment, management has the ability through the schematic to assess the impact of changes in various elements of sales, costs and asset components upon the final measure of corporate success—return on investment. Where a company breaks down its organization by profit centers, each division can be analyzed on a similar basis, either with the "du Pont" formula or as shown in Exhibit 1 (XVI).

We now depart from this over-all approach of appraising company performance and discuss profit performance standards for divisions. In making this transition it is well to keep in mind the material which we have already presented on the significance of the over-all company returns on various bases on the liability side, such as long-term capital, as compared with returns on assets.

## DIVISIONAL PROFIT PERFORMANCE STANDARDS

The philosophy underlying the use of return on investment to evaluate subordinate management level performance is straightforward. Top corporate management is concerned with achieving a satisfactory return on the total corporate investment. Attaining this objective is facilitated if each responsible subordinate level executive focuses on the same criterion—if he attempts to achieve a satisfactory return on the investment for which he

is responsible. Ideally, companies would develop return on investment measures not only for divisions of corporations but also for separate profit centers within those divisions and still further for individual product lines and individual products within those divisions. As will be discussed subsequently, there are often severe practical constraints on how far down in the organization the return on investment measure is significant. However, the philosophy is clear. Using return on investment throughout the organization would permit performance standards to be set in a consistent fashion throughout the corporation. The total corporate return on assets employed would be developed by merely summing the individual returns on the individual components making up the corporate whole.

Used as a performance standard, return on investment is helpful in two ways. First, divisional operating results can be expressed in terms of the experienced return on investment. The individual division manager has done an excellent, a satisfactory, or a poor job depending upon his operating results thus expressed. Secondly, the concept of return on investment can be useful in testing whether or not the proposed profit plan set forth by a division manager is satisfactory, that is, it can be tested against whether it produces the desired return on investment. If not, then revisions in the profit plan are called for until the desired results are produced.

How useful return on investment is as a top management tool, both to evaluate segments of the business and to guide and stimulate subordinate level executives to improve upon profit performance, depends upon the basic organizational structure of the company and the particular responsibilities assigned to subordinate level executives.

### Defining Profit Centers

Return on investment is primarily helpful as a performance standard in those companies which are organized into profit centers, where each profit center manager has a certain investment entrusted to his care and is respon-

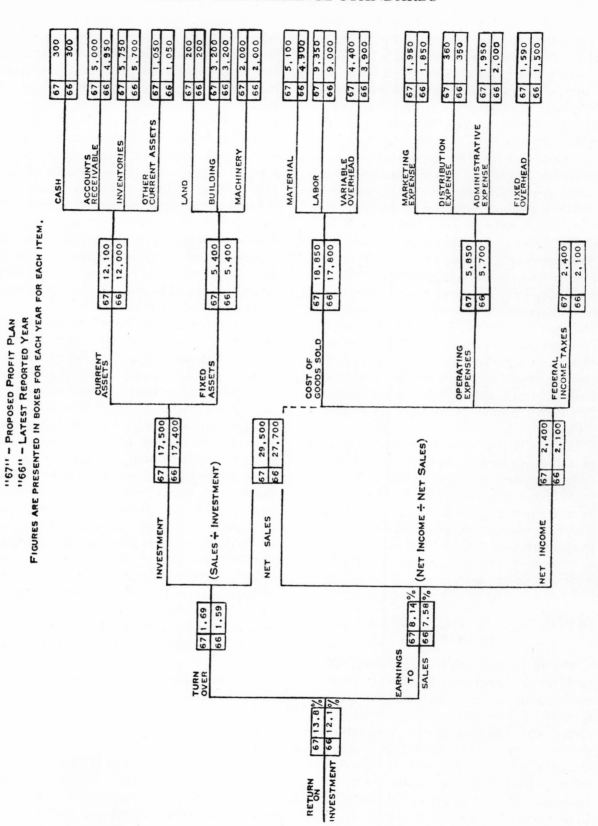

EXHIBIT 1 (XVI)

RETURN ON INVESTMENT WITH COMPONENT BREAKDOWN

"67" – PROPOSED PROFIT PLAN
"66" – LATEST REPORTED YEAR

FIGURES ARE PRESENTED IN BOXES FOR EACH YEAR FOR EACH ITEM.

sible for producing a satisfactory return on that investment. This profit center concept is widely employed in American business. Many, if not most, large corporations and quite a few of those of medium and small size are organized divisionally, and each division manager or vice president is responsible for producing satisfactory profits on the investment entrusted to his care.

Whether the profit center concept is useful in particular company situations and, if so, how the company should be divided into most meaningful profit centers must be assessed by each company in light of its own situation and management philosophy. A full discussion of the considerations involved is obviously beyond the scope of this chapter. However, two principles do deserve comment here, particularly if return on investment is to be used as a performance standard for these profit centers.

First, the return on investment measure is most meaningful if it relates to a particular responsible manager who has full control over both the income and investment base associated with his profit center. The more control the profit manager has over his center's revenues, its costs, and its investment, the more effective is return on investment both as a measure of the manager's historical and planned performance and as a device to stimulate him to seek added profits. This is because return on investment thereby focuses more directly on results achieved by a specific responsible manager.

Of course, in defining profit centers, corporate management customarily does not give profit center managers full autonomy to control all factors bearing on their returns on investment. This is because it is essential to overall corporate success to assure that actions taken at the divisional or profit center level are consistent with total corporate objectives. To accomplish this, corporate management typically retains for itself control over certain factors bearing upon divisional return on investment. This fact does not of itself mean that return on investment is unsatisfactory as a

profit center performance standard. The principle remains, however, that the more control the profit center manager has over his return on investment, the more effective is return on investment as a performance standard. Exactly how much control the divisional manager must retain over the factors bearing on his return on investment for the measure to be meaningful as a performance standard is a matter of judgment requiring resolution in each individual case.

For example, one problem frequently encountered by companies wishing to employ the return on investment concept as a divisional performance standard relates to the question of how to price goods transferred among divisions. In some cases one division transfers all or substantially all of its production to another division of the company. In such cases it seems quite questionable as to whether the transferring division can meaningfully be considered a profit center at all and therefore it is questionable whether return on investment is useful as the divisional performance standard. This is because the division manager does not in any meaningful sense "sell" his product to the receiving divisions; he thus has virtually no control over his revenues, however defined, which of course are a key determinant of return on investment.

Other multi-divisional companies have divisions which transfer a significant, but not dominant, portion of their production to other corporate divisions. In these cases meaningful prices must be set defining the value at which one division "sells" to other divisions if the profit center concept is to be introduced. Different pricing concepts such as market prices, negotiated prices, or cost plus prices may be appropriate depending upon the individual corporate circumstance. It is generally essential, however, for corporate management, as distinguished from divisional management, to retain final control over the pricing mechanism by which inter-divisional transfers are made. This is to assure that divisional decisions are made on a basis consistent with total corporate welfare. The point to be emphasized here is that the inter-divisional pricing problem is one that can be satisfactorily resolved, and the fact that corporate management retains control over establishing inter-divisional prices does not necessarily mean that the profit center concept cannot be employed or that return on investment is not in these cases a meaningful performance standard.

The second problem concerning establishing profit centers is that the return on investment measure is most meaningful if both the income and the investment base are specifically identifiable with the operating unit being measured. Arbitrary allocations of either income or of investment to the unit being measured are to be avoided if at all possible. This is because a divisional manager can generally exert control only over those factors which are specifically identifiable with his division. Arbitrarily allocating elements of corporate income, over-all overhead costs and certain corporate investments not identifiable divisionally tends to dilute the meaning of a return on investment measure as an index of specific divisional performance.

Because of this second problem, return on investment tends to lose its significance as a primary performance standard as it is applied to lower organizational levels. Thus, for example, a national retailing chain can fairly well identify the return on assets related to its autonomous store groups. As the return on investment concept is applied to the next lower level—to appraise individual store performance—certain difficulties arise. Specifically, identifying cash, accounts receivable and inventories to particular stores sometimes becomes difficult. Any method of allocating these assets to individual stores must be arbitrary. As the concept is applied to still the next lower level—to the individual departmental level— identifying the investment base accurately is usually impossible except for the investment in inventory. Accordingly, to appraise departmental performance, a return measure which relates departmental margins with departmental inventories is more appropriate than a measure attempting to relate net allocated income to allocated total assets employed.

## Using the Profit Performance Standard

As mentioned previously, return on investment is helpful as a profit performance standard for top management use in two ways. First, it can be useful as a control device to appraise division managers: the profit center manager has done a good or poor job depending upon his operating results expressed in return on investment terms. Secondly, return on investment can be useful in testing whether or not a division manager's proposed profit plan produces the results desired by top management.

Properly designed, and based upon meaningful profit center definitions, return on investment can thus be one of top management's most effective control tools. It can be one of the primary measures by which division management's success is appraised by top management. Indeed, a number of companies have successfully linked division management compensation with the management's ability to meet or surpass the targets established in return on investment terms by top management. By directly coupling monetary rewards to a division manager's success in meeting return on investment targets, corporate management can assure that subordinate management levels are focusing upon not only profit margins but also capital turnover. Divisional attention is focused upon effective employment of capital—a key measure of total corporate success.

A word of caution is in order. Return on investment cannot be utilized as the sole measure of divisional success. Other factors [2] such as share of market enjoyed, funds expended on research and development and the number of new products introduced, all of which bear upon the long-term return on assets employed,

[2] Because of these other factors, return on investment as a performance measure has been criticized and alternative methods suggested. See "New System For Divisional Control" by Bruce D. Henderson and John Deardon, *Harvard Business Review*, Sept.–Oct. 1966. However, it is felt that no purely mathematical formula can take into account all of the other factors and that, properly applied, return on assets is probably the easiest to use and understand in most situations.

must also be taken into account in evaluating performance. Experience suggests that it is all too easy for a division manager to improve upon his return on investment for a year or two at the expense of long-term corporate success. Thus, for example, a division manager can postpone certain expenses, thereby improving his return on the short term. However, long-term success of the division may thereby be impaired. Therefore, in a divisional review of return on investment top management should also cover the factors which will make for long-term as well as short-term success.

At least four other questions arise in deciding upon how to use return on investment as an effective divisional profit performance standard. One of these relates to exactly how to define the investment on which the return on investment measure is computed. A second relates to what elements of income should be included for individual divisions or profit centers. A third relates to the usefulness of the measure in cases where capital is not the important income producing factor. And the fourth relates to the question of how a satisfactory return on investment goal should be computed for specific divisions.

*Investment Base*

Used to appraise divisional performance, return on investment can probably best be measured as the relationship between division income and the total *assets employed* by that divisional unit. Assets employed is preferable to either equity or long-term capital as the investment base. Since division managers have typically little control over the sources of outside capital, it seems logical that the base to use in measuring their performance should be the total of the assets under their direction, regardless of the sources from which these funds were derived.

Differences of opinion exist concerning whether the asset base on which the rate of return is calculated should be the gross asset figure or the net figure after allowances for depreciation or whether the figure should represent replacement cost of assets. There is, fur-

thermore, the question as to whether leased facilities should be reflected for rate of return calculation purposes as if they were owned facilities. A number of companies use the gross value of assets, that is, original book value, in order to inject a rough equalization factor between older assets which are substantially depreciated and new assets. On the other hand, net book value figures are commonly used as the asset base so that the base agrees with reported balance sheet asset figures. A number of variations concerning how the investment base should be measured are in existence: consistency in company practice is non-existent.

There is no absolutely right or wrong way to measure assets to be included in the investment base. Those who argue against using the net book value figures which appear on the balance sheet do so on the grounds that adjustments to the net book figures tend to place asset values among divisions on a more equal basis, thus facilitating meaningful comparisons among return on asset employed measures among divisions. To the extent that adjustments can be meaningfully made, this is all to the good. But it should be recognized, as will be pointed out subsequently, that developing investment bases among divisions so that direct comparisons can be made is virtually impossible. Circumstances will differ from one division to another and making adjustments to reflect assets on an equal basis is a cumbersome and time-consuming process. Further, it may tend to cause confusion among executives looking at the asset figures as adjusted and then trying to relate these figures to the asset figures appearing on the balance sheet.

Each company must decide for itself whether replacement cost, gross book value, or net book value is the best measure of the investment base. All will be satisfactory, provided that the measure is used appropriately to motivate divisional executives. The disadvantage of making adjustments is that it tends to confuse executives and is a time-consuming process. In the author's estimation, companies beginning to use return on investment as a performance tool would be well advised to use the net book values as reflected on the financial statement as the investment base. This has the advantage of being simple and of assuring that when executives look at the sum of the asset bases used for various divisions, the total is the same as total assets appearing on the balance sheet.

## Divisional Income

The question of what income should be assigned to divisional units is directly related to the question of what assets are assigned to these units and how these assets are measured. Certainly, income must relate to the figure used for investment. Thus, for example, if the investment base includes fixed assets at net book value, then depreciation should be related to those assets in computing the income derived from their use. On the other hand, if it is decided to value fixed assets at their gross book value, then depreciation should not be assigned to the assets in deriving an income figure on which to compute return on assets employed. Similarly, if it is decided that corporate marketable securities should not be assigned to individual divisions since divisions have no control over the size of the corporate marketable securities investment, then interest income derived from these securities should not be assigned to individual divisions.

The question of defining what income should relate to divisional units is, in summary, a straightforward one. The principle involved is that income should be identified with those assets involved in producing that income.

Pre-tax operating income is sometimes a very worthwhile measure. Removing income tax considerations from the measure is helpful because different items may be handled differently from a tax viewpoint among divisions. Comparability is thus sometimes better achieved if income tax considerations are removed from the measure.

## Where Capital Is Not a Significant Income Producing Factor

We have already noted that return on assets employed is not a satisfactory *exclusive* measure of management performance. This is so for a number of reasons: particular among them is the fact that divisional management can maximize short term returns at the expense of long term corporate welfare. In addition, however, there are certain cases where return on assets employed is not even a prime performance standard. This is so in those cases where capital is not a significant income producing factor.

Such situations arise in service organizations. For a law firm or an accounting firm, return on assets employed is not a good measure by which to judge success economically. This is obviously because the prime income producing factor, or scarce resource, is not capital but competent individuals. In a similar fashion, there are some profit centers or units within large corporations where return on assets employed is not a meaningful measure because the limiting factor is not capital. In such cases, adjustments must be made to the return expected from these segments of the organization in order to get meaningful return on assets employed comparisons among the organizational units.

## Setting Divisional Profit Standards

There are at least two fairly common fallacies involved in applying return on assets employed as a performance standard. One of these might be called the "higher the better" philosophy or fallacy. This states that the higher a division's return, the better is the performance of the division manager. Accordingly, a division manager should strive to maximize the return on his assets employed.

Some reflection will illustrate the fallacy of this approach in setting a goal. To achieve the highest return, a division manager can completely eliminate credit, thereby eliminating the investment in accounts receivable, and can reduce inventory to a bare cash and carry minimum, ignoring the question of customer service, because he will thus reduce his investment base. Further, he can allow his investment in equipment to wear out, thus further reducing the investment base. All of these actions, obviously absurd from a corporate point of view, will have the short-term effect of increasing divisional return on assets employed. All a division manager needs to do is to so reduce his investment base as to maximize the return he can earn on that investment base. What corporate management desires, of course, is for subordinate managers to continue to make investments until the point where the additional investment will earn a return just equal to the company's Profit Goal. In this fashion, divisional and corporate profit maximization is assured. But this result is not obtained if divisional management is urged constantly to increase its return on assets employed. Care must be taken to establish the divisional profit standard in such a way as not to encourage maximization but rather to encourage the earning of a corporate approved target return on assets employed.

Another common top management fallacy is to attempt to compare the returns on assets employed from one division to another. Certain comparisons are inevitable. However, the goal established for an individual division should reflect corporate expectations concerning what that particular division should do. Short-term comparisons from one division to another can lead to inequitable and disruptive situations. This is so for several reasons.

First, as mentioned previously, it is almost impossible to assure that the way in which assets are measured from one division to another is such as to produce strictly comparable investment bases. For example, the manager of Division A may be dealing with a plant exactly similar to that of Division B. However, Division B had its plant built two years after that of Division A and at that point in time construction costs were significantly higher. Thus, Division B has a higher asset base, however measured. Strict return on asset employed measures will always lead to an unfavorable comparison of Division B versus Division A.

Second, the importance of capital as an income producing factor can vary from one division to another, as suggested above. Commonly, management would expect a higher return on that division with a lower required capital base than on the one where capital was a more important income-producing element. Third, it is unrealistic in any one year to expect that all divisions will earn approximately equal returns. In today's diversified corporations, inevitably one division will find itself in a different phase in either the growth cycle or the economic cycle. Thus, corporate management should establish divisional goals to reflect what can reasonably be expected.

## PERFORMANCE STANDARDS AND LONG-RANGE PLANNING

We have mentioned the fact that divisional returns on assets employed cannot be directly compared one with the other nor can they be meaningfully trended from year to year with a view toward continually increasing returns on assets employed. Rather they should be tested against top management's reasonable expectations as to what the division should do in light of its products' positions in the economic environment and in light of its stage in the growth cycle. Effectively implementing this comparison against plan implies that a meaningful long-term plan for each divisional segment has been constructed.

The concept of return on assets employed can be very constructively utilized to express in summary form management's thinking on where capital should be employed in the corporation over the longer term as well as the returns expected from each division within this long-term corporate plan.

A number of companies which have given serious thought and study to the development of long-range corporate plans have found the use of return on assets employed effective as a device to summarize the results of this planning. In abbreviated form Exhibit 2 (XVI) illustrates such a presentation. This exhibit summarizes the Z Corporation's long-range financial plan for the years 1967 through 1971.

Z Corporation has three major divisions. Additionally, there are certain amounts of assets

## EXHIBIT 2 (XVI)

## Z CORPORATION

### Five Year Plan of Assets Employed and Expected Returns
### (000's omitted)

| DIVISION | 1967 A | % | 1968 A | % | 1969 A | % | 1970 A | % | 1971 A | % |
|---|---|---|---|---|---|---|---|---|---|---|
| A | $100 | 10% | $100 | 10% | $100 | 10% | $100 | 10% | $100 | 10% |
| B | 230 | 12.4% | 225 | 11.3% | 210 | 11.8% | 195 | 9.9% | 190 | 9.0% |
| C | 50 | 15% | 75 | 20% | 100 | 20% | 130 | 22% | 140 | 24% |
| Corp. | 20 | - | 20 | - | 20 | - | 20 | - | 20 | - |
| | $400 | 11.5% | $420 | 12.0% | $430 | 12.5% | $445 | 13.0% | $450 | 13.5% |

employed which are not specifically identifiable with any one division but rather are corporate in nature. In columnar form for each year are shown the amount of assets employed in each of the divisions together with the assets not identifiable to any single division. Also shown are the anticipated returns on assets employed for each of the individual divisions. The Z Corporation anticipates earning an 11.5% return on total assets employed in 1967. Both the assets employed as well as the anticipated return on the investment of these assets are expected to increase over the ensuing four years.

A format similar to Exhibit 2 (XVI) focuses management's attention on both the amount of asset investment and the earnings expected on these divisional investments over time. Such a discipline permits top management assessment of those divisions where earnings are expected to climb as well as to discern opportunities for profitable investment of new capital. Such a format permits management to explore the consequences on total corporate return on assets employed of different ration-

ing schemes by assigning assets to various divisions in the future.

The planning process lying behind the results expressed in Exhibit 2 (XVI) assures that appropriate goals are established both for the employment of assets by division and for the earnings rates to be expected for each division. The earnings rates displayed in Exhibit 2 (XVI) represent the appropriate earnings goals by which to measure divisional performance on a year-to-year basis.

## COMPARED WITH PROFITABILITY RATE

Chapter XV explained the use of profitability rate in appraising the economic worth of new investments. So far in this chapter, we have discussed the use of a related return on investment concept as a device for both appraising subordinate level performance and for long-range planning.

We now hasten to point out that the two measures are not directly comparable one to the other. There are at least three reasons for this. First, Time Value Profitability Rate is developed for an individual proposed new project. Return on assets employed is related to the performance of the total organization or a particular segment of the organization; each organizational segment consists of a number of individual projects, some undertaken this year but a number undertaken in previous years. Secondly, profitability rate depicts the average annual earnings rate for a proposed new project over its entire economic life. Return on assets employed, on the other hand, depicts an earnings rate for a particular time period, usually a year. Thirdly, profitability rate is correctly computed on a cash flow basis. Return on assets employed, on the other hand, depicts the relationship of accrual—not cash—earnings to book assets.

For the above three reasons, the measure of profitability rate and the measure of assets employed are not directly comparable on a year-to-year basis. This lack of comparability over the long run is not important. This is because if a division manager continues to accept only those new investments which meet the corporate criterion of the correct Profit Goal, he will also, over time, achieve a return on assets employed which will also achieve the corporate Profit Goal. However, for any short-term period of time it is important that top management recognize the differences inherent in concept between profitability rate and return on assets employed. Serious administrative difficulties can arise if top management does not recognize these differences. These comments are in line with previous words of caution about utilizing return on investment as the sole measure of divisional success.

For example, let us suppose a division manager of a highly profitable division earning a very large return on assets employed is being encouraged to improve still further on this percentage return. This manager would be extremely reluctant, particularly if he were evaluated for compensation or otherwise on the basis of whether he improved on last year's return, to accept any new investment which would have the effect of reducing his return. Specifically, let us suppose that the corporate Profit Goal is 15%. The division manager is presently earning a 30% return on assets employed. He is considering a new project which has a prospective profitability rate of 20%. From the corporate viewpoint, the project is desirable since 20% exceeds the 15% Profit Goal. The division manager, however, understandably would be reluctant to accept the 20% project if he is told to improve upon his already high 30% return on assets employed. His required return on assets employed must be tempered by corporate management to encourage him to accept this sort of project.

A similar problem may arise in the case where a proposed new investment has a very high profitability rate, say 25%, over its entire project life but has negative earnings in the first year or two of its life because of heavy start-up costs. Corporate management must expect its performance standards for a particular division to be lowered for the first two years of a new project of this type if it anticipates a division manager's accepting such a new project.

The point to note is that while the profitability rate and return on assets employed, correctly defined, will, over the long run, lead to consistent corporate results as measured against Profit Goals, in the short term, administrative difficulties can arise if the use of both measures is not judicious. Coping with these short-term problems requires intelligent administration of the rate of return control mechanism. This implies intelligent setting of the performance standards for particular organization segments and an educational process so as to assure that divisional managers, in appraising new investments, will take actions consistent with total long-range corporate welfare.

## APPENDIX A

# Summarizing a Balance Sheet
# and Income Statement
# with Financial Ratios
# and List of Analytical Questions

# APPENDIX A

### BALANCE SHEET AND INCOME STATEMENTS - ALL
### MANUFACTURING COMPANIES

#### Balance Sheet - December 31, 1966
#### (in billions)

| Assets | | | Liabilities | | |
|---|---|---|---|---|---|
| Cash on hand and in bank | $ 21.2 | | Short-term loans from banks | $ 15.6 | |
| U.S. Government securities | 8.5 | | Advances and repayment by U.S. Government | 4.7 | |
| Receivables from U.S. Government | 4.1 | | Trade accounts and notes payable | 35.0 | |
| Other notes and accounts receivable (net) | 67.5 | | Federal income taxes accrued | 13.5 | |
| Inventories | 98.2 | | Current installments due on long-term debts | 4.0 | |
| Other current assets | 12.6 | $212.1 | Other current liabilities | 25.7 | |
| Property, plant, and equipment | $307.9 | | Total current liabilities | | $ 98.5 |
| Deduct: Reserve for depreciation and depletion | 149.2 | | Long-term debt | 56.3 | |
| Total property, plant, and equipment (net) | | $158.7 | Other non-current liabilities | 11.2 | |
| Other non-current assets | | 32.0 | Total liabilities | | $166.0 |
| | | | Capital stock, capital surplus and minority interest | $ 83.0 | |
| Total Assets | | $402.8 | Earned surplus and surplus reserves | 153.8 | |
| | | | Total stockholders' equity | | $236.8 |
| | | | Total liabilities and stockholders' equity | | $402.8 |

#### Income Statement - 1966
#### (in billions)

| | |
|---|---|
| Sales (net of returns, allowances, and discounts) | $554.3 |
| Deduct: Costs and expenses (net of purchase discounts) | 503.0 |
| Net profit from operations | $ 51.3 |
| Add: Other income or deductions (net) | 0.5 |
| Net profit before Federal income taxes | $ 51.8 |
| Deduct: Provision for Federal income taxes | 20.8 |
| Net profit after taxes | $ 31.0 |
| Deduct: Cash dividends charged to surplus | 13.0 |
| Net profit retained in business | $ 18.0 |
| Depreciation and depletion included above, including accelerated amortization of emergency facilities | $ 17.6 |

For all manufacturing corporations except newspapers. Quarterly Financial Report for Manufacturing Corporations-Fourth Quarter 1966. Federal Trade Commission-Securities and Exchange Commission.

## BALANCE SHEETS AND INCOME STATEMENTS
## SUMMARIZED - ALL MANUFACTURING COMPANIES

### Balance Sheet Summarized - December 31, 1966

|   |   |   |   |
|---|---|---|---|
| Current Assets | $212.1 | Current Liabilities | $ 98.5 |
| Plant, Net | 158.7 | Long-Term Capital | |
| | | Debt | $ 56.3 |
| A | | Common Equity | 236.8[a] |
| B | | Total Long-Term | |
| | | Capital | 293.1 |
| Other Items | $ 32.0 | | |
| Total | $402.8 | Other Items | 11.2 |
| | | Total | $402.8 |

### Income Statement Summarized - 1966

| | | |
|---|---|---|
| C | Sales | $554.3 |
| | Costs and expenses | 500.2[b] |
| | Net profit from operations | $ 54.1 |
| | Other Income | 0.5 |
| | Net Profit before Federal Income Taxes | $ 54.6 |
| D | Interest | 2.8[b] |
| | Federal Income Taxes | 20.8 |
| E | Net profit after taxes | $ 31.0 |
| F | Dividends | 13.0 |
| | Net profit retained in business | $ 18.0 |
| G | Depreciation and depletion, included above | $ 17.6 |

[a] The figure for capital stock was not broken down into preferred and common but the amount of preferred is relatively small.

[b] The amount of interest expense was not given. The figure used above was estimated by applying a rate of 5% to the long-term debt and a like amount was eliminated from operating expenses.

OVERALL FINANCIAL RATIOS - ALL MANUFACTURING COMPANIES - 1966

---

Current Assets to Current Liabilities                    2.2 to 1
Long-Term Capital

|  | Amount |  |
|---|---|---|
| Debt | $ 56.3 | 19% |
| Common Equity | 236.8 | 81 |
| Total | $293.1 | 100% |

Long-Term Capital of $293.1 provides:

| | |
|---|---|
| Plant, net | $158.7 |
| Working Capital (current assets less current liabilities) | 113.6 |
| Other Items, net | 20.8 |
| | $293.1 |

| | | |
|---|---|---|
| Net profit after taxes as % of sales | $E \div C$ | 5.6% |
| Net profit plus interest as a % of sales | $(E + D) \div C$ | 6.1% |
| Return on common equity | $E \div A$ | 13.1% |
| Return on long-term capital | $(E + D) \div B$ | 11.5% |
| Sales per $ of long-term capital | $C \div B$ | $1.89 |
| Percent of earnings paid out in dividends | $F \div E$ | 41.9% |
| Depreciation and depletion as a % of sales | $G \div C$ | 3.2% |

$$\frac{\text{Sales}}{\text{Long-term capital}} \times \frac{\text{Net Profit + Interest}}{\text{Sales}} = \text{Return on Long-Term Capital}$$

$$\frac{C}{B} \times \frac{E + D}{C} = \frac{E + D}{B}$$

$$\frac{\$554.3}{\$293.1} \times \frac{\$31.0 + \$2.8}{\$554.3} = \frac{\$31.0 + \$2.8}{\$293.1}$$

$$\$1.89 \times 6.1\% = 11.5\%$$

---

## BALANCE SHEET AND INCOME STATEMENT SUMMARIZED AND ADJUSTED FOR LONG-TERM CAPITAL EQUAL 100—ALL MANUFACTURING COMPANIES

In our simplified balance sheet in the text of the book, we have shown the long-term capital as 100. If the items in the above statements are adjusted proportionately so that long-term capital equals 100, the figures would be as shown below. This is accomplished simply by dividing all numbers by the number we wish to represent as 100, that is, the total long-term capital $293.1. The relationships of the figures are close to those we used in our summarized statements throughout the book.

From these summarized and adjusted figures we see that $100 Long-Term Capital supplies Working Capital (current assets less current liabilities) $39, Plant, net $54 and Other Items net $7. Since these figures have been rounded, ratios calculated from them do not come out

### Balance Sheet Summarized and Adjusted - December 31, 1966

| | | | |
|---|---|---|---|
| Current Assets | $ 72 | Current liabilities | $ 33 |
| Plant, net | 54 | Long-Term Capital | |
| | | Debt | $19 |
| | | Common Equity | 81 |
| | | Total | $100 |
| Other Items | 11 | Other Items | 4 |
| Total | $137 | Total | $137 |

### Income Statement Summarized and Adjusted - 1966

| | |
|---|---|
| Sales | $189 |
| Costs and expenses | 170 |
| Net profit from operations | $ 19 |
| Other income | 0 |
| Net profit before Federal income taxes | $ 19 |
| Interest | 1 |
| Federal income taxes | 7 |
| Net profit after taxes | $ 11 |
| Dividends | 5 |
| Net profit retained in business | $ 6 |

exactly the same as when calculated from the detailed statements.

## LIST OF ANALYTICAL QUESTIONS FOR ITEMS IN BALANCE SHEET AND INCOME STATEMENT

A complete evaluation of a company requires a review of all factors that may affect future profits and investments so that a forecast can be made. This will include a study of the financial statements. They should be subjected to analysis by numerous financial ratios and viewed for trends, for vulnerability to adverse developments and in comparison with other companies in the industry. Such studies are only helpful in revealing strengths and weaknesses if there is complete information about the figures in the financial statements. We should have answers to many questions about each item: some of these are listed below.

*Balance Sheet Questions:*

Current assets

What is the make-up of the current assets?

Are there any large amounts of cash or short-term investments?

What is the composition of the inventories? How are they valued? Do inventories include readily marketable commodities or is it made to order special equipment? How much research and development expense, overhead, etc. is absorbed in inventory?

Are receivables good? What has been the loss experience?

## Plant, net

How is the plant stated? Is it over- or under-valued? Is there any unused plant?

Is the depreciation reserve adequate?

If there is a significant change from the previous year: When did it occur? What was its nature? How did it affect earnings?

## Other asset items

What is the nature of the investments in subsidiaries and companies which are not controlled?

Are there any non-productive assets?

What about intangible items such as good will?

## Current liabilities

What policy does the company use in paying bills? Are trade creditors being paid on time? Is the company taking advantage of discounts available?

Are there short-term loans in current liabilities which are regularly renewed and should be treated as long-term debt? What are the loan restrictions?

Are there any contingent liabilities as revealed in the footnotes?

## Long-term capital

What are the repayment schedules and maturities of the debt?

Are there any signficant restrictive terms in the senior securities which will hinder the company's freedom in financial decisions?

Are there any important leases which should be capitalized?

If there are convertible securities what is the conversion price and what is the potential dilution? Are there any stock options and if so what is the effect on dilution?

## *Income Statement Questions*

What is the make-up of sales and are there any long-term contracts? What are the returns and allowances on sales? Do they indicate that there is an unusual amount of defective merchandise being shipped which will result in disputed accounts receivable and which may indicate obsolete manufacturing equipment?

What is the nature of the expense items and are there any long-term contracts with escalation clauses?

Are officers' salaries in closely held companies in line with publicly-owned companies?

Were there any changes in prices or costs during the year, and, if so, when and how much?

Is the allowance for depreciation adequate?

What is the basis for tax accruals? When was the last Internal Revenue clearance? Are there any disputed items?

Are there any non-recurring expenses or income items?

How is good will being amortized, if at all?

How are such costs as research, development, drilling, etc., handled? Are they expensed or capitalized?

## APPENDIX B

# Senior Capital
# Cost Details

## BOND QUALITY RATINGS

Throughout the book, we refer to ratings to indicate the quality of debt securities. Ratings are assigned to debt securities[1] by the three rating agencies, Fitch Investors Service, Moody's Investors Service, and Standard and Poor's Corporation. Ratings signify the quality or inherent risk in securities.

Ratings are generally limited to publicly-held issues. That means that the agencies do not rate issues sold privately.

Issues of new and untried companies usually are not rated because there is no record on which to base a rating. A company usually must have an operating record for at least three years in order to be rated, but this does not al-

ways hold for Standard. It depends on the character of the company. Corporate debt issues are generally not rated by Fitch if they are under $500,000, not by Moody's if under $600,000, as a class, and not by Standard if under $2,000,000. There are a few types of companies having large enough issues and a sufficiently long record which are not rated for special reasons.

Ratings in each agency are the considered opinion of a rating committee. They are based on a careful analysis of all factual information amassed by the agencies and on their experience. They study all the statistics, ratios, history of the company and the industry; talk with management and even competitors; and then arrive at a rating on the basis of judgment.

The rating agencies attempt, insofar as possible, to make ratings comparable not only among companies of the same industry but among industries.

[1] Fitch Investors Service rates preferred and common stocks. Standard and Poor's Corporation also rates preferred and common stocks, but on a somewhat different basis. Our interest is primarily in bond rather than stock ratings.

The agencies have selected numerous statistical tests to serve as points of comparison between one issue and another. But the weight given to each one may vary with the circumstances, and for this reason the agencies themselves will not say specifically what the ratios should be. There are various factors involved which cannot be reduced to figures. For certain types of companies, where there is relative uniformity of operations and risk, there may be some recognizable correlation between ratings and such a ratio as debt to total capital structure, but it is up to you to make some comparative analysis to find it out.

Junior debt will generally be graded at least one notch lower than the senior debt, even if there is a smaller amount of junior debt and even if it matures before the senior debt. Maturity does not affect Moody's ratings. If the maturity is very short, it sometimes may influence a rating by Fitch and Standard. If there is a large amount of junior debt, it may be rated more than one notch lower. Junior debt may reduce the rating on the senior debt if it adds to the total debt burden of the company so as to adversely affect the company's financial strength.

The market price of securities does not have any effect on ratings. The agencies may note any substantial change in the market price of a company's securities and it may suggest to them to look into the matter of ratings, but it is not taken into account in assigning the rating. In other words, the reverse is the case: ratings affect the market, rather than the market affecting the rating.

The ratings are continuously under review by all the agencies. When there is new debt financing, close attention is paid to the effect on the capital structure, and at such times a special review is made. However, ratings are not changed unless there is a definite, nontransitory change in factors affecting the rating. This is because the ratings are established for lasting quality. The theory is that if the ratings are soundly arrived at, then they should be rather constant, unless there is a marked permanent change in the company's position. The analysts have carefully reviewed a company's financial policy and character before assigning the rating. They do not find it necessary to modify the rating whenever a few figures get out of line. Some investors buy securities by their ratings and would be confused if there were rapid changes. The agencies recognize their responsibility to investors and try to decide upon a rating with the long-range view in mind.

Ratings are not an exact guide to quality because they cannot be determined on a mathematical basis, but the long experience of the agencies does minimize the possibility of error. Their ratings are widely accepted by investors and by the financial community.

Ratings reflect in part the financial policy followed by the management. They give a good indication of the company's ability to borrow and the approximate cost of debt money. When a company sells a bond, the management, the underwriters and the potential buyers of the securities are all vitally interested in the rating assigned to it. Indirectly, debt ratings are a clue to the quality of equity securities. In all, they are a valuable tool in various phases of finance. They have become so much a part of finance that they are an integral part of financial jargon.

The symbols which Moody's uses for the first four ratings and excerpts from their definitions are as follows:

*Aaa* ". . . the best quality . . . 'gilt edge' . . ."

*Aa* ". . . high quality by all standards . . ."

*A* ". . . higher medium grade . . . elements may be present which suggest a susceptibility to impairment some time in the future."

*Baa* ". . . lower medium grade . . . lack outstanding investment characteristics, and, in fact, have speculative characteristics as well."

We will not be concerned with the lower ratings and therefore will omit their definitions.

The other agencies use different symbols, but their approach to bond ratings is basically the same. The following language is used in financial circles to represent the four quality ratings discussed above without reference to any one of the agencies: Triple A, Double A, Single A, Triple B.

For a particular company the rating decreases as the debt is increased, because the debt burden becomes heavier and the risk greater. All other factors are constant; the amount of debt is the only variable. But between companies other factors are not equal, and there may be considerable difference in debt ratios for the same rating. In order to get some idea of the relationship of debt ratio and rating for a particular type of company, it is necessary to make a study of other companies as nearly similar as possible. How close the correlation is between debt ratios and ratings will depend on the nature of the business.[2]

The quality of a bond does not depend as much on assets as it does on earnings. However, if two companies earn the same rate on the capital structure and otherwise have the same characteristics, then the one with the lower debt ratio would obviously have the better earnings protection for debt service.

In the industrial field, where there is much variation in the factors that affect the quality of a company's securities, there may be a wide spread in bond ratings between two companies with the same debt ratio. Or conversely, there may be a wide spread in debt ratio between two companies with the same rating. Furthermore, since there are relatively few ratings to cover a wide variation in quality, there is a band of debt ratios within which a rating may fall, rather than a specific percentage.

## AMOUNTS AT WHICH TO STATE SENIOR SECURITIES

At maturity, a company has to pay 100% of principal amount to bondholders. The net amount the company receives when the debt issue is sold, which is available for corporate purposes, may be more or less than 100% for two reasons.

1. The bonds may have been sold at a slight discount or premium.
2. The net amount of money the company receives is after deducting financing costs.

Bonds are carried on the balance sheet at 100% with the difference between 100% and the net price the company receives being stated as debt discount and expense, or premium. Since the company must pay off the bonds at 100% at maturity, this represents the extent of the ultimate claim ahead of the common stock. For purposes of security analysis in figuring capital structure ratios, the bonds are stated at 100%. The same principle applies to other types of debt. We are interested in determining costs as viewed in the securities markets. Therefore, we calculate the capital structure ratios with debt being stated at 100%.

Preferred stocks may be par or no par. Preferred stocks generally have no maturity. One evidence of the claim of a preferred stock ahead of the common stock is the amount it receives in event of liquidation of the company. For purposes of security analysis, preferred stocks may be stated at liquidating value. If the liquidating value is above the stated or par value, the preferred may be increased accordingly and the common stock figure reduced by a like amount.

There is one very limited situation in which rates for senior securities should be applied to the net amounts a company receives from the

[2] Average Debt Ratios, Interest Coverage Ratios and Bond Ratings for companies in Moody's Industrial Common Stock Average which have rated securities.

### 1961–1965

| Rating | No. Companies | Average Debt as % of Total Term Capital | Average Times Fixed Charges Earned after Taxes |
|--------|---------------|------------------------------------------|-------------------------------------------------|
| Aaa | 6 | 10 | 35 |
| Aa | 17 | 16 | 21 |
| A | 20 | 22 | 10 |

Source: Moody's Industrial Manual, Moody's Investors Services, Inc.—June, 1966.

sale of the securities rather than 100% principal amount for bonds and liquidating value for preferred stock. This is the case of the regulated industries, such as the public utility companies in states which incorrectly regulate on the basic historical cost rather than current cost. In order to be consistent, in those jurisdictions it is necessary to apply the historical rates to the actual amounts of money a company received from the sale of the securities, adjusted for the amount of the discounts or premiums already amortized at the particular date.

## YIELD—ITS RELATION TO PRICE

If you are rusty on the idea of yield to maturity for debt, we give you a brief review. It can be explained by the following example. If a bond sells at 102, has a 5% interest coupon, and is due in two years, the approximate yield to maturity is 4%. The company pays 100 at maturity. Therefore, when an investor buys a bond at 102, he loses the $2 premium at maturity. Spread over the life of the issue this $2 premium amounts to $1 each year. He gains $5 in interest each year and loses $1 in premium each year. His true return is $4 or 4%; this is known as yield to maturity. Conversely, if the same bond, which will be paid off at 100 in two years sells for 98, the approximate yield to maturity would be 6%: $5 in interest each year plus $1 each year for the discount below 100.

These figures are helpful for illustrative purposes, but they are only approximations. To obtain correct yields to maturity, you will have to refer to the Bond Value Tables which accurately spread the premium or discount on a compound interest basis over the life of the bonds.

There is a rough rule of thumb that 1 point in the price of a bond ($1 for a $100 bond) is equivalent to 0.05% in yield to maturity. This 0.05% in yield is referred to as 5 basis points: one basis point is 0.01% in yield.

This rule of thumb is very rough because the effect of price on yield depends on the size of the coupon, the maturity, and the amount that the price is above or below 100. The excerpts from the Bond Value Table, shown in Exhibit 1 (B), illustrate this idea except for the effect of prices being far above or below 100.

## EXHIBIT 1 (B)

### BOND VALUE TABLE, EXCERPTS[a]

| Column | 1 | 2 | 3 | 4 | 5 | 6 |
|---|---|---|---|---|---|---|
| | 4% Interest Coupon | | 5% Interest Coupon | | 6% Interest Coupon | |
| Maturity | Yield | Price | Yield | Price | Yield | Price |
| 20 Years | 3.95% | 100.69 | 4.95% | 100.63 | 5.95% | 100.58 |
| | 4.00 | 100.00 | 5.00 | 100.00 | 6.00 | 100.00 |
| 30 Years | 3.95% | 100.87 | 4.95% | 100.78 | 5.95% | 100.70 |
| | 4.00 | 100.00 | 5.00 | 100.00 | 6.00 | 100.00 |

[a] Financial Publishing Company, Boston, Massachusetts.

These figures show the spread in price for a difference in yield of 0.05% or 5 basis points. It can be seen that with a 20-year maturity and a 4% interest coupon, a difference in yield of 0.05% means a price differential of 0.69. With a 30-year maturity and a 6% interest coupon a difference in yield of 0.05% means a price differential of 0.70. This gives you an idea of the extent of the accuracy of our rule of thumb. As the maturity becomes shorter, the inaccuracy increases. Nevertheless, it is handy to have in mind the general relationship in order to be able to translate the approximate effect of a difference in price into yield or vice versa.

When a bond has a sinking fund, the buyers of the bond will figure the yield to final maturity because the sinking fund is drawn by lot. There is no way for any one buyer to know whether his bond would be retired through sinking fund before maturity. However, the issuing company will have to calculate the cost rate based on the yield with the average maturity giving effect to the sinking fund.

In a serial type of issue, in which there are many different maturities for a single issue, it is necessary to calculate the weighted average rate for the various maturities.

For a preferred stock which does not have any maturity, there is a reasonably close relationship between the rule of thumb of 5 basis points in yield being equivalent to $1 in price. For example, a preferred with a $5 dividend yields 5% at a price of 100. For a price of 99, the yield is 5.05%.

If a preferred stock has an appreciable sinking fund which is fixed in amount, it may be necessary for the company to figure the yield with weight being given to the effect of sinking fund payments. A purchase fund, which requires purchase of stock in the market only if the price falls below a stipulated price, may be disregarded.

## INDEXES OF YIELDS ON OUTSTANDING BONDS AND PREFERRED STOCKS OF INDUSTRIAL COMPANIES

In Chapter IV there are given the five- and ten-year averages for Moody's Indexes of Yields for outstanding bonds of industrial companies for various quality of ratings, and also the index of yields for outstanding preferred stocks. The figures for each year, on which these averages are based, are given in Exhibits 2 (B) and 3 (B).

## FINANCING COSTS

In using the yields on outstanding issues to obtain cost rates, adjustments must be made for financing costs. The size of both parts of financing costs—underwriter's commission and financing expenses—depends on many factors. The principal factor is the size of the issue. Next in importance is its quality. Other factors are the type of security, the type of business, the condition of the security market, and the method of sale. The effect of size is shown in Exhibit 4 (B). The figures are not of recent vintage, but they are the best comprehensive ones available and satisfactorily illustrate the point. If you are doing a very refined job, you may wish to estimate closely the amount to allow as it may be affected not only by size but also by quality of issue and all the other factors.

Our discussion of costs thus far has referred to issues sold publicly, which are underwritten. In contrast to an underwritten financing is a private sale. This is also referred to as a direct or private placement. In such a financing the issue is not underwritten. A company may eliminate the services of the underwriter entirely, or use an underwriter as the company's agent to place the issue. An agent's fee is far less than an underwriter's commission. When the underwriter acts as an agent, he does not take the risk of ownership. The financing expenses are lower for a private sale because there is no need to have a prospectus, etc. One reason why small issues are sold privately is to avoid financing costs which run proportionately higher for small issues.

Many factors may affect the size of the agent's fee and the financing expenses, but again size of issue is generally dominant. The effect of size and type of security is shown in Exhibit 5 (B).

In connection with a private sale, it should be noted that much of the savings of a private sale may be absorbed by the investors' obtaining a better price. The investors are aware of this savings and bargain accordingly. Whether the yield for a private sale, based on the net proceeds for the company, will be

## EXHIBIT 2 (B)

## INDEX OF YIELDS TO MATURITY FOR OUTSTANDING BONDS OF INDUSTRIAL COMPANIES
Moody's Investors Service, Inc.

| Year | Aaa | Aa | A | Baa |
|---|---|---|---|---|
| 1966 | 5.12% | 5.15% | 5.26% | 5.68% |
| 1965 | 4.45 | 4.50 | 4.55 | 4.92 |
| 1964 | 4.32 | 4.41 | 4.47 | 4.87 |
| 1963 | 4.14 | 4.29 | 4.37 | 4.90 |
| 1962 | 4.18 | 4.30 | 4.43 | 4.98 |
| 5 year average 1962-1966 | 4.44 | 4.53 | 4.62 | 5.07 |
| 1961 | 4.21 | 4.33 | 4.50 | 5.10 |
| 5 year average 1961-1965 | 4.26 | 4.37 | 4.46 | 4.95 |
| 1960 | 4.28 | 4.39 | 4.58 | 5.11 |
| 1959 | 4.27 | 4.36 | 4.49 | 4.91 |
| 1958 | 3.61 | 3.78 | 3.91 | 4.59 |
| 1957 | 3.76 | 3.89 | 4.03 | 4.79 |
| 10 year average 1957-1966 | 4.23 | 4.34 | 4.46 | 4.99 |
| 1956 | 3.30 | 3.39 | 3.47 | 3.84 |
| 10 year average 1956-1965 | 4.05 | 4.16 | 4.28 | 4.80 |

lower than the yield for a public offering depends on all the circumstances surrounding the financing at the particular time. As a practical matter, for Cost-of-Capital purposes, estimates for senior capital costs can be based on public offerings.

## YIELD ON NEW ISSUES
## VERSUS OUTSTANDING ISSUES

In Chapter IV we explained why new issues represent the best sources of data of debt cost

if such information can be obtained. For bond cost purposes, the yield must be based on the net proceeds the company receives after all financing costs, including underwriter's commissions and financing expenses. However, there are relatively few industries which do sufficient financing so that an adequate sample is available over an extended period.

It was pointed out that a new issue will generally have to be sold at a higher yield than a similar outstanding issue in order to absorb the added supply. Thus, if the yield on outstanding bonds is used for determining bond

## EXHIBIT 3 (B)

## INDEX OF YIELDS FOR OUTSTANDING PREFERRED STOCKS OF INDUSTRIAL COMPANIES

### Moody's Investors Service, Inc.
### Low Dividend Series

| Year | High Grade | Medium Grade |
|------|------------|--------------|
| 1966 | 4.67% | 4.95% |
| 1965 | 4.07 | 4.38 |
| 1964 | 4.05 | 4.38 |
| 1963 | 4.04 | 4.41 |
| 1962 | 4.21 | 4.60 |
| 5 Year Average 1962-1966 | 4.21 | 4.54 |
| 1961 | 4.36 | 4.68 |
| 5 Year Average 1961-1965 | 4.15 | 4.49 |
| 1960 | 4.48 | 4.80 |
| 1959 | 4.45 | 4.80 |
| 1958 | 4.24 | 4.70 |
| 1957 | 4.36 | 4.89 |
| 10 Year Average 1957-1966 | 4.29 | 4.66 |
| 1956 | 3.90 | 4.37 |
| 10 Year Average 1956-1965 | 4.22 | 4.60 |

cost, it must be adjusted to approach the yield on new issues.

The utility industry is one of the few industries which has done so much financing that there is a good sample of new issues. We can use this industry to indicate the difference in yield on new issues versus outstanding issues of a similar quality. We can use bond ratings to indicate general quality comparability.

These figures are shown in Exhibit 6 (B).

The two groups of issues are not strictly comparable, so that the difference in yield may not be due entirely to the new issue effect. However, the figures indicate the general picture.

The spread not only depends on the condition of the bond market, but is also affected by other factors such as the quality of the is-

## EXHIBIT 4 (B)

## FINANCING COSTS AS A PERCENT OF PROCEEDS-ISSUES OFFERED PUBLICLY
All Types of Industries - Classified by Type of Security and Size
of Issue - 1951, 1953 and 1955[a]

| Size of Issue ($ Millions) | Underwriters' Commission | Expenses |
|---|---|---|
| **Bonds, Notes and Debentures** | | |
| Under $0.5 | ----- | ----- |
| 0.5 - 0.9 | 7.53% | 3.96% |
| 1.0 - 1.9 | 5.80 | 2.37 |
| 2.0 - 4.9 | 2.37 | 1.41 |
| 5.0 - 9.9 | 1.01 | 0.82 |
| 10.0 - 19.9 | 0.88 | 0.64 |
| 20.0 - 49.9 | 0.85 | 0.48 |
| 50.0 and over | 0.88 | 0.32 |
| **Preferred Stocks** | | |
| Under $0.5 | ----- | ----- |
| 0.5 - 0.9 | 8.67% | 3.96% |
| 1.0 - 1.9 | 5.98 | 2.09 |
| 2.0 - 4.9 | 3.83 | 1.05 |
| 5.0 - 9.9 | 2.93 | 0.79 |
| 10.0 - 19.9 | 2.40 | 0.52 |
| 20.0 - 49.9 | 2.84 | 0.35 |
| 50.0 and over | 2.12 | 0.38 |

[a]"Cost of Flotation of Corporate Securities 1951-1955," pages 38 and 39. Securities and Exchange Commission, Washington, D.C., June 1957.

## EXHIBIT 5 (B)

## FINANCING COSTS AS A PERCENT OF PROCEEDS-ISSUES SOLD PRIVATELY
### All Types of Industries - Classified by Type of Security and Size of Issues - 1951, 1953 and 1955[a]

| Size of Issue ($ Millions) | Fees | Expenses |
|---|---|---|
| **Bonds, Notes and Debentures** | | |
| Under $0.3 | 1.86% | 1.49% |
| 0.3 - 0.4 | 1.60 | 1.06 |
| 0.5 - 0.9 | 1.31 | 0.83 |
| 1.0 - 1.9 | 0.97 | 0.59 |
| 2.0 - 4.9 | 0.69 | 0.43 |
| 5.0 - 9.9 | 0.49 | 0.34 |
| 10.0 - 19.9 | 0.31 | 0.22 |
| 20.0 and over | 0.22 | ----- |
| **Preferred and Common Stock** | | |
| Under $0.3 | 4.15% | 1.25% |
| 0.3 - 0.4 | 3.15 | 0.13 |
| 0.5 - 0.9 | 1.46 | 0.53 |
| 1.0 - 1.9 | 1.48 | 0.61 |
| 2.0 - 4.9 | 1.02 | 0.50 |
| 5.0 - 9.9 | 0.62 | 0.38 |
| 10.0 - 19.9 | 1.10 | 0.14 |
| 20.0 and over | ----- | ----- |

[a]"Cost of Flotation of Corporate Securities 1951-1955," pages 64 and 66, Securities and Exchange Commission, Washington, D.C., June 1957. Separate information is not available for preferred and common, but it is believed that the figures are dominated by preferred stock data.

EXHIBIT 6 (B)

## COMPARISON OF YIELDS ON NEW ISSUES WITH OUTSTANDING ISSUES

Yields to Maturity Based on Prices to the Public for New Issues of Bonds
over $10,000,000 in size Rated A by Moody's Investors Service, Inc., for
Companies serving Principally Electricity
compared with
Moody's Investors Service, Inc. Index of Yields to
Maturity for Outstanding Public Utility Bonds Rated A

| Column | 1 | 2 | 3 |
| --- | --- | --- | --- |
| | Monthly Average[a] Yields for | Yields for | Column 1 less Column 2 Increase in Yield for New Issues Over |
| Year | New Issues | Outstanding Issues[a] | Outstanding Issues |
| 1966 | 5.60% | 5.43% | 0.17% |
| 1965 | 4.71 | 4.60 | 0.11 |
| 1964 | 4.55 | 4.53 | 0.02 |
| 1963 | 4.42 | 4.39 | 0.03 |
| 1962 | 4.39 | 4.51 | -0.12 |
| 5 Year Average 1962-1966 | 4.73 | 4.69 | 0.04 |
| 1961 | 4.74 | 4.58 | 0.16 |
| 5 Year Average 1961-1965 | 4.56 | 4.52 | 0.04 |
| 1960 | 5.04 | 4.82 | 0.22 |
| 1959 | 5.14 | 4.81 | 0.33 |
| 1958 | 4.11 | 4.00 | 0.11 |
| 1957 | 4.87 | 4.24 | 0.63 |
| 10 Year Average 1957-1966 | 4.76 | 4.59 | 0.17 |
| 1956 | 3.79 | 3.51 | 0.28 |
| 10 Year Average 1956-1965 | 4.58 | 4.40 | 0.18 |

[a]New issues were offered only in certain months.  In order to make the figures comparable, the yields on outstanding issues
were included for those months for which new issues were available.

sue. The lower the quality the greater the spread.

The yield on the new issues averaged 0.18% greater than the yield on outstanding issues for the ten year period. It showed considerable variation as would be expected. When the buyers are eager the spread narrows. Under unusual circumstances buyers may be so hard put to invest their money that they will pay a premium for new issues. This occurred in 1962, according to the figures.

In 1957 the new issues showed a 0.63% greater yield than the outstandings. In that year conditions in the bond market were unusual and yields on outstanding bonds were of little use in estimating the yields on new issues.

In Exhibit 1 (IV), Chapter IV, we adjusted the yields on outstanding senior issues to obtain cost rates based on net proceeds. The basis on which these adjustments were made is shown in Exhibit 7 (B).

For the bonds, the financing costs were estimated in terms of points and these were translated into basis points of yield by referring to Bond Value Tables. This was added to an estimated adjustment for added yield for new issues over outstanding issues. The same approach was used for preferred stocks except that the dividend rates corresponded to the yields on the outstanding issues.

## IMBEDDED COSTS AS
## PART OF SENIOR CAPITAL COST

For regulated industries, such as the electric, gas and telephone utilities, some regulatory authorities erroneously use historical cost for rate-making purposes. If such a procedure is forced on a company, there are sometimes special costs which must be included. They are called imbedded costs. Imbedded costs refer to costs incurred when a senior security is refunded with another security.

These costs may include the unamortized discounts (less any premiums) and expenses incurred in the issuance of the redeemed securities, the call premium on the redeemed securities, the cost to call, such as duplicate interest and the cost of the call notice, etc. They are applicable to the new refunding issue. They can be applied by deducting them from the net proceeds received for the new refunding issue and then calculating the yield to maturity based on the net proceeds less these deductions. For regulatory purposes, the calculations should be made without allowing for tax savings because the return used for regulatory purposes is the To Investor Rate. These costs should be allowed for as part of the senior capital cost whether or not they have been written off the balance sheet.

If a utility company has historical cost forced on it by regulation, then theoretically it should use historical cost of common. This would require an analysis of the common cost at each time some was sold and also the cost each year of the earned surplus as it was retained. This would require a study which would go so many years back that the results would be meaningless. This highlights the inappropriateness of the historical cost approach.

## EXHIBIT 7 (B)

ADJUSTMENTS MADE IN EXHIBIT 1 (IV), CHAPTER IV, TO
OBTAIN YIELDS AT NET PROCEEDS FOR NEW ISSUES
FROM YIELDS ON OUTSTANDING BONDS

---

BONDS
(To translate points into yield, Bond Value Tables
were used, assuming 25 year maturity and interest
coupons to closest 1/8% to the yields on the outstanding issues.)

|  | AAA | | AA | | A | | Baa | |
|---|---|---|---|---|---|---|---|---|
|  | Points | Yield | Points | Yield | Points | Yield | Points | Yield |
| **5 Year Average 1961 - 1965** | | | | | | | | |
| Underwriter's Commission | 0.80) | 0.09% | 0.85) | 0.09% | 0.90) | 0.10% | 1.00) | 0.11% |
| Expenses | 0.50) | | 0.50) | | 0.50) | | 0.60) | |
| Allowance above outstandings | | 0.02 | | 0.03 | | 0.04 | | 0.06 |
| Adjustment | | 0.11% | | 0.12% | | 0.14% | | 0.17% |
| **10 Year Average 1956 - 1965** | | | | | | | | |
| Underwriter's Commission | 0.90) | 0.09% | 0.95) | 0.09% | 1.00) | 0.10% | 1.10) | 0.12% |
| Expenses | 0.50) | | 0.50) | | 0.50) | | 0.60) | |
| Allowance above outstandings | | 0.14 | | 0.16 | | 0.18 | | 0.20 |
| Adjustment | | 0.23% | | 0.25% | | 0.28% | | 0.32% |

PREFERREDS
(Calculations, as shown below, to translate points
into yield, assume that the dividend rate is the
same as the yield on the outstanding issues.)

|  | High Grade | | Medium Grade | |
|---|---|---|---|---|
|  | Points | Yield | Points | Yield |
| **5 Year Average 1961 - 1965** | | | | |
| Underwriter's Commission | 1.60) | 0.09%[a] | 1.75) | 0.11%[b] |
| Expenses | 0.60) | | 0.60) | |
| Allowance above outstandings | | 0.04 | | 0.06 |
| Adjustment | | 0.13% | | 0.17% |
| **10 Year Average 1956 - 1965** | | | | |
| Underwriter's Commission | 1.85) | 0.11%[c] | 2.00) | 0.12%[d] |
| Expenses | 0.60) | | 0.60) | |
| Allowance above outstandings | | 0.18 | | 0.20 |
| Adjustment | | 0.29% | | 0.32% |

---

[a] $\dfrac{4.15}{100 - 1.60 - 0.60} = \dfrac{4.15}{97.80} = 4.24\%$    Subtract 4.15% to get 0.09%

[b] $\dfrac{4.49}{100 - 1.75 - 0.60} = \dfrac{4.49}{97.65} = 4.60\%$    Subtract 4.49% to get 0.11%

[c] $\dfrac{4.22}{100 - 1.85 - 0.60} = \dfrac{4.22}{97.55} = 4.33\%$    Subtract 4.22% to get 0.11%

[d] $\dfrac{4.60}{100 - 2.00 - 0.60} = \dfrac{4.60}{97.40} = 4.72\%$    Subtract 4.60% to get 0.12%

# Leases

## NATURE OF LEASES

Leases on real property [1] may be classified in two forms—the gross lease and the net lease.

The gross lease calls for one total payment, generally on the first of each month. From this rent, the lessor, or owner of the property, must pay all operating expenses and taxes. What is left over must take care of both depreciation of the property, which provides return of his investment, and also return or yield on his investment. Unless there is a "tax stop" clause or other escalation clauses concerning operating expenses, etc., the lessor runs the risk of having his net income curtailed by any increases in taxes or expenses.

A net lease generally calls for the lessee to pay all taxes and operating expenses, thereby assuming responsibility for any increase that may occur during the term of the lease. The net lease payments cover just the financing charges for the property. Generally, institutional investors prefer net leases.

In order to analyze the financial aspects of a gross lease, it is necessary to separate the part of the lease payments which go for taxes and expenses, etc., and the part which, in effect, represents the financing of the property.

[1] Leases may be made for many types of property such as equipment, fixtures, automobiles, etc. The features of leases may vary widely, depending to some extent on the nature of the property leased.

Leases may include many features such as additional payments above the fixed minimum payments based on a per cent of sales and renewal provisions for a certain period. While leases generally have equal monthly payments, they may be set up so that higher payments are at the beginning of the lease with correspondingly lower payments towards the end. Henceforth, in our comments on leasing, we will refer to leases with equal payments.

In general financial terminology, it may be said that the net lease payments and the part of the gross lease which covers the financing of the property include two elements: interest and repayment of principal. Generally, they provide for full repayment of the cost of the leased asset over the term of the lease plus an interest payment. As stated above, the combined dollar amount of these two elements is generally equal annually; the proportion of interest and principal will vary each year. During the early years of the lease the amount of interest will be larger, while the principal installments will increase towards the end of the lease.

The lessor or owner of the property will divide up the rental payments between interest and repayment of principal on the most advantageous basis allowed for tax purposes. Lease terminology usually describes these two elements as yield which represents the interest, and principal reduction which represents

## EXHIBIT 1 (C)

### ILLUSTRATION OF NET LEASE PAYMENTS
For Lease Paid Monthly.  Rentals Represent Total
Rentals Paid in a Year

| Column | 1 | 2 | 3 |
|---|---|---|---|
| Year | Yield or Interest | Write-off or Principal Payment | Total Net Lease Payments |
| 1 | $1,159,048 | $ 1,505,444 | $ 2,664,492 |
| 2 | 1,066,195 | 1,598,297 | " |
| 3 | 967,616 | 1,696,876 | " |
| 4 | 862,956 | 1,801,536 | " |
| 5 | 751,841 | 1,912,651 | " |
| 6 | 633,873 | 2,030,619 | " |
| 7 | 508,629 | 2,155,863 | " |
| 8 | 375,660 | 2,288,832 | " |
| 9 | 234,490 | 2,430,002 | " |
| 10 | 84,613 | 2,579,879 | " |
|  | $6,644,921 | $20,000,000 | $26,644,920 |

the depreciation and other write-offs, if any. To simplify our explanation, we will use the term interest and principal repayment but, in the tables, we include both terminologies.

Given in Exhibit 1 (C) is an example of lease payments on a property worth $20,000,-000 with the final maturity of the lease in 10 years and the interest rate at 6%.

We have referred to leases as net and gross. Some types of leases for some types of property also may be classified as operating and financial. An operating lease is one which is made primarily for reasons other than financial, such as: the property cannot be obtained except by lease, or it is desired to have maintenance furnished, or the lessor is better able to dispose of secondhand equipment, etc. A financial lease is one that is made primarily for financial reasons, as a substitute for another form of debt financing. A financial lease is generally a net lease.

There has been much controversy and consideration misconception about the nature of leasing.[2] It has been argued that a lease is not a debt security because a lessee who goes bankrupt is only responsible for a limited number of lease payments. The important point is not

[2] "Illusion in Lease Financing," an article written in 1959 by Donald R. Gant, Partner, Goldman Sachs & Co., New York City, helped to clarify the true nature of leases. *Harvard Business Review*, March–April 1959. Vol. 37, No. 2.

what happens after bankruptcy but that non-payment of a lease will put a company into bankruptcy just like any other debt. It has also been contended that investors do not give the same weight to a lease as they do to straight debt from the point of view of the effect on the company's credit; therefore, a company can have more obligations in the form of leases than in straight debt. Perhaps some naive investors may overlook the leverage effect of a lease, but experienced financial analysts generally will give effect to leases just as they do to debt, regardless of what ratios they use to analyze it.

We feel strongly that any financial lease should be treated like other forms of debt.

Lease payments are an alternative to payments of interest and principal on a debt. Capitalizing the lease and putting the property and lease obligation on the balance sheet puts a lease transaction into its true perspective.

For example, if the property described above had been purchased for $20,000,000 and financed with a $20,000,000 bond with a sinking fund retiring the entire issue by maturity, the payments (paid semi-annually) with a 6% interest rate, would have been as shown in Exhibit 2 (C).

The dollar interest or yield payments for a lease with equal monthly payments may be higher than for the debt security, because with the lease the write-off, or principal payments,

## EXHIBIT 2 (C)

### ILLUSTRATION OF BOND PAYMENTS
Interest Paid Semi-Annually.  Sinking Fund Payable Annually

| Column | 1 | 2 Sinking Fund | 3 |
|---|---|---|---|
| Year | Interest | Principal Payments | Total[a] |
| 1 | $1,200,000 | $ 2,000,000 | 3,200,000 |
| 2 | 1,080,000 | " | 3,080,000 |
| 3 | 960,000 | " | 2,960,000 |
| 4 | 840,000 | " | 2,840,000 |
| 5 | 720,000 | " | 2,720,000 |
| 6 | 600,000 | " | 2,600,000 |
| 7 | 480,000 | " | 2,480,000 |
| 8 | 360,000 | " | 2,360,000 |
| 9 | 240,000 | " | 2,240,000 |
| 10 | 120,000 | " | 2,120,000 |
| | $6,600,000 | $20,000,000 | 26,600,000 |

[a]Lease payments can be graduated downward in this same manner. In some situations this may be advantageous to the user of the property.

in the early years are generally not as great as the sinking fund payments for the debt security.[3] However, even allowing for this difference, the comparison between financing the $20,000,000 property with a lease or debt is not complete, because with a lease the residual value of the property may be lost [4] at the end of a lease.

## CAPITALIZING LEASES

The principal portion of net lease payments can be calculated by applying capitalization factors. The known quantities must be the equal annual rental, the effective interest rate and the final maturity. If the interest rate is unknown an approximate rate can be used.

A capitalization factor gives the present value, at a certain interest rate, of annual payments of $1 over a certain period of years. The reciprocal of this figure gives the constant percentage payment rate to provide both interest at the specified rate and principal payments for the number of years indicated.

Exhibit 3 (C) gives capitalization factors for certain interest rates and maturities. For example, if the lease rentals were $2,664,492 annually and the interest component of the leases were 6% with the final payment of the lease at the end of 10 years, multiply by 7.51 to obtain an equivalent principal of $20,000,000.

All leases need not necessarily be capitalized in making a financial analysis. In order to be consistent in financial analysis, we are primarily interested in capitalizing only financial leases, those which are a substitute for some other form of debt financing. This is not to say that operating leases are not just as much a form of debt, but they may be analyzed from the point of view of their effect on operating expenses. Some leases are quite complicated and, as noted above, may contain such provisions as a minimum payment and an additional payment dependent on sales. Generally, only the minimum payments are capitalized.

## COST RATES FOR LEASES

With a known principal amount for which the lease is made, a known schedule of equal dollar payments, and a known final maturity, it is possible to obtain the nominal interest rate for a lease by referring to the proper tables. However, the true cost of a lease cannot be determined that simply. Lease renewal charges and loss of residual value of the asset to the lessor at the end of the lease may be important costs needing careful consideration. Where significant, an additional allowance must be made for any financing costs in connection with lease financing. For example, there may be a payment to an agent for arranging the deal. These are all additional costs as compared to ownership of the asset and financing with straight debt.

A very approximate method of handling such costs is to divide the total amount of financing costs, lease renewal costs, and loss of residual value, by the number of years to the maturity of the lease before any renewal options and to add these annual amounts to the annual lease payments. Then calculate the interest rate with these new total annual payments. This method does not give effect to the time value of money for these costs and is erroneous for this reason. It makes the lease cost rate appear higher than it actually is. The financing costs are payable immediately, whereas the lease renewal costs and loss of residual value do not occur until some time in the future. The method of calculating an accurate cost rate for a lease, when there are additional costs, is by the Time Value Profitability Rate explained in Chapter XIII. Given

[3] For the point of view of the books of the lessor or owner of the property, the apportionment between yield and write-off will depend, as previously pointed out, on the circumstances surrounding the lessor.

[4] The effect of the loss of residual value may be minimized by a purchase or repurchase option, or by lease renewal options at token rentals.

Loss of residual value may be avoided entirely by having the property owned by a subsidiary of the lessee. The property is leased by the parent of the subsidiary. The subsidiary arranges debt financing for approximately the full value of the property, based on the credit of the parent company. The lease payments must be at least sufficient to take care of both interest and principal payments on the debt. This type of financing is known as a high credit corporate lease obligation.

# APPENDIX C

## EXHIBIT 3 (C)

## CAPITALIZATION FACTORS[a]

### For Leases Paid Monthly

To apply:   Multiply total rental paid in a year by the appropriate factor.

| Final Maturity of Lease in Years | 5% | 6% | 7% | 8% | 9% | 10% |
|---|---|---|---|---|---|---|
| 1 | .97 | .97 | .96 | .96 | .95 | .95 |
| 2 | 1.90 | 1.88 | 1.86 | 1.84 | 1.82 | 1.81 |
| 3 | 2.78 | 2.74 | 2.70 | 2.66 | 2.62 | 2.58 |
| 4 | 3.62 | 3.55 | 3.48 | 3.41 | 3.35 | 3.29 |
| 5 | 4.42 | 4.31 | 4.21 | 4.11 | 4.01 | 3.92 |
| 6 | 5.17 | 5.03 | 4.89 | 4.75 | 4.62 | 4.50 |
| 7 | 5.90 | 5.70 | 5.52 | 5.35 | 5.18 | 5.02 |
| 8 | 6.58 | 6.34 | 6.11 | 5.89 | 5.69 | 5.49 |
| 9 | 7.24 | 6.94 | 6.66 | 6.40 | 6.15 | 5.92 |
| 10 | 7.86 | 7.51 | 7.18 | 6.87 | 6.58 | 6.31 |
| 11 | 8.45 | 8.04 | 7.66 | 7.30 | 6.97 | 6.66 |
| 12 | 9.01 | 8.54 | 8.10 | 7.70 | 7.32 | 6.97 |
| 13 | 9.54 | 9.01 | 8.52 | 8.07 | 7.65 | 7.26 |
| 14 | 10.05 | 9.46 | 8.91 | 8.41 | 7.94 | 7.52 |
| 15 | 10.54 | 9.88 | 9.27 | 8.72 | 8.22 | 7.75 |
| 16 | 11.00 | 10.27 | 9.61 | 9.01 | 8.46 | 7.97 |
| 17 | 11.44 | 10.64 | 9.92 | 9.28 | 8.69 | 8.16 |
| 18 | 11.85 | 10.99 | 10.22 | 9.52 | 8.90 | 8.33 |
| 19 | 12.25 | 11.32 | 10.49 | 9.75 | 9.09 | 8.49 |
| 20 | 12.63 | 11.63 | 10.75 | 9.96 | 9.26 | 8.64 |
| 21 | 12.99 | 11.92 | 10.99 | 10.16 | 9.42 | 8.76 |
| 22 | 13.33 | 12.20 | 11.21 | 10.34 | 9.57 | 8.88 |
| 23 | 13.65 | 12.46 | 11.42 | 10.50 | 9.70 | 8.99 |
| 24 | 13.96 | 12.70 | 11.61 | 10.66 | 9.82 | 9.08 |
| 25 | 14.26 | 12.93 | 11.79 | 10.80 | 9.93 | 9.17 |

[a]Figures provided by the Financial Publishing Company, Boston, Massachusetts.

in Exhibit 4 (C) is a calculation of the cost rate for a lease based on this approach. The example refers to the same figures we previously used for the $20,000,000 of property with two additions: one, the lease can be renewed for 5 years at one-half the rental figure; and two, at the end of the renewal period the property is estimated to have a residual value of $1,000,000 which the lessee will lose at that time. The calculations are based on the as-sumption that the lessee considers it advantageous to renew the lease at the end of the tenth year. Note that if the property were financed with a $20,000,000 bond issue, there would be no renewal rental cost and the residual value would not be lost.

The purpose of calculating the full cost rate for a lease is to determine whether financing with a lease is appropriate. The true cost rate for this lease is about 8½%. In such a decision

EXHIBIT 4 (C)

NET LEASE COST CALCULATION[a]

| Year | Principal Value of Leased Property | Lease Payments | Renewal Payments | Loss of Residual Value[b] | Net Cash Flow | Discounted at 8-1/2% Factor | Amount |
|---|---|---|---|---|---|---|---|
| 0 | $20,000,000 | | | | | | |
| 1 | | $ 2,664,492 | | | $ 2,664,492 | .9217 | $ 2,455,862 |
| 2 | | " | | | " | .8495 | 2,263,486 |
| 3 | | " | | | " | .7829 | 2,086,031 |
| 4 | | " | | | " | .7216 | 1,922,697 |
| 5 | | " | | | " | .6650 | 1,771,887 |
| 6 | | " | | | " | .6129 | 1,633,067 |
| 7 | | " | | | " | .5649 | 1,505,172 |
| 8 | | " | | | " | .5207 | 1,387,401 |
| 9 | | " | | | " | .4799 | 1,278,690 |
| 10 | | " | | | " | .4423 | 1,178,505 |
| 11 | | | $1,332,246 | | 1,332,246 | .4076 | 543,023 |
| 12 | | | " | | " | .3757 | 500,525 |
| 13 | | | " | | " | .3463 | 461,357 |
| 14 | | | " | | " | .3191 | 425,120 |
| 15 | | | " | $1,000,000 | 2,332,246 | .2941 | 685,914 |
| | | $26,644,920 | $6,661,230 | $1,000,000 | $34,306,150 | | $20,098,737 |
| | | | | $1,000,000 | | | |

[a] The calculations are based on all payments being made on an annual basis, with the first payment made at the end of the first year. If the calculations were made on a monthly basis to conform to rental payments the result would be slightly different.

[b] If the lessee decided not to renew at the end of the tenth year, there will be no renewal payments and the calculations for the lease cost would have to be based on the estimated cost of residual value at the end of ten years.

the question is whether the lease rate is a reasonable rate for debt financing; the rate should be compared with the interest rate on other forms of debt. For a strict comparison with debt financing, the debt should have the same repayment schedule as the principal payments for the lease and the compounding period should be the same. Whether refinement of the calculations to this degree is necessary will depend on the circumstances.

## PROFITABILITY ANALYSIS FOR PROPERTY LEASED

Quite a different question from whether lease financing is an appropriate method of financing arises in determining the profitability of a project which is financed with a lease. Some companies have well-established standards for capital expenditure approval. However, sometimes companies do not require similar approval for leased property on the false assumption that no capital is required.

The lease rate should not be used as the Cost-of-Capital for determining the feasibility of such a project. This would be the same as making the mistake of applying a debt rate to a project which happens to be financed with a bond issue. The composite rate should be applied to all projects no matter how financed. Leasing requires common equity to support the credit just as does debt. Determining the desirability of a project using leased property requires starting with the value of the property under lease, as well as whatever working capital the project may require, and then calculating a Time Value Profitability Rate as with any other type of project. This rate must be compared with a Profit Goal commensurate with the risk of the project.

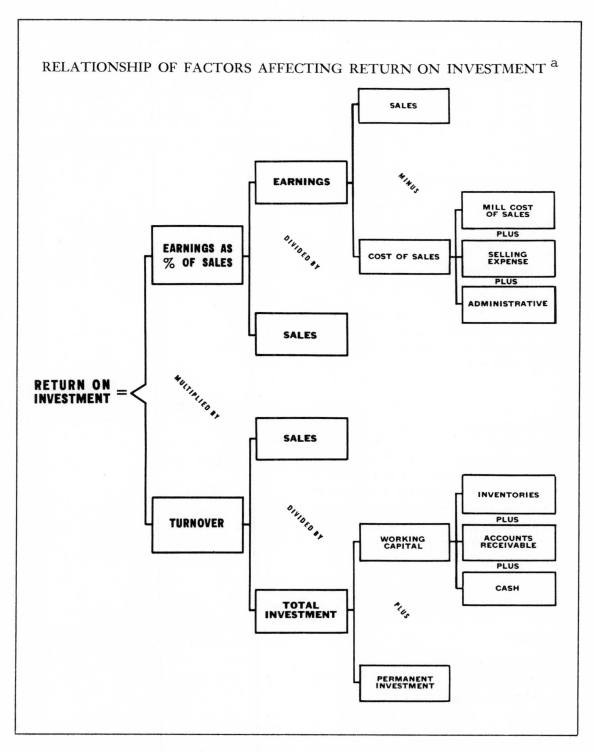

RELATIONSHIP OF FACTORS AFFECTING RETURN ON INVESTMENT [a]

[a] Reprinted by permission of E. I. du Pont de Nemours & Co., Inc., Wilmington, Delaware 19898, from its publication *Executive Committee Control Charts*.

# Illustrative Applications of
# Time Value Profitability Rate and
# Explanation of Other Correct Techniques [1]

The first part of this appendix sets forth three examples of how the Time Value Profitability Rate Technique can be applied. The examples include a plant opening, a division liquidation and a company acquisition. The second part of the appendix covers an explanation and comparison of other correct techniques of profitability analysis which allow for the time value of money.

## ILLUSTRATIVE APPLICATIONS OF TIME PROFITABILITY RATE

### Plant Opening

The management of Dairy Products Company is considering opening a new plant to provide additional production capacity for the company's new product line of premixed for-

[1] This appendix was contributed by Dr. Victor H. Brown, Partner, Touche, Ross, Bailey & Smart, 80 Pine Street, New York, New York.

mulas. It is estimated that this will require an initial investment of $1,550,000 comprising the following:

| | |
|---|---|
| Working Capital | $ 550,000 |
| Land | 200,000 |
| Building (estimated 40 year life) | 600,000 |
| Fixtures (estimated 10 year life) | 200,000 |
| | $1,550,000 |

Forecasts of growth in sales volume indicate that an additional $150,000 working capital investment will be required at the end of the fifth year. It is estimated that, on the average, plant fixtures will require complete replacement every ten years. For both book and tax purposes the company uses the sum-of-the-digits method in computing depreciation. Estimates of expected sales and profit results are shown in Columns 3–5 in Exhibit 1 (E).

EXHIBIT 1 (E)

ANALYSIS OF PROPOSED NEW PLANT
EVALUATION OF EXPECTED OPERATION
CASH FLOW SCHEDULE
(Dollars in thousands)

| COL. | 1 | 2 | 3 | 4 | 5 | 6 | 7 (2 + 5 + 6) | 8 | 9 (7 x 8) | 10 | 11 (7 x 10) |
|---|---|---|---|---|---|---|---|---|---|---|---|
| LINE | | | | | EXPECTED CASH FLOWS | | | EXPECTED CASH FLOWS DISCOUNTED | | | |
| | Year | Investment | Sales | Profit (% of sales) | Profit after depreciation and taxes | Depreciation | Net cash flow | Discounted at 8% Factor | Amount | Discounted at 10% Factor | Amount |
| 1 | 0 | $(1,550)ᵃ | | | | | $(1,550.0) | 1.000 | $(1,550.0) | 1.000 | $(1,550.0) |
| 2 | 1 | - | $2,000 | - % | $ (10) | $65.7 | $ 55.7 | .926 | $ 51.6 | .909 | $ 50.6 |
| 3 | 2 | - | 2,500 | 2.0 | 30 | 61.2 | 91.2 | .857 | 78.2 | .826 | 75.3 |
| 4 | 3 | - | 2,750 | 4.0 | 55 | 56.9 | 111.9 | .794 | 88.8 | .751 | 84.0 |
| 5 | 4 | - | 3,000 | 5.0 | 75 | 52.5 | 127.5 | .735 | 93.7 | .683 | 87.1 |
| 6 | 5 | $ (150)ᵇ | 3,250 | 6.0 | 97.5 | 48.1 | (4.4) | .681 | (3.0) | .621 | (2.7) |
| 7 | 6 | - | 3,500 | 8.0 | 140 | 43.8 | 183.8 | .630 | 115.8 | .564 | 103.7 |
| 8 | 7 | - | 3,750 | 8.0 | 150 | 39.4 | 189.4 | .583 | 110.4 | .513 | 97.2 |
| 9 | 8 | - | 4,000 | 10.0 | 200 | 35.0 | 235.0 | .540 | 126.9 | .467 | 109.7 |
| 10 | 9 | - | 4,000 | 10.0 | 200 | 30.7 | 230.7 | .500 | 115.4 | .424 | 97.8 |
| 11 | 10 | $ (200)ᶜ | 4,000 | 10.0 | 200 | 26.3 | 26.3 | .463 | 12.2 | .386 | 10.2 |
| 12 | 11 | - | 4,000 | 10.0 | 200 | 58.4 | 258.4 | .429 | 110.9 | .350 | 90.4 |
| 13 | 12 | - | 4,000 | 10.0 | 200 | 53.9 | 253.9 | .397 | 100.8 | .319 | 81.0 |
| 14 | 13 | - | 4,000 | 10.0 | 200 | 49.6 | 249.6 | .368 | 91.9 | .290 | 72.4 |
| 15 | 14 | - | 4,000 | 10.0 | 200 | 45.3 | 245.3 | .340 | 83.4 | .263 | 64.5 |
| 16 | 15 | - | 4,000 | 10.0 | 200 | 40.8 | 240.8 | .315 | 75.9 | .239 | 57.6 |
| 17 | 16 | - | 4,000 | 10.0 | 200 | 36.5 | 236.5 | .292 | 69.1 | .218 | 51.6 |
| 18 | 17 | - | 4,000 | 10.0 | 200 | 32.1 | 232.1 | .270 | 62.7 | .198 | 46.0 |
| 19 | 18 | - | 4,000 | 10.0 | 200 | 27.7 | 227.7 | .250 | 56.9 | .180 | 41.0 |
| 20 | 19 | - | 4,000 | 10.0 | 200 | 23.4 | 223.4 | .232 | 51.8 | .164 | 36.6 |
| 21 | 20 | $1,200.9ᵈ | 4,000 | 10.0 | 200 | 19.0 | 1,419.9 | .215 | 305.3 | .149 | 211.6 |
| 22 | | | | | $3,137.5 | | | | $1,798.7 | | $1,465.6 |

ᵃInitial investment.
ᵇAdditional working capital.
ᶜReplacement of fixtures.
ᵈResidual value.

CALCULATIONS

Time value profitability rate:  8% + 2% × $\left(\dfrac{\$1,798.7 - \$1,550.0}{\$1,798.7 - \$1,465.6}\right)$ = 9.5%

Return on average book value:  $\dfrac{\$3,137.5/20}{\$1,294.2}$ = 12.1%

Return on total book value:  $\dfrac{\$3,137.5/20}{\$1,700}$ = 9.2%

Management estimates the company's Cost-of-Capital [2] at approximately 9% and that this new investment would have about the same risk thus requiring a similar rate of return. Accordingly, management wishes to assess whether or not the new plant will generate a return sufficiently above this Cost-of-Capital to justify the undertaking.

Estimates of investments and cash flows are set forth in Columns 2–7 in Exhibit 1 (E). If the expansion is successful, sales and earnings are expected to continue for an indefinite period of time—certainly for more than twenty years. However, for evaluation purposes a twenty-year economic life is arbitrarily assumed. This assumption produces satisfactory results provided the remaining value of plant investment at the end of twenty years is estimated and considered in the profitability evaluation. In this case, it is estimated that the residual value of the investment at the end of twenty years, after considering applicable income taxes, will comprise the following:

| | |
|---|---|
| Working Capital | $ 700,000 |
| Land and Building (after taxes on gain from disposal) | 500,900 |
| | $1,200,900 |

This amount is considered in the cash flow analysis as a cash receipt at the end of the twentieth year.

If it is felt that other terminal values should be estimated, additional calculations should be made. In principle, the terminal value should be the higher of these two figures: the liquidating value of the investment (net of taxes), or the value of the investment to the company on a going concern basis at the chosen terminal date. An alternative evaluation procedure would consist of forecasting cash flows from the plant for an indefinite life, whereupon the above terminal value estimate would not be required. However, computational simplicity results from considering the investment to have a twenty-year life. Ordinarily, neg-

ligible differences in Time Value Profitability Rates obtain under either method of analysis. Because of the discounting procedure, relatively little weight is assigned to cash flow estimates made for more than twenty years in the future. The effect of the terminal value on the rate, of course, depends on its relative size and the chosen terminal date.

By trial and error, the prospective Time Value Profitability Rate is found to be 9.5%. Relevant computations are shown in Column 8–11 and in the calculations at the bottom of the table.[3] This return is slightly above the 9% Cost-of-Capital for the proposal.

However, one of the company's top officers suggests that there are risks inherent in this proposed expansion and that further analysis appears desirable before proceeding. He specifically mentions two risks: first, changing technology in the preparation of premixed formula may make present equipment obsolete at the end of, perhaps, ten years; and second, the sales and profit projections used in deriving the 9.5% Time Value Profitability Rate may prove unduly optimistic, especially considering the possible introduction of similar product lines by competitors. Accordingly, he suggests that the proposal's Profitability Rate be estimated under alternative assumptions concerning economic life and estimated future profits.

In Exhibit 2 (E), the plant's Time Value Profitability Rate is computed, assuming premature liquidation of operations at the end of ten years. It is estimated that the residual value of the plant at the end of ten years will be $1,322,600 after considering applicable income taxes. The proposal's Time Value Profitability Rate under this pessimistic assumption is found to be 7.5%, an amount below the Cost-of-Capital.

Exhibit 3 (E) sets forth the derivation of the proposal's Time Value Profitability Rate under conservative assumptions concerning fu-

[2] This rate is the After Tax Equivalent Cost-of-Capital.

[3] Trial and error use of discount tables shows that the rate lies between 8% and 10%. The figure of 9.5% is obtained by interpolating between these figures on a straight line basis.

## EXHIBIT 2 (E)

### ANALYSIS OF PROPOSED NEW PLANT
### EVALUATION OF POSSIBLE PREMATURE LIQUIDATION

CASH FLOW SCHEDULE
(Dollars in thousands)

| COL. | 1 | 2 | 3 | 4 | 5 | 6 | 7 | 8 | 9 | 10 | 11 |
|---|---|---|---|---|---|---|---|---|---|---|---|
| | | | | | | | (2 + 5 + 6) | | (7 × 8) | | (7 × 10) |
| | | | | | EXPECTED CASH FLOWS | | | | EXPECTED CASH FLOWS DISCOUNTED | | |
| | | | | | | | | Discounted at 6% | | Discounted at 8% | |
| LINE | Year | Investment | Sales | Profit (% of sales) | Profit after depreciation and taxes | Depreciation | Net cash flow | Factor | Amount | Factor | Amount |
| 1 | 0 | $(1,550)a | | | | | $(1,550.0) | 1.000 | $(1,550.0) | 1.000 | $(1,550.0) |
| 2 | 1 | – | $2,200 | – | $ (10) | $65.7 | $ 55.7 | .943 | $ 52.5 | .926 | $ 51.6 |
| 3 | 2 | – | 2,500 | 2.0 | 30 | 61.2 | 91.2 | .890 | 81.2 | .857 | 78.2 |
| 4 | 3 | – | 2,750 | 4.0 | 55 | 56.9 | 111.9 | .840 | 94.0 | .794 | 88.8 |
| 5 | 4 | – | 3,000 | 5.0 | 75 | 52.5 | 127.5 | .792 | 101.0 | .735 | 93.7 |
| 6 | 5 | $ (150)b | 3,250 | 6.0 | 97.5 | 48.1 | (4.4) | .747 | (3.3) | .681 | (3.0) |
| 7 | 6 | – | 3,500 | 8.0 | 140 | 43.8 | 183.8 | .705 | 129.6 | .630 | 115.8 |
| 8 | 7 | – | 3,750 | 8.0 | 150 | 39.4 | 189.4 | .665 | 126.0 | .583 | 110.4 |
| 9 | 8 | – | 4,000 | 10.0 | 200 | 35.0 | 235.0 | .627 | 147.3 | .540 | 126.9 |
| 10 | 9 | – | 4,000 | 10.0 | 200 | 30.7 | 230.7 | .592 | 136.6 | .500 | 115.4 |
| 11 | 10 | $ 1,322.6c | 4,000 | 10.0 | 200 | 26.3 | 1,548.9 | .558 | 864.3 | .463 | 717.1 |
| 12 | | | | | $1,137.5 | | | | $ 1,729.2 | | $ 1,494.9 |

a Initial investment.
b Additional working capital.
c Residual value.

### CALCULATIONS

Time value profitability rate:  $6\% + 2\% \times \dfrac{(\$1,729.2 - 1,550.0)}{(\$1,729.2 - 1,494.9)} = \underline{\underline{7.5\%}}$

Return on average book value:  $\dfrac{\$1,137.5/10}{\$1,369.2} = \underline{\underline{8.3\%}}$

Return on total book value:  $\dfrac{\$1,137.5/10}{\$1,700.0} = \underline{\underline{6.7\%}}$

## EXHIBIT 3 (E)

### ANALYSIS OF PROPOSED NEW PLANT
### EVALUATION OF OPERATION - CONSERVATIVE BASIS
### CASH FLOW SCHEDULE
(Dollars in thousands)

| COL. | 1 | 2 | 3 | 4 | 5 | 6 | 7 | 8 | 9 | 10 | 11 |
|---|---|---|---|---|---|---|---|---|---|---|---|
| | | | | | EXPECTED CASH FLOWS | | (2 + 5 + 6) | EXPECTED CASH FLOWS DISCOUNTED | | | |
| | | | | | | | | Discounted at 6% | (7 x 8) | Discounted at 8% | (7 x 10) |
| LINE | Year | Investment | Sales | Profit (% of sales) | Profit after depreciation and taxes | Depreciation | Net cash flow | Factor | Amount | Factor | Amount |
| 1 | 0 | $(1,550)a | | | | | $(1,550.0) | 1.000 | $(1,550.0) | 1.000 | $(1,550.0) |
| 2 | 1 | - | $1,800 | - | $ (67) | $65.7 | $ (1.3) | .943 | $ (1.2) | .926 | $ (1.2) |
| 3 | 2 | - | 2,350 | 1.5 | 35 | 61.2 | 96.2 | .890 | 85.6 | .857 | 82.4 |
| 4 | 3 | - | 2,560 | 3.0 | 54.5 | 56.9 | 111.4 | .840 | 93.6 | .794 | 88.5 |
| 5 | 4 | | 2,625 | 4.0 | 52.5 | 52.5 | 105.0 | .792 | 83.2 | .735 | 77.2 |
| 6 | 5 | $ (150)b | 2,730 | 5.0 | 68.3 | 48.1 | (33.6) | .747 | (25.1) | .681 | (22.9) |
| 7 | 6 | - | 3,260 | 6.0 | 98 | 43.8 | 141.8 | .705 | 100.00 | .630 | 89.3 |
| 8 | 7 | - | 3,340 | 6.3 | 105 | 39.4 | 144.4 | .665 | 96.0 | .583 | 84.2 |
| 9 | 8 | - | 3,500 | 8.0 | 140 | 35.0 | 175.0 | .627 | 109.7 | .540 | 94.5 |
| 10 | 9 | | 3,500 | 8.0 | 140 | 30.7 | 170.7 | .592 | 101.1 | .500 | 85.4 |
| 11 | 10 | $ (200)c | 3,500 | 8.0 | 140 | 26.3 | (39.7) | .558 | (18.8) | .463 | (15.6) |
| 12 | 11 | - | 3,500 | 8.0 | 140 | 58.4 | 198.4 | .527 | 104.6 | .429 | 85.1 |
| 13 | 12 | - | 3,500 | 8.0 | 140 | 53.9 | 193.9 | .497 | 96.4 | .397 | 77.0 |
| 14 | 13 | - | 3,500 | 8.0 | 140 | 49.6 | 189.6 | .469 | 88.9 | .368 | 69.8 |
| 15 | 14 | - | 3,500 | 8.0 | 140 | 45.3 | 185.3 | .442 | 81.9 | .340 | 63.0 |
| 16 | 15 | - | 3,500 | 8.0 | 140 | 40.8 | 180.8 | .417 | 75.4 | .315 | 57.0 |
| 17 | 16 | - | 3,500 | 8.0 | 140 | 36.5 | 176.5 | .394 | 69.5 | .292 | 51.5 |
| 18 | 17 | - | 3,500 | 8.0 | 140 | 32.1 | 172.1 | .371 | 63.8 | .270 | 46.5 |
| 19 | 18 | - | 3,500 | 8.0 | 140 | 27.7 | 167.7 | .350 | 58.7 | .250 | 41.9 |
| 20 | 19 | - | 3,500 | 8.0 | 140 | 23.4 | 163.4 | .331 | 54.1 | .232 | 37.9 |
| 21 | 20 | $1,200.9d | 3,500 | 8.0 | 140 | 19.0 | 1,359.9 | .312 | 424.3 | .215 | 292.4 |
| 22 | 21 | | | | $2,166.3 | | | | $1,741.7 | | $1,383.9 |

a Initial investment.
b Additional working capital.
c Replacement of fixtures.
d Residual value.

### CALCULATIONS

Time value profitability rate: 
$$6\% + 2\% \times \frac{(\$1,741.7 - 1,550.0)}{(\$1,741.7 - 1,383.9)} = 7.1\%$$

Return on average book value: 
$$\frac{\$2,166.3/20}{\$1,294.2} = 8.4\%$$

Return on total book value: 
$$\frac{\$2,166.3/20}{\$1,700.0} = 6.4\%$$

ture revenues and earnings. Management feels that the earnings estimates in Exhibit 3 (E) reflect conservative assumptions concerning anticipated sales. The resulting 7.1% return thus measures the lower limit of expected earning power.

Equipped with these estimates—9.5%, 7.5% and 7.1%—of the project's anticipated profitability, management must decide whether to open the plant.[4] In this case, the only forecast which shows a return even slightly above Cost-of-Capital is the optimistic one. Since a Profit Goal should be above the Cost-of-Capital, management decided against opening the plant.

Note in this example that the Time Value Profitability Rate is computed on the total of working capital and fixed assets, rather than on the total current and fixed assets. This is because corporate Cost-of-Capital is ordinarily computed on long-term capital which provides plant and working capital. Profitability rates, to be comparable, should be computed on the long-term capital invested in projects, or appropriate adjustments should be made in the rate.

Exhibits 1 (E), 2 (E), 3 (E), also show rates of return by using both accounting methods—return on average and total investment. The

following figures are used in deriving the investment base for calculating these measures.

*Average Book Value*

The most straightforward method of making this calculation is to total the net book investment for the beginning of each year and the end of the last year and then dividing by the number of years plus one. For Exhibits 1 (E) and 3 (E) it is $1,294,190, and for Exhibit 2 (E) it is $1,369,200.

*Total Book Value*

| Initial investment | $1,550,000 |
|---|---|
| Additional working capital | 150,000 |
| Total | $1,700,000 |

Since the $200,000 of fixtures in the tenth year are replacements for the $200,000 of fixtures in the first year, they do not add to total book value. The total is the same for all three exhibits.

The rates of return for the three forecasts for the new plant opening, on the basis of the different methods of calculations, are as follows:

|  | Time Value Profitability Rate | Accounting Methods | |
|---|---|---|---|
|  |  | Return on Total Book Value | Return on Average Book Value |
| Exhibit 1 (E) Expected Operation | 9.5% | 9.2% | 12.1% |
| Exhibit 2 (E) Premature Liquidation | 7.5% | 6.7% | 8.3% |
| Exhibit 3 (E) Conservative Basis | 7.1% | 6.4% | 8.4% |

The extent of the possible error in the use of one of the accounting methods in this example is as much as 2.6%—a significant amount in a close case like this one. The extent of the error will depend on the cash flows of each

project. The returns on average book value might erroneously induce some managements to go ahead with the project whereas the Time Value Profitability Rates suggest more caution.

*Division Liquidation*

Dairy Products Company has one division which has been showing poor earnings. Re-

[4] Methods have been suggested for arriving at a single rate whereby it is possible to assign weights representing the probability of each individual profitability rate's occurring.

turns on this division's total book investment for the last three years have been 1.3%, 1.1% and 1.0% respectively. Management attention has been directed toward improving the situation, but detailed studies suggest that little can be done. Accordingly, management wishes to evaluate the desirability of closing the division. It is believed that closing this division would have little, if any, effect upon the profitability of the remaining divisions.[5]

First, estimates are made of the income which may be expected from continuing to operate the division for a reasonable number of years. It is expected that the division, after depreciation and taxes, can at best be expected to earn the amounts set forth in Exhibit 4 (E), Column 3, over the next seven years. These projected earnings will produce an apparently unattractive annual return on a $725,000 total book investment of less than 1%.

However, the book value of the permanent capital invested in the division is not a valid measure of the economic investment in the division. The economic value of the capital invested in the division is its value in best alternative use. Typically, this is its liquidating value since sale of the investment is typically its best alternative use. In a few cases, however, when facilities can be diverted to some other corporate use, the value of the investment for such purpose may be higher than resale value. Dairy Products Company would liquidate divisional assets if the division were shut down and thus prepared divisional balance sheets on both a book and a liquidating basis, as shown in Exhibit 5 (E).

The liquidating value of the division is estimated to be considerably less than its book value. Upon liquidation, it is expected that accounts receivable collection losses will mount, that inventory losses will be suffered and that prepaid items will have a zero value.

The Time Value Profitability Rate which could be earned on the $365,000 economic in-

vestment in the division by continuing operations is computed in Exhibit 4 (E). The resulting 9.1% rate is the appropriate measure of financial worth to use in deciding upon whether or not to liquidate the division. If this is above the company's Cost-of-Capital and the risk of the division is the same as that for the company, continuing to operate the division is slightly more profitable than liquidating it. This is true despite the fact that the division's prospective rate of return on total book value is less than 1.0%. However, management estimates that the risk of this division is somewhat greater than the risk of the business as a whole. On the basis of this judgment, Cost-of-Capital of 9% for the company as a whole should be increased to at least 10% for this division. Thus liquidation may be appropriate.

*Company Acquisition*

Dairy Products Company's management is currently considering the acquisition of a small candy manufacturing company. It is estimated that an initial cash investment of $325,000 will be required, comprising the following:

| | |
|---|---|
| Cash purchase | $275,000 |
| Working Capital | 50,000 |
| | $325,000 |

Management feels that the risk in the candy business is about in line with its existing business and, therefore, it can employ a 9% After Tax Equivalent Cost-of-Capital.

The candy manufacturer has not shown an increasing level of sales and profits in recent years. The following table indicates the pertinent data for the last five years.

| Year | Sales | Earnings | Cash Flow |
|---|---|---|---|
| 1961 | $190,000 | $5,500 | $25,500 |
| 1962 | 195,000 | 5,700 | 25,700 |
| 1963 | 200,000 | 6,000 | 26,000 |
| 1964 | 200,000 | 6,000 | 26,000 |
| 1965 | 200,000 | 6,000 | 26,000 |

However, the management of Dairy Products Company believes that a major reason for this

---

[5] If a division closing does affect the profits or expenses of other divisions, these effects must be included in the evaluation of the profitability of the division under consideration.

EXHIBIT 4 (E)

ANALYSIS OF POSSIBLE DIVISIONAL LIQUIDATION
EVALUATION OF PROFITABILITY OF CONTINUED OPERATION
CASH FLOW SCHEDULE

| COL. | 1 | 2 | 3 | 4 | 5 | 6 | 7 | 8 | 9 |
|---|---|---|---|---|---|---|---|---|---|
| LINE | | | EXPECTED CASH FLOWS | | (2 + 3 + 4) | EXPECTED CASH FLOWS DISCOUNTED | (5 × 6) | | (5 × 8) |
| | Year | Investment | Profit after depreciation and taxes | Depreciation[b] | Net cash flow | Discounted at 8% Factor | Amount | Discounted at 10% Factor | Amount |
| 1 | 0 | $(365,000)[a] | | | $(365,000) | 1.000 | $(365,000) | 1.000 | $(365,000) |
| 2 | 1 | – | $ 7,000 | $ 31,500 | $ 38,500 | .926 | $ 35,651 | .909 | $ 34,997 |
| 3 | 2 | – | 7,000 | 31,000 | 38,000 | .857 | 32,566 | .826 | 31,388 |
| 4 | 3 | – | 7,000 | 31,000 | 38,000 | .794 | 30,172 | .751 | 28,538 |
| 5 | 4 | – | 6,500 | 31,000 | 37,500 | .735 | 27,563 | .683 | 25,613 |
| 6 | 5 | – | 6,500 | 30,500 | 37,000 | .681 | 25,197 | .621 | 22,977 |
| 7 | 6 | – | 6,000 | 30,500 | 36,500 | .630 | 22,995 | .564 | 20,586 |
| 8 | 7 | $ 325,000[c] | 5,500 | 30,500 | 361,000 | .583 | 210,463 | .513 | 185,193 |
| 9 | | | $45,500 | $216,000 | $586,500 | | $384,607 | | $349,292 |

CALCULATION

$$\text{Time value profitability rate} = 8\% + 2\% \times \frac{(\$384,607 - \$365,000)}{(\$384,607 - \$349,292)} = 9.1\%$$

[a] Equivalent investment.
[b] Depreciation is based on stated book value of the investment.
[c] Residual value.

## EXHIBIT 5 (E)

## DIVISIONAL BALANCE SHEET

|  | Book Value | Liquidating Value |
|---|---|---|
| **Current Assets:** | | |
| Cash | $100,000 | $100,000 |
| Accounts Receivable | 150,000 | 120,000[a] |
| Inventory | 175,000 | 120,000[a] |
| Prepaid Expenses | 25,000 | -------[a] |
| Total | $450,000 | $340,000 |
| Less Current Liabilities | 200,000 | 200,000 |
| Working Capital | $250,000 | $140,000 |
| **Property, Plant and Equipment:** | | |
| Land | $200,000 | |
| Plant and Equipment ($1,000,000 less $725,000 accumulated depreciation) | 275,000 | $225,000[a] |
| Total | $475,000 | $225,000 |
| Permanent Capital | $725,000 | $365,000[a] |

[a] Amounts are after adjustment for applicable tax credits.

apparent lack of growth has been a reluctance to supply additional working capital for operations.

More important, management feels that the candy manufacturer has failed to utilize the proper distribution channels and promotional techniques necessary for growth. Since there is a marked similarity between Dairy Products Company's channels of distribution and advertising and those necessary for growth of the candy manufacturer, substantially increased sales and earnings can reasonably be expected to result through the proposed acquisition.

Estimates of investments and anticipated cash flows are set forth in Exhibit 6 (E). The resulting Time Value Profitability Rate from the proposed acquisition is shown to be 8.7%, based on the assumption that sales volume and cash flow will increase for the reasons stated above. This figure suggests that the acquisition should be turned down, whereas both of the accounting methods show returns which suggest that the acquisition might be worthwhile. Note that the Time Value Profitability Rate is based on an estimated liquidating value no greater than the initial investment. If the ac-

## EXHIBIT 6 (E)

### ANALYSIS OF PROPOSED ACQUISITION
### EVALUATION OF EXPECTED OPERATIONS
### CASH FLOW SCHEDULE

| Col.<br>Line | 1 | 2 | 3 | 4 | 5 | 6<br>(4 x 5) | 7 | 8<br>(4 x 7) |
|---|---|---|---|---|---|---|---|---|
| | | | EXPECTED CASH FLOWS | | | EXPECTED CASH FLOWS DISCOUNTED | | |
| | | | Profit after<br>depreciation<br>and taxes | Net cash<br>flow[b] | Discounted at 8% | | Discounted at 10% | |
| | Year | Investment | | | Factor | Amount | Factor | Amount |
| 1 | 0 | $(325,000)[a] | | $(325,000) | 1.000 | $(325,000) | 1.000 | $(325,000) |
| 2 | 1 | | $ 10,000 | $ 10,000 | .926 | $ 9,260 | .909 | $ 9,090 |
| 3 | 2 | | 12,000 | 12,000 | .857 | 10,284 | .826 | 9,912 |
| 4 | 3 | | 14,000 | 14,000 | .794 | 11,116 | .751 | 10,514 |
| 5 | 4 | | 18,000 | 18,000 | .735 | 13,230 | .683 | 12,294 |
| 6 | 5 | | 20,000 | 20,000 | .681 | 13,620 | .621 | 12,420 |
| 7 | 6 | | 24,000 | 24,000 | .630 | 15,120 | .564 | 13,536 |
| 8 | 7 | | 26,000 | 26,000 | .583 | 15,158 | .513 | 13,338 |
| 9 | 8 | | 30,000 | 30,000 | .540 | 16,200 | .467 | 14,010 |
| 10 | 9 | | 33,000 | 33,000 | .500 | 16,500 | .424 | 13,992 |
| 11 | 10 | | 36,000 | 36,000 | .463 | 16,668 | .386 | 13,896 |
| 12 | 11 | | 39,000 | 39,000 | .429 | 16,731 | .350 | 13,650 |
| 13 | 12 | | 42,000 | 42,000 | .397 | 16,674 | .319 | 13,398 |
| 14 | 13 | | 44,000 | 44,000 | .368 | 16,192 | .290 | 12,760 |
| 15 | 14 | | 46,000 | 46,000 | .340 | 15,640 | .263 | 12,098 |
| 16 | 15 | | 48,000 | 48,000 | .315 | 15,120 | .239 | 11,472 |
| 17 | 16 | | 50,000 | 50,000 | .292 | 14,600 | .218 | 10,900 |
| 18 | 17 | | 50,000 | 50,000 | .270 | 13,500 | .198 | 9,900 |
| 19 | 18 | | 50,000 | 50,000 | .250 | 12,500 | .180 | 9,000 |
| 20 | 19 | | 50,000 | 50,000 | .232 | 11,600 | .164 | 8,200 |
| 21 | 20 | $ 325,000[c] | 50,000 | 375,000 | .215 | 80,625 | .149 | 55,875 |
| 22 | | | $692,000 | | | $ 350,338 | | $ 280,255 |

### CALCULATIONS

Time value profitability rate: $8\% + 2\% \times \dfrac{\$(350,338 - 325,000)}{\$(350,338 - 280,255)} = 8.7\%$

Return on average book value: $\dfrac{\$692,000/20}{\$325,000} = 10.6\%$

Return on total book value: $\dfrac{\$692,000/20}{\$325,000} = 10.6\%$

[a] Initial investment.

[b] It is estimated that capital replacements will approximately equal depreciation charges.

[c] Residual value is estimated to be about the same as the initial investment value with capital replacements approximately equal to depreciation charges.

quisition proved successful the liquidating value might be substantially higher. For example, if the liquidating value were double, or 12½ times estimated earnings at the end of the 20th year, the Time Value Profitability Rate would be about 10%. However, this possibility is sufficiently uncertain so it is decided that the prospective acquisition should be dropped.

## OTHER CORRECT TECHNIQUES

We now discuss briefly two other correct capital budgeting techniques. They are the Excess Present Value Method and the Annual Excess Value Method.

### Excess Present Value

Of the three correct capital budgeting techniques, Excess Present Value is probably the simplest to complete. Two steps are required once a proposal's initial investment and expected cash flows have been estimated. First, the investment's projected cash flows are discounted, at the Profit Goal rate, back to the present "zero point" (or discounted or compounded to some "zero point" other than the present). Secondly, the investment required at the "zero point" (usually the initial investment) is subtracted from the sum of discounted cash flows to determine the dollar excess (or deficiency) in present value. An excess present value signals a profitable investment, a deficiency in present value indicates an investment which fails to meet the Profit Goal.

For illustration purposes, we will use the same Project A that we used to illustrate the Time Value Profitability Rate. That project required an initial investment of $100,000 and was expected to generate four annual cash returns of $35,000 each, with no salvage value left at the end of its four year economic life. Assume that management has established a Profit Goal of 10% for this type of investment.

Exhibit 7 (E) is in the form that might be used for the necessary computations. Column 1 shows the net cash flows; Column 2 gives the factors for 10% from a discount table; and

Column 3 is filled in by multiplying Column 1 by Column 2 for each year. Column 3 is then totaled; the sum is $110,915. Comparing this sum to the $100,000 initial investment, shown at the "zero point" in time in the Exhibit, we see that Project A's proposal has a $10,915 Excess Present Value—the sum of Column 3 is $10,915 higher than the $100,000 initial investment. This means that the proposed investment is expected to return more than the 10% profit goal that management has set for this type of project. Therefore, all other things being equal, this proposal should be accepted. If the proposal's total present value had been below $100,000, then the deficit present value figure would have indicated that the project failed to meet the 10% Profit Goal, and the investment would not be desirable.

In actual use for capital budgeting decision-making, the raw $10,915 Excess Present Value is not as useful as the ratio of the total Present Value to the initial investment—that is, $110,915 divided by $100,000 which equals 1.11. This ratio of 1.11, usually called the "Excess Present Value Index," enables decision-makers to rank projects with different initial investment. To explain, we might assume another project which has the same raw $10,915 Excess Present Value—but which requires an initial investment of $1,000,000 or ten times as much. While the Excess Present Value is the same, the second project's Excess Present Value Index is only 1.01 ($1,010,915 divided by $1,000,000). The Excess Present Value Index, therefore, correctly ranks the second project as having a lower profitability rate. So long as a proposal shows an Excess Present Value Index greater than 1.00 however, the proposal's return exceeds the Profit Goal and is economically desirable, all other things being equal. But an Excess Present Value Index of less than 1.00 would indicate a project which fails to meet the 10% Profit Goal.

### Annual Excess Value

The third of the three correct capital budgeting techniques is the Annual Excess Value Method. To explain this technique, we will

## EXHIBIT 7 (E)

## EXCESS PRESENT VALUE TECHNIQUE ILLUSTRATION

## PROJECT A

| Column / Year | 1 Net Cash Flow | 2 10% Discounts Factors | 3 Present Value (1 x 3) |
|---|---|---|---|
| 0 | $(100,000) | 1.000 | $(100,000) |
| 1 | $ 35,000 | .909 | $ 31,815 |
| 2 | 35,000 | .826 | 28,910 |
| 3 | 35,000 | .751 | 26,285 |
| 4 | 35,000 | .683 | 23,905 |
| Total | $ 140,000 | | $ 110,915 |
| Excess Present Value | | | $ 10,915 |

Excess Present Value Index = $\frac{\$110,915}{\$100,000}$ = 1.11

again use Project A. Its Excess Present Value amounted to $10,915; dividing by four gives $2,729 per year for the four year life of the project. However, this $2,729 simple annual figure is not an adequate measure of the annual excess value; it fails to consider that the Excess Present Value could be invested at interest so that it could be amortized over the four year project life to return an aggregate amount of more than the $10,915 principal amount. In fact, if the $10,915 is invested at the project's 10% Profit Goal rate, it will produce $3,438 per year for four years. This $3,438 Annual Excess Value is the annual amount that will return $10,915 over a four year period plus a return of 10%.

In other words, the Excess Present Value of $10,915 represents the excess above the Profit Goal at the "zero point" in time; the Annual Excess Value of $3,438 represents the annual amount which would amortize the $10,915 over the four year project life at the Profit Goal rate.

To calculate the Annual Excess Value, first calculate the Excess Present Value. Then multiply by a factor similar to interest and discount factors, which gives the annual amount that the Excess Present Value will produce so as to return the principal amount and income at the applicable rate. These factors are known as annuity factors or Capital Recovery factors. A sample of annuity factors is shown in Exhibit 8 (E). For example, at a 10% rate for four years the factor is 0.315. This means that an annual receipt of $0.315 for four years would return to an investor his initially in-

## EXHIBIT 8 (E)

### SAMPLE TABLE OF ANNUITY FACTORS[a]
(Annual amounts, including principal and interest, which
will be provided by $1 invested today at compound interest)

| i<br>n | 4% | 6% | 8% | 10% | 15% |
|---|---|---|---|---|---|
| 1 | 1.040 | 1.060 | 1.080 | 1.100 | 1.150 |
| 2 | .530 | .545 | .560 | .576 | .615 |
| 3 | .360 | .374 | .388 | .402 | .438 |
| 4 | .275 | .288 | .302 | .315 | .350 |

$$\text{Formula:} \quad f = \frac{i}{1 - (1+i)^n}$$

f = Annuity factor
n = Number of compounding periods
i = Interest rate per period

[a]For complete tables see footnote reference to table "Sample Table of Compound Interest Factors," Exhibit 3 (XV), in Chapter XV.

vested $1.00 amount plus an annual return of 10% on his unrecovered principal. Multiplying the $10,915 Excess Present Value for Project A by the 0.315 factor gives $3,438, Project A's Annual Excess Value.

The Annual Excess Value method is also referred to as the Equivalent Uniform Annual Cost technique. To explain the method more fully, we will explain it in the same way as do those who refer to it by this latter term. In its simplest form, for a project with equal annual net cash flows, this technique merely subtracts one year's capital charge from one year's Net Cash Flow. If the remainder is positive, the investment meets the Profit Goal established; if the remainder is negative, however, the investment should not be made. The capital charge in the Excess Annual Value or Equivalent Uniform Annual Cost technique

is that uniform, annual amount which will both amortize the initial investment and also provide a return at the Profit Goal rate. This capital charge can be determined by referring to annuity factors described above.

To illustrate, we will again use Project A. Each year's Net Cash Flow was $25,000. The economic life was four years; from annuity tables we would find that the capital charge for $1 is 0.315 for a 10% return over four years. This means that $0.315 paid at the end of each of the four years would pay back the $1 plus a return of 10% on each year's unrecovered balance. Since Project A requires an investment of $100,000, its capital charge is therefore $31,500 each year. The Equivalent Uniform Annual Cost technique would be applied to the project as shown in Exhibit 9 (E). The fact that there is an equivalent uniform

EXHIBIT 9 (E)

ANNUAL EXCESS VALUE

| | |
|---|---:|
| Annual Net Cash Flow | $35,000 |
| Equal annual payments required to amortize $100,000 initial investment over 4 year life and return 10% on unrecovered balance | 31,500 |
| Equivalent uniform annual revenue (or Annual Excess Value) | $ 3,500[a] |

[a] This $3,500 would be equal to the $3,438 as previously calculated from the Excess Present Value if the factors used in making the calculations were carried out more decimal places. The figure by both methods would then be $3,453.

annual remainder of $3,500[6] left, after the annual capital charge, signifies that this project more than meets the Profit Goal of 10%.

All four of the annual net cash flows in our example conveniently are equal, which makes the application of the technique with this method of calculation quite simple. In actual evaluations, this uniformity is somewhat rare. The calculation can be done this way even with unequal cash flows, but the preferable method of calculation is, as explained above, to determine the Excess Present Value at the "zero point" in time and then convert it to the Annual Excess Value by applying annuity factors.

## COMPARISON OF THE THREE CORRECT TECHNIQUES

There are numerous variations[7] and modifications of the three techniques described

above, but these three are basic. The Time Value Profitability Rate, as the title suggests, solves for the rate that a project is expected to return. The Excess Present Value technique solves for the excess present dollar equivalent, or a ratio of the total present value dollar to the initial investment, that the project will return above the Profit Goal. The annual Excess Value technique solves for the excess dollars per year that the project will return above the Profit Goal.

Correctly applied, all three techniques will give correct answers. That is, they will properly combine all three of the factors which basically determine the financial worth of the project—1) the initial investment, 2) the net cash flows and 3) the timing of the net cash flows. Why, then, do we specifically recommend the Time Value Profitability Rate?

We suggest that the Time Value Profitability Rate is preferable for most companies because it has two practical advantages in assisting top management in formulating capital budgeting decisions. First, it is the only one of the three techniques which supplies an answer in terms of a rate. Usually this is easier for management to comprehend. For example, if management has set a Profit Goal of 12% it is easy to grasp the significance of a 15% Time Value Profitability Rate for a proposed project.

The second advantage is that the technique does not require the pre-establishment of the appropriate Profit Goal. A proposal's Time Value Profitability Rate can be calculated by staff analysts before the proposed project is presented to the capital budgeting decision-makers. The decision-makers can then compare the Time Value Profitability Rate against that Profit Goal they believe necessary to allow for risk. In each of the other two correct techniques, a pre-established Profit Goal must

[6] This $3,500 would be equal to the $3,438 as previously calculated from the Excess Present Value if the factors used in making the calculations were carried out more decimal places. The figure by both methods would then be $3,453.

[7] For example, a variation on the Annual Excess Value technique, developed by the Machinery and Allied Prod-

ucts Institute and known as "the MAPI System," offers a very structured method of deriving an "urgency rating" for equipment replacement and (as revised in 1958) for more unsophisticated capital budgeting proposals. Although very simple to apply, the system is difficult to understand. This often leads to mechanical applications of the system to project analyses, which may be undesirable in any but the simplest proposals.

be used in arriving at the final answer. If the decision-makers decide the pre-established goal was inappropriate for the project's risk, it is necessary to redo the calculations.

The principal advantage of Excess Present Value is that it is simple to compute. In the Time Value Profitability Rate, the trial and error work necessary in the calculation is more arduous than the original calculations for Excess Present Value. If the forecast figures change, it is much less time consuming to recalculate the result for the Excess Present Value. New figures can be added or subtracted after discounting at the Profit Goal rate used in the original calculation. This makes it possible readily to test the sensitivity of project profitability to changes in expected revenues, costs and required investment. Furthermore, if a company wishes its division managers to perform the calculations, it can furnish just one table with discount factors for the Profit Goal the company has established for that division. These can be applied directly to the cash flows. These advantages however may be outweighed by the two disadvantages mentioned above—the necessity of pre-establishing Profit Goals for each project, and the difficulty of grasping the significance of, say, a $10,915 Excess Present Value or even of a 1.11 Excess Present Value Index.

The same advantages and disadvantages generally apply to the Annual Excess Value technique although it requires one more step in calculation than the Excess Present Value method. The technique can be used wherever the other methods can be used and some people prefer this one for all purposes.

As pointed out in Chapter XV, critics of the Time Value Profitability Rate commonly raise the objection of "the implied reinvestment assumption" when the method is used to make a choice between mutually exclusive projects. This will now be discussed more fully. Both the Excess Present Value and the Excess Annual Value techniques avoid this objection because they both directly assume a required earnings, or reinvestment rate, making it somewhat easier to compare one project directly with another. For the same reason,

they also avoid the multiple rate problem which we will discuss subsequently.

*Implied Reinvestment Assumption—Unequal Cash Flows*

In directly comparing one project with another on the basis of Time Value Profitability Rates, an assumption concerning the profitability of cash throwoff reinvestments is always made. If there is no specific different assumption made, profitability conclusions drawn from rate comparisons are based upon the assumption that each project's cash flows will be reinvested at the same rate that is shown for the project itself. By this we do not mean that Time Value Profitability Rate calculation itself includes any such asumption for any project. What we are saying is that in deciding on which of two projects to accept, a straight rate comparison assumes that the cash available for reinvestment will be invested at the project rate. For projects which have unequal cash flows, a straight rate comparison presents a problem for this reason.

For example, suppose that a choice must be made between Project M and Project N, both of which have the same $100,000 initial investment and Time Value Profitability Rate of 50%, but which have different cash flows as shown in Exhibit 10 (E).

Which project is more attractive depends upon the rates at which cash flows can be reinvested. Project M would be the more attractive if all cash flows were reinvested at greater

## EXHIBIT 10 (E)

### UNEQUAL NET CASH FLOWS

| Year | Project M | Project N |
|------|-----------|-----------|
| 0 | ($100,000) | ($100,000) |
| 1 | 150,000 | 54,800 |
| 2 | | 54,800 |
| 3 | | 54,800 |
| 4 | | 54,800 |
| 5 | | 54,800 |
| 6 | | 54,800 |

than a 50% rate because we would get the money back quicker to reinvest at the higher rate. Conversely, it would be less attractive if the reinvestment rate were less than 50%.[8] The inference that the proposals are equally attractive because each has a 50% rate is valid only if indefinite cash flow reinvestments at 50% rates are presumed.

Recognizing the need for making some reinvestment rate assumption is of particular practical importance in evaluating conflicting, or mutually exclusive, projects. Such proposals are alternative to one another so that the acceptance of one automatically triggers the rejection of the other(s); for example, a company considering whether to make or buy an item is confronted with two conflicting proposals. Direct profitability comparisons among conflicting projects are essential; thus, the reinvestment assumption is important.

While precision in forecasting reinvestment rates is admittedly impossible, management may, in comparing conflicting proposals, wish to make reinvestment rate assumptions different from those implicitly made in direct Time Value Profitability Rate comparisons. For example, management may have definite expectations concerning the profitability of projects that it believes are feasible for the near future;

these expectations may be substituted for the rate which the project shows as the Time Value Profitability Rate. An alternative approach is to calculate the Time Value Profitability Rate for conflicting projects using the Company's Profit Goal rate as the reinvestment rate.

In evaluating independent projects—those which are not conflicting or mutually exclusive—it is generally impossible, even with the best of forecasts, to estimate the profitability of cash flow reinvestments on an individual project basis. This is because cash flows available for reinvestment at any point in time are typically derived from numerous projects and constitute a homogeneous pool of capital at management's disposal; identification of specific segments of this pool with individual investments is possible only on an arbitrary basis. Thus, in appraising most independent proposals, the reinvestment assumption at the project's own rate is unimportant in making project decisions. Ignoring the reinvestment assumptions, a company will accept, after due consideration to risks and intangibles, all projects with Time Value Profitability Rates equal to or greater than the company's Profit Goal. This course of action will lead to best results from the shareholder viewpoint.

[8] To illustrate, assume a 10% reinvestment rate. If Project M's $150,000 cash throwoff were reinvested at 10%, a capital sum of $241,577 would accumulate six years after the project's adoption. This amount is derived by multiplying the $150,000 by the compounding factor of 1.610,510 for 10% for the remaining years, which equals $241,577. The formula is $S \times (1+i)^n$, or $150,000 \times (1 + 0.10)^5 = \$241,577$.

If Project N's cash flow were reinvested at 10%, a capital sum of $422,815 would accumulate six years after the project's adoption. This amount is derived by multiplying each $54,800 amount by the compounding factor for 10% for the period remaining. $54,800 \times 1.610,510,000 + \$54,800 \times 1.464,100,000 + \$54,800 \times 1.331,000 + \$54,800 \times$ 1.210,000,000 + 54,800 \times 1.100,000,000 + 54,800 = \$422,815$. It can also be obtained by multiplying the $54,800 annual cash flow by the factor 7.715,610. This is the factor which shows how much $1 deposited for each of six annual periods at 10% compound interest will grow. The formula is $S \times \frac{(1+i)^n - 1}{i}$ or $54,800 \times \frac{(1 + 0.10)^6 - 1}{10} = \$422,815$.

Considering the two projects over a six year period and taking account of the 10% reinvestment rate, the Time Value Profitability Rate for the projects can be determined to be 16% for Project M and 27% for Project N as follows:

| | | PROJECT M | | | | PROJECT N | | |
| | | Cash Flow with 10% Reinvestment Rate | Cash Flow Discounted at 16% | | | Cash Flow with 10% Reinvestment Rate | Cash Flow Discounted at 27% | |
| Yr. | Investment | | Factor | Amount | Investment | | Factor | Amount |
|---|---|---|---|---|---|---|---|---|
| 0 | $100,000 | | 1.0000 | ($100,000) | $100,000 | | 1.0000 | ($100,000) |
| 1 | | | | | | | | |
| 2 | | | | | | | | |
| 3 | | | | | | | | |
| 4 | | | | | | | | |
| 5 | | | | | | | | |
| 6 | | $241,577 | .4104 | $99,143 | | $422,815 | .2383 | $100,757 |

However, in certain appraisals of independent projects, the reinvestment assumption at the project's own rate may be important and lead to incorrect decisions. For example, the feasibility of certain foreseeable future projects may be contingent on adopting certain present alternatives. For example, a plan to construct a plant one year hence may require the present reservation of liquid capital. Account should be taken of this fact in determining the Time Value Profitability Rate for the present alternative.

The point to note is that while management may be satisfied with the assumption that the reinvestment rate is the same as the project rate in many cases, in other cases this assumption may be unsatisfactory. In such situations, a more appropriate assumption should be made.

*Implied Reinvestment Assumption*
*Unequal Initial Investment*

In a comparison of one project with another on the basis of Time Value Profitability Rates, a problem of the implied reinvestment assumption also arises when the initial investments are unequal. Here again, the problem is important only when conflicting proposals are being evaluated. For example, Project X, shown in Exhibit 11 (E) with a 10% rate, cannot directly be compared with the 15% rate for Project Y if the projects require initial investments of $100,000 and $60,000 respectively.

## EXHIBIT 11 (E)

### UNEQUAL INITIAL INVESTMENTS

| | PROJECT X | | | | PROJECT Y | | | |
|---|---|---|---|---|---|---|---|---|
| | | Cash | Cash Flow Discounted at 10% | | | Cash | Cash Flow Discounted at 15% | |
| Yr. | Investment | Flow | Factor | Amount | Investment | Flow | Factor | Amount |
| 0 | $100,000 | | 1.000 | ($100,000) | $60,000 | | | ($60,000) |
| 1 | | $40,000 | .909 | 36,360 | | $25,000 | .885 | 22,125 |
| 2 | | $40,000 | .826 | 33,040 | | 25,000 | .783 | 19,575 |
| 3 | | $40,000 | .751 | 30,040 | | 25,000 | .693 | 17,325 |
| | | | | $ 99,440 | | | | $59,025 |

Which project is more attractive depends upon the rate that would be earned upon the differential $40,000 that would be available if Project Y were accepted. Only if this differential rate were 6% would the two projects be equally profitable.[9] And this is true only if the cash flows from each project were reinvested at the particular project's rate.

The Time Value Profitability Rate can be

adapted satisfactorily to evaluate such conflicting proposals by means of the "incremental added investment method." This procedure involves comparing all of a set of conflicting proposals that show Time Profitability Rates higher than the Profit Goal in order of size, from the smallest to the largest, in the following two steps.

1. Determine the Time Value Profitability Rate for the proposal requiring the smallest initial investment.
2. Compute the Time Value Profitability Rate implied by the incremental original capital and the incremental cash flows needed to adapt the proposal requiring the next largest investment. If the result-

[9] This is illustrated below.

| Year | Differential Investment | Differential Cash Flow | Cash Flow Discounted at 6% | |
|---|---|---|---|---|
| | | | *Factor* | *Amount* |
| 0 | $40,000 | | | ($40,000) |
| 1 | | $15,000 | .943 | 14,145 |
| 2 | | 15,000 | .890 | 13,350 |
| 3 | | 15,000 | .840 | 12,600 |
| | | | | $40,095 |

ing rate exceeds the Profit Goal, drop the first project from further consideration. Using the second project as a new standard, repeat this incremental approach until only one proposal remains. This is financially the most attractive.

This adaptation of the Time Value Profitability Rate analysis is straightforward and can serve satisfactorily to evaluate such conflicting investment opportunities. Care, however, is required in measuring the differential cash flows expected from successive incremental investments. This can be a somewhat complicated process involving initially a recognition of the appropriate alternatives to include within a set of conflicting proposals.

*Multiple Rate Problem*

Some incremental investments and, less frequently, some individual proposals can have more than one Time Value Profitability Rate. Appropriate reinvestment assumptions must be made in developing usable rate measures in these instances.

An investment expected to produce cash flows of both positive and negative amounts can have more than one Time Value Profitability Rate; the maximum number of rates is equal to the number of sign changes in the total net cash flows, including the initial investment.[10] For example, Project Z requires a $10,000 initial outlay (a negative cash flow) and will produce three cash flows as follows: Year 1, $60,000; Year 2, $110,000 (negative); and Year 3, $60,000. This project has three rates (0%, 100% and 200%)—the maximum number possible since there are three reversals of cash flow signs. This is shown in Exhibit 12 (E) figures by applying discount rates for 0%, 100% and 200% to the cash flows.

## EXHIBIT 12 (E)

### MULTIPLE RATE PROBLEM

| Year | Net Cash Flows | Discounted at 0% | | Discounted at 100% | | Discounted at 200% | |
|---|---|---|---|---|---|---|---|
| | | Factor | Amount | Factor | Amount | Factor | Amount |
| 0 | ($10,000) | 1 | ($10,000) | 1.000 | ($10,000) | 1.00000 | ($10,000) |
| 1 | 60,000 | 1 | 60,000 | .500 | 30,000 | .33333 | 20,000 |
| 2 | -110,000 | 1 | -110,000 | .250 | -27,500 | .11111 | -12,222 |
| 3 | 60,000 | 1 | 60,000 | .125 | 7,500 | .037037 | 2,222 |

Manifestly, this illustrative proposal does not have three different valid indexes of profitability. Valid rate measures can be developed for

projects with multiple rates by initially assuming appropriate reinvestment rates. To illustrate, the proposal cited above has a 4½% rate if a 10% reinvestment rate is assumed.[11] With an assumed 50% reinvestment rate, the project has a 44% rate of return.[12] These resultant

---

[10] The point that proposals may have more than one implied rate of return is made and more fully discussed by James H. Lorie and Leonard J. Savage in their article, "Three Problems in Rationing Capital," *Journal of Business*, October, 1955, pp. 236–38. These authors also discuss the procedure outlined above for evaluating conflicting proposals (Ibid., p. 239). The points that proposals can conceivably have more than two directly implied rates of return and that the number of possible rates depends upon the number of sign reversals in the estimated cash flow stream are made by Jack Hirshleifer, *An Isoquant Approach to Investment Decision Problems* (Santa Monica: Rand Corporation, Report P-1158, August, 1957), p. 38.

[11] The cash flows reinvested at a 10% rate would be as follows: $60,000 × 1.210 — $110,000 × 1.1 + $60,000 = $11,600. With an initial investment of $10,000, this $11,600 at the end of the three year period would produce a Time Value Profitability Rate of 4½%.

[12] The cash flows reinvested at a 50% rate would be as follows: $60,000 × 2.250 — $110,000 × 1.500 + $60,000 = $30,000. With an initial investment of $10,000, this $30,-000 at the end of the three year period would produce a Time Value Profitability Rate of 44%.

rates are valid profitability indexes. Individual proposals with multiple rates of return are relatively rare. Differential cash flows developed for incremental investments, however, may well assume peculiar shapes through time. If projected cash flows alternate between positive and negative amounts, care must be taken to use a specific reinvestment rate in solving for the profitability rate.

We have tried to indicate in this technical discussion that the problems involved with the Time Value Profitability Rate should not be viewed as hurting its effectiveness. These problems were included for the purpose of presenting a complete picture. When a management reaches the point of choosing a method for profitability analysis of projects which includes the time value of money technique, it will have to choose the one best suited to its particular situation. However, one technique should be used consistently, since all users should be thoroughly familiar with the concepts of the application and the meaning of the answers. The technique chosen should be the one which permits management to grasp the results most readily, and it should be consistent with the way in which they are most accustomed to consider capital expenditures.

# INDEX

# INDEX